Module
7

Christian Ministry

Foundations *of* Christian Leadership

The Christian Leader as Deacon:

DIAKONOI

. . . .

The Christian Leader as Elder:

PRESBYTEROI

. . . .

The Christian Leader as Pastor:

POIMENES

. . . .

The Christian Leader as Bishop:

EPISKOPOI

Capstone Module 7: Foundations of Christian Leadership Student Workbook

ISBN: 978-1-62932-007-6

Contents

About the Instructor

Rev. Dr. Don L. Davis is the Executive Director of The Urban Ministry Institute and a Senior Vice President of World Impact. He attended Wheaton College and Wheaton Graduate School, and graduated summa cum laude in both his B.A. (1988) and M.A. (1989) degrees, in Biblical Studies and Systematic Theology, respectively. He earned his Ph.D. in Religion (Theology and Ethics) from the University of Iowa School of Religion.

As the Institute's Executive Director and World Impact's Senior Vice President, he oversees the training of urban missionaries, church planters, and city pastors, and facilitates training opportunities for urban Christian workers in evangelism, church growth, and pioneer missions. He also leads the Institute's extensive distance learning programs and facilitates leadership development efforts for organizations and denominations like Prison Fellowship, the Evangelical Free Church of America, and the Church of God in Christ.

A recipient of numerous teaching and academic awards, Dr. Davis has served as professor and faculty at a number of fine academic institutions, having lectured and taught courses in religion, theology, philosophy, and biblical studies at schools such as Wheaton College, St. Ambrose University, the Houston Graduate School of Theology, the University of Iowa School of Religion, the Robert E. Webber Institute of Worship Studies. He has authored a number of books, curricula, and study materials to equip urban leaders, including *The Capstone Curriculum*, TUMI's premiere sixteen-module distance education seminary instruction, *Sacred Roots: A Primer on Retrieving the Great Tradition*, which focuses on how urban churches can be renewed through a rediscovery of the historic orthodox faith, and *Black and Human: Rediscovering King as a Resource for Black Theology and Ethics*. Dr. Davis has participated in academic lectureships such as the Staley Lecture series, renewal conferences like the Promise Keepers rallies, and theological consortiums like the University of Virginia Lived Theology Project Series. He received the Distinguished Alumni Fellow Award from the University of Iowa College of Liberal Arts and Sciences in 2009. Dr. Davis is also a member of the Society of Biblical Literature, and the American Academy of Religion.

Introduction to the Module

Greetings, in the strong name of Jesus Christ!

The leaders of the Church of God are his precious gift to his people throughout the ages. The evidence that Jesus loves his people dearly is that he has granted unto them apostles, prophets, evangelists, pastors and teachers to equip his people to represent the Kingdom of God in this fallen and soon-to end world (Eph. 4.9-16). This module highlights the various roles and offices associated with this high and important task in the Kingdom of God.

To begin with, in Lesson 1, *The Christian Leader as Deacon (Diakonoi)* we will probe the foundations of Christian leadership as it relates to the offices and functions of leadership in the local church. We will explore the ministry of deacons, or, in the Greek, *diakonoi*, examining its meaning in the Greek NT, and its probable origins in the Jewish synagogue. We will also look at the *diaconate*, or ministry of deacons, and comment on the authority and functions of this ministry through three models of the Deacon's role: as a servant, as a steward, and as an assistant.

Next, in our second lesson, *The Christian Leader as Elder (Presbyteroi)* we will trace the notion of elder from its OT root in the tribal system and synagogue, to the Sanhedrin, and to the NT Church. We'll then give careful consideration to the calling of and the criteria for becoming an elder in the NT Church, and will complete our brief study by examining several analogies to help us understand the nature of biblical eldership; that of an overseer, a father or parent, a colleague or team member, and finally a representative. We will consider these in order to discover new ways we can put the principles of eldership into practice in our own lives and ministries.

In Lesson 3, *The Christian Leader as Pastor (Poimenes)*, we will outline the biblical context of the idea of the pastorate, starting with the definition of the Greek term for pastoring, and tracing historically the development of the idea of a formal office of the pastorate. We will then highlight the calling and the criteria for representing God as an undershepherd of the flock. We will close our section with a discussion of pastoral authority, along with a look at three biblical models and analogies of pastoral care: that of a nurturer and care giver, a protector and guardian, and a leader of the flock of God.

Finally, in Lesson 4, *The Christian Leader as Bishop (Episkopoi)*, we will provide a broad definition and overview to this dynamic concept of bishop or overseer. Beginning with a consideration of the NT language, we will trace its probable context from the council of elders in Jewish rulership, including the development of the concept, through the history of the Church. After considering the calling and criteria of the bishop's office, we will examine the concept of bishop through the images of supervisor, apostle, and spiritual director. We hope our study will show how the very nature of Christian leadership and Christian community demands bishop-level oversight and relationship which goes beyond just the local body itself.

It is hard to imagine a more wonderful gift to an assembly or group of assemblies than godly, Christlike leadership, true shepherds who guard and protect the flock of God. May God use this study to inspire you to nurture and care for his people, to emulate the Good Shepherd who laid down his life for his sheep.

- Rev. Dr. Don L. Davis

Course Requirements

Required Books and Materials

- Bible (for the purposes of this course, your Bible should be a translation [ex. NIV, NASB, RSV, KJV, NKJV, etc.], and not a paraphrase [ex. The Living Bible, The Message]).

- Each Capstone module has assigned textbooks which are read and discussed throughout the course. We encourage you to read, reflect upon, and respond to these with your professors, mentors, and fellow learners. Because of the fluid availability of the texts (e.g., books going out of print), we maintain our *official* Capstone Required Textbook list on our website. Please visit *www.tumi.org/books* to obtain the current listing of this module's texts.

- Paper and pen for taking notes and completing in-class assignments.

Suggested Readings

- Hyde, Douglas. *Dedication and Leadership*. Notre Dame: University of Notre Dame Press, 2001.

- Sanders, J. Oswald. *Spiritual Leadership*. Chicago: Moody Press, 1994.

- Carter, Kenneth H., Jr. *The Gifted Pastor: Finding and Using Your Spiritual Gifts*. Nashville: Abingdon Press, 2001.

Summary of Grade Categories and Weights

Attendance & Class Participation	30%	90 pts
Quizzes	10%	30 pts
Memory Verses	15%	45 pts
Exegetical Project	15%	45 pts
Ministry Project.	10%	30 pts
Readings and Homework Assignments.	10%	30 pts
Final Exam	10%	30 pts
	Total: 100%	300 pts

Grade Requirements

Attendance at each class session is a course requirement. Absences will affect your grade. If an absence cannot be avoided, please let the Mentor know in advance. If you miss a class it is your responsibility to find out the assignments you missed, and to talk with the Mentor about turning in late work. Much of the learning associated with this course takes place through discussion. Therefore, your active involvement will be sought and expected in every class session.

Every class will begin with a short quiz over the basic ideas from the last lesson. The best way to prepare for the quiz is to review the Student Workbook material and class notes taken during the last lesson.

The memorized Word is a central priority for your life and ministry as a believer and leader in the Church of Jesus Christ. There are relatively few verses, but they are significant in their content. Each class session you will be expected to recite (orally or in writing) the assigned verses to your Mentor.

The Scriptures are God's potent instrument to equip the man or woman of God for every work of ministry he calls them to (2 Tim. 3.16-17). In order to complete the requirements for this course you must select a passage and do an inductive Bible study (i.e., an exegetical study) upon it. The study will have to be five pages in length (double-spaced, typed or neatly hand written) and deal with the principles surrounding the foundations of Christian leadership highlighted in this course. Our desire and hope is that you will be deeply convinced of Scripture's ability to change and practically affect your life, and the lives of those to whom you minister. As you go through the course, be open to finding an extended passage (roughly 4-9 verses) on a subject you would like to study more intensely. The details of the project are covered on pages 10-11, and will be discussed in the introductory session of this course.

Ministry Project

Our expectation is that all students will apply their learning practically in their lives and in their ministry responsibilities. The student will be responsible for developing a ministry project that combines principles learned with practical ministry. The details of this project are covered on page 12, and will be discussed in the introductory session of the course.

Class and Homework Assignments

Classwork and homework of various types may be given during class by your Mentor or be written in your Student Workbook. If you have any question about what is required by these or when they are due, please ask your Mentor.

Readings

It is important that the student read the assigned readings from the text and from the Scriptures in order to be prepared for class discussion. Please turn in the "Reading Completion Sheet" from your Student Workbook on a weekly basis. There will be an option to receive extra credit for extended readings.

Take-Home Final Exam

At the end of the course, your Mentor will give you a final exam (closed book) to be completed at home. You will be asked a question that helps you reflect on what you have learned in the course and how it affects the way you think about or practice ministry. Your Mentor will give you due dates and other information when the Final Exam is handed out.

Grading

The following grades will be given in this class at the end of the session, and placed on each student's record:

A - Superior work   D - Passing work

B - Excellent work   F - Unsatisfactory work

C - Satisfactory work   I - Incomplete

Letter grades with appropriate pluses and minuses will be given for each final grade, and grade points for your grade will be factored into your overall grade point average. Unexcused late work or failure to turn in assignments will affect your grade, so please plan ahead, and communicate conflicts with your instructor.

Exegetical Project

Purpose

As a part of your participation in the Capstone module *Foundations of Christian Leadership,* you will be required to do an exegesis (inductive study) on one of the following passages on the biblical meaning and definitions of Christian leadership in the Church and community:

- ❏ Matthew 20.20-28
- ❏ Jeremiah 23.1-4
- ❏ John 13.1-17
- ❏ Matthew 23.8-12
- ❏ 1 Peter 5.1-4
- ❏ Acts 20.24-28
- ❏ Ezekiel 34.2-10

The purpose of this exegetical project is to give you an opportunity to do a detailed study of a major passage on the nature of Christian leadership. Using the text as a base and lens, you will be called to think critically about the nature of your duty, privilege, and responsibility to lead others according to the structure of Christ's own leadership. Our desire is that you will glean new insights into the whats and wherefores of leading others as Christ leads his Church through your meditation and study of the text. We are convinced that strong, ongoing, exegesis of the Word of God can enhance every dimension of your personal walk of discipleship, as well as enrich you in your current ministry and leadership role in your church and ministry.

Outline and Composition

This is a Bible study project, and, in order to do *exegesis,* you must be committed to understand the meaning of the passage in its own setting. Once you know what it meant, you can then draw out principles that apply to all of us, and then relate those principles to life. A simple three step process can guide you in your personal study of the Bible passage:

1. What was *God saying to the people in the text's original situation*?

2. What principle(s) does *the text teach that is true for all people everywhere,* including today?

3. What is *the Holy Spirit asking me to do with this principle here, today,* in my life and ministry?

Once you have answered these questions in your personal study, you are then ready to write out your insights for your *paper assignment.*

Here is a *sample outline* for your paper:

1. List out what you believe is *the main theme or idea* of the text you selected.

2. *Summarize the meaning* of the passage (you may do this in two or three paragraphs, or, if you prefer, by writing a short verse-by-verse commentary on the passage).

3. *Outline one to three key principles or insights* this text provides on the nature of Christian leadership.

4. Tell how one, some, or all of the principles may relate to *one or more* of the following:

   a. Your personal spirituality and walk with Christ

   b. Your life and ministry in your local church

   c. Situations or challenges in your community and general society

As an aid or guide, please feel free to read the course texts and/or commentaries, and integrate insights from them into your work. Make sure that you give credit to whom credit is due if you borrow or build upon someone else's insights. Use in-the-text references, footnotes, or endnotes. Any way you choose to cite your references will be acceptable, as long as you 1) use only one way consistently throughout your paper, and 2) indicate where you are using someone else's ideas, and are giving them credit for it. (For more information, see *Documenting Your Work: A Guide to Help You Give Credit Where Credit Is Due* in the Appendix.)

Make certain that your exegetical project, when turned in meets the following standards:

- It is legibly written or typed.

- It is a study of one of the passages above.

- It is turned in on time (not late).

- It is 5 pages in length.

- It follows the outline given above, clearly laid out for the reader to follow.

- It shows how the passage relates to life and ministry today.

Do not let these instructions intimidate you; this is a Bible study project! All you need to show in this paper is that you *studied* the passage, *summarized* its meaning, *drew out* a few key principles from it, and *related* them to your own life and ministry.

Grading   The exegetical project is worth 45 points, and represents 15% of your overall grade, so make certain that you make your project an excellent and informative study of the Word.

Ministry Project

Purpose

The Word of God is living and active, and penetrates to the very heart of our lives and innermost thoughts (Heb. 4.12). James the Apostle emphasizes the need to be doers of the Word of God, not hearers only, deceiving ourselves. We are exhorted to apply the Word, to obey it. Neglecting this discipline, he suggests, is analogous to a person viewing our natural face in a mirror and then forgetting who we are, and are meant to be. In every case, the doer of the Word of God will be blessed in what he or she does (James 1.22-25).

Our sincere desire is that you will apply your learning practically, correlating your learning with real experiences and needs in your personal life, and in your ministry in and through your church. Therefore, a key part of completing this module will be for you to design a ministry project to help you share some of the insights you have learned from this course with others.

Planning and Summary

There are many ways that you can fulfill this requirement of your study. You may choose to conduct a brief study of your insights with an individual, or a Sunday School class, youth or adult group or Bible study, or even at some ministry opportunity. What you must do is discuss some of the insights you have learned from class with your audience. (Of course, you may choose to share insights from your Exegetical Project in this module with them.)

Feel free to be flexible in your project. Make it creative and open-ended. At the beginning of the course, you should decide on a context in which you will share your insights, and share that with your instructor. Plan ahead and avoid the last minute rush in selecting and carrying out your project.

After you have carried out your plan, write and turn in to your Mentor a one-page summary or evaluation of your time of sharing. A sample outline of your Ministry Project summary is as follows:

1. Your name

2. The place where you shared, and the audience with whom you shared

3. A brief summary of how your time went, how you felt, and how they responded

4. What you learned from the time

Grading

The Ministry Project is worth 30 points and represents 10% of your overall grade, so make certain to share your insights with confidence and make your summary clear.

LESSON
1

The Christian Leader as Deacon
Diakonoi

page 331 📖 1

Lesson Objectives

page 333 📖 2

Welcome in the strong name of Jesus Christ! After your reading, study, discussion, and application of the materials in this lesson, you will be able to:

- Articulate the foundations of Christian leadership as it relates to the offices and functions of leadership in the local church (deacons, elders, pastors, and bishops).

- Define one of the foundations of Christian leadership from the standpoint of the ministry of deacons, or, in the Greek, *diakonoi*, giving evidence of the meanings of the term *diakonoi* in the Greek NT.

- Trace the origins and development of the role of the deacon from its parallel role in the Jewish synagogue, the *hazzan*.

- Lay out clearly the key issues related to the call to the diaconate, or ministry of deacons, and the various biblical criteria and qualifications connected to being a deacon in the Church of God.

- Outline the authority of the deacon's office in both Scripture and history, and elaborate on some of the functions of this important ministry among the people of God.

- Unpack the data on three images or models of the deacon's role, i.e., the roles of servant, steward, and assistant.

- Define the kinds of issues and concepts involved in equipping deacons for urban congregations, as well as the various principles and practices associated with the office.

- Recognize the importance of the diaconate for urban congregations, both in terms of meeting practical needs as well as dividing the labor amongst the leaders to ensure that the congregation's full priorities are not neglected.

1

Who Is the Greatest?

Devotion

page 333 📖 3

Mark 9.33-37 - And they came to Capernaum. And when he was in the house he asked them, "What were you discussing on the way?" [34] But they kept silent, for on the way they had argued with one another about who was the greatest. [35] And he sat down and called the twelve. And he said to them, "If anyone would be first, he must be last of all and servant of all." [36] And he took a child and put him in the midst of them, and taking him in his arms, he said to them, [37] "Whoever receives one such child in my name receives me, and whoever receives me, receives not me but him who sent me."

There is something oddly comforting about the unclarity of the apostles. If Christ was able to use them in the remarkable way he did, even in spite of the kinds of weird and ungodly attitudes they had on a wide range of issues, then there is hope for us! The above text is significant because of its occurrence in the journey of the Lord Jesus. It took place after Peter made the God-inspired confession of the Messianic identity of Jesus of Nazareth, and our Lord further revealed that he would be betrayed, be handed over by the scribes and chief priests, and be crucified. In some way, the episodes which preceded this incident were the defining moment in our Lord's self-revelation about his identity and his intention and work in the world. The Messiah of God would be shamed, tortured, humiliated, and crucified, but three days later he would rise. What an amazing teaching, filled to the brim with implications about the humility of Jesus Christ, and his willingness to follow his Father's will to the utmost extremity. What a revelation: the anointed of God would be humiliated for the sake of redeeming his own!

On the heels of this remarkable disclosure, the apostles were accompanying our Lord to his hometown, Capernaum. On the way, the disciples' conversation must have been animated enough that it intrigued our Lord who asked them what was the subject of conversation on the way to the house. The apostles' silence must have been deafening, for they knew what they had been talking about, and were ashamed of both its content and form. The text is clear in verse 34: "But they kept silent, for on the way they had argued with one another about who was the greatest." The apostles had just learned that their master, Jesus of Nazareth was in fact the long-awaited Messiah, and their minds turned immediately to their place with him, the "pecking order" they enjoyed and would enjoy perhaps in the coming Kingdom. How inappropriate and shameful, on the very doorstep of our Lord's clearest teaching about his upcoming humiliation and death, that the apostles would be talking about their own blessing, greatness, and significance.

Rather than berate them, Jesus sits down, calls the twelve to him, and teaches them the heart of kingdom greatness. "If anyone would be first, he must be last of all and servant of all." This principle of greatness through service, being first by becoming last and servant of all, marks every dimension of our Lord's life. From his birth, his adolescence and adulthood, in every phase of his life and ministry, our Lord had proven the truth of this dynamic principle. In a real sense, he calls the disciples to imitate his own life, and to embody in their characters and practices the same lowliness and humility that characterized his own dealings. Greatness is not about comparing our abilities, significance, resources, achievements and talents to others. Greatness, by Christ's definition, is available to anyone who is willing to become last, to become the servant of all.

And what is the concrete image of this humility. Jesus takes a child and placed him in the midst of the apostles, and *taking the little one in his arms*, he gave the sense of lowliness required. "Whoever receives one such child in my name receives me, and whoever receives me, receives not me but him who sent me." This links the lowliness that we express to the most humble person to the very person of the King himself. Truly, our Messiah cannot be approached or received on any other ground than lowly ground. Humility is the only doorway to receiving him.

To what extent does your life and ministry reflect the wisdom and revelation that Jesus gave to his disciples that day. Do you flesh out in your life the reality that to become first, you must become last, the servant of all? This is both a revelation of God, and a standard of leadership. Without lowliness and humility, without servanthood and submission, there can be no leadership, no maturity, no representation of Christ. This is precisely why there are so few true Christian leaders. Many (if not most) are not willing to go so low in order to be raised high.

Commit yourself afresh to the this basic but revolutionary redefinition of the meaning of greatness. "If anyone would be first, he must be last of all and servant of all." Would you like to be first, too?

1

After reciting and/or singing the Nicene Creed (located in the Appendix), pray the following prayer:

God of all grace who by your Holy Spirit has appointed the orders of ministry in the Church: Look with favor on your servants now called to the Order of Deacons: Maintain them in your truth and renew in them your holiness that they may faithfully serve you to the glory of your Name and the benefit of your Church; through the merits of our Savior Jesus Christ.

~ The Church of the Province of South Africa.
Minister's Book for Use with the Holy Eucharist and Morning and Evening Prayer.
Braamfontein: Publishing Department of the Church of the Province of South Africa. p. 111.

Nicene Creed and Prayer

No quiz this lesson

Quiz

No Scripture memorization this lesson

Scripture Memorization Review

No assignments due this lesson

Assignments Due

CONTACT

The Bigger the Better

Many define their ministries in the church by tangible, quantifiable markers, all of which speak of broad impact. All too often, success in ministry is measured by the *numbers* of people associated with our church and ministry, by the *size* of our facilities, and how posh they are, by the *amount* of money we collect through our collections and offerings, and by the *reputation* we hold with others who use these same markers as the sign of authentic success in ministry. By definition, the person who serves the Lord in a church with few members, a modest church, with little financial resources, and who is unknown among the "name recognition" crowd–such a person cannot be considered successful. In what sense, according to your own opinion, are these markers true indicators of success of ministry? Can they be, and if so, where and how so?

page 335 📖 4

That Message Won't Work Here

2 ▶ Many in the city are attracted to a kind of Christian image and vision that emphasizes victory, triumph, and success. Arguably the most popular teachers of the Bible in the city emphasize the promise of abundance, prosperity, and health for the obedient disciple of Jesus. The tonic of servanthood, sacrifice, and self-forgetful care has never been a popular message, and it appears, in many urban situations, to be equally difficult to accept. Why would we emphasize such a message among those whose entire lives have been known by being the proverbial last in society, the most ignored and from the least adored neighborhoods on earth? Many preachers would say that such a message, in the face of ongoing trouble and need is pouring the proverbial salt on the wounds of the needy. A message that focuses on self-death and being the last will not work here, they would suggest. What do you think of this emphasis on servanthood and its implications for neighborhoods which have *always* been on the bottom?

A Way of Controlling Those on the Bottom

3 ▶ In response to the biblical teaching with its emphasis on the lowliness and humility of Christ, and that as a model for Christian leaders, some have suggested that this has been used historically to silence opposition and relegate the poor to the bottom. For instance, the ethic of submission was a popular ethical topic of instruction during the American slavery era, and for those slaves who responded favorably to the Gospel, they were often exhorted to follow the example of Christ in lowly submission, along with the Pauline instruction to remain in the position in which you came into the faith, even if, in fact, it were slavery. Unfortunately, the Bible has been interpreted to mean that women, minorities, and others on the bottom must embrace the ethic of servanthood and submission, and find ways to live peacefully in their status. The ethic of Jesus and his standard for servanthood was made the foundation for a kind of social conservatism that allowed neither protest, self-assertion, or any attempt at self-determination, even in the midst of real oppression. Is the ethic of Jesus *passé* (that is, over and unworkable for the poor), or is his teaching the most revolutionary vision for leaders among the poor?

The Christian Leader as Deacon (*Diakonoi*)

Segment 1: Definition and Overview

Rev. Dr. Don L. Davis

Christian leadership can be understood clearly through the foundations of service outlined in the biblical offices and functions of leadership in the Church. These include the roles of deacon, elder, pastor, and bishop. The fundamental principle of all Christian leadership is servanthood, which is embodied directly in both the terminology and position of the ministry of deacons, or, as it is phrased in the Greek, *diakonoi*. The development of the diaconate (the ministry of deacons) may have its origins and development based on the role of the assistant in the traditional Jewish synagogue called the *hazzan*. The NT outlines carefully the calling and qualifications of the ministry of the diaconate, or ministry of deacons, a ministry involving both the administration of care among the members of the body, as well as spiritual outreach and instruction.

Our objective for this segment, *The Christian Leader as Deacon: Definition and Overview*, is to enable you to see that:

- The New Testament underscores the idea of Christian leadership on the foundation of the offices and roles of leaders as they provided care and instruction for the Church. These roles and offices include the position of deacons, elders, pastors, and bishops.

- The fundamental principle of all Christian leadership is servanthood, which is embodied directly in both the terminology and position of the ministry of deacons, or, as it is phrased in the Greek, *diakonoi*. The role of deacon is directly related to the role of offering selfless service to other members of the body of Christ, and it is this meaning that the term *diakonoi* captures in the Greek NT.

- The parallel of the NT ministry of deacons may be traced back to the development of the role of the assistant in the Jewish synagogue, the *hazzan*.

- Historically, the role of the deacon has been established formally in the Church, a ministry which in many traditions is referred to as the diaconate, or ministry of deacons. The NT pastoral epistles provide us with clear criteria and qualifications for both men and women to exercise their responsibility as deacons in the Church of God.

Summary of Segment 1

- The primary service of the office of deacon involved charitable works among the believers, supplying the needs of the saints, and administrating resources for the benefit of the community, especially those who were neediest and most vulnerable among them. The office, however, cannot be limited only to doing works of charity and compassion. The deacons of the NT were deeply spiritual individuals who functioned in the whole range of evangelism, teaching, and ministry.

Video Segment 1
Outline

page 336 📖 5

Appoint, therefore, for yourselves, bishops and deacons worthy of the Lord—men who are meek, truthful and tested, and are not lovers of money. For they also render to you the service of prophets and teachers. Therefore, do not despise them, for they are your honored ones, together with the prophets and teachers.
~ Didache (c. 80-140, E), 7.381. David W. Bercot, ed. *A Dictionary of Early Christian Beliefs*. Peabody, MA: Hendrickson, 1998, p. 190.

I. NT Meanings of the Term *Diakonoi* (plural for *diakonos*)

A. Word meanings for *diakonoi* (deacon, one called to serve and help)

1. References in the extra-biblical literature writings of the word meant "waiter," "servant," "steward," or "messenger."

2. The term *diakonos*, and its cognates occur many times in the New Testament, as do its synonyms. *Diakonos* and its related terms speak of the service or outward duty of a bondservant *doulous*—those who are committed to service and help.

3. *Diakonoi* was used often in the NT context, but later came to be applied to a distinct group of officers who served in the context of the Church.

4. Before the term came to refer to Christian leaders performing the work of service in the Church, it was used in a general sense of believers who were called to live as servants (*diakonoi*).

B. Broad general usage for the term *"diakonoi"* (plural for *diakonos*)

1. A waiter at meals, John 2.5, 9

2. The attendant of a king, Matt. 22.13

3. A servant of Satan, 2 Cor. 11.15

4. A servant of Christ, 2 Cor. 11.23

5. A servant of God, 2 Cor. 6.4

6. A political ruler, Rom. 13.4

7. A servant of the Church, Col. 1.24-25

C. Being a bond servant of Jesus Christ and a servant to others is a hallmark of being a Christian; to serve is a normative standard for all disciples of Jesus.

1. We are to be servants even as the Son of Man came not to be served but to serve, and give his life as a ransom for many.

   a. Matt. 20.26-28

   b. Luke 22.27

It would behoove you, as a church of God, to elect a deacon to act as the ambassador of God.
~ Ignatius (c. 105, E), 1.85., Ibid.

c. John 13.12-17

2. The greatest in the Kingdom of God is the one who is the servant of all, Mark 9.35.

3. It is in our humbling of ourselves in service that we are exalted by God.

    a. Luke 14.10-11

    b. James 4.6

4. To be a Christian is to become a servant of Jesus Christ, John 12.25-26.

5. The heart of the final judgment for disciples is understood in how a living faith demonstrated itself in feeding the hungry, welcoming strangers, visiting the sick and the prisoner, clothing the naked, and providing drink for the thirsty, Matt. 25.31-46.

D. Servanthood is foundational to any Christian understanding of leadership.

Many Christian leaders are referred to as members of this diaconate (fellowship of servants). One way to understand this is to see that every Christian leader is involved in "deaconing."

1. Timothy

    a. 1 Thess. 3.2

b.   1 Tim. 4.6

2.   Tychicus, Col. 4.7

3.   Epaphras, Col. 1.7-8

4.   Paul, 1 Cor. 3.5

5.   Messiah Jesus, Rom. 15.8

II. Origins and Development of the Office of Deacon

A. *Hazzan* of the Jewish synagogue: a possible Jewish precedent of the office of deacon

   1.   Charged with the care for the synagogue

   2.   Opened the doors, kept it clean, passed out books for reading, closed the synagogue after services, etc.

   3.   Jesus probably handed his scroll to a *hazzan* after he read the Isaiah 61 text, inaugurating his Messianic kingdom ministry, cf. Luke 4.20.

B. Historical development of the office (Philippian citation, Phil. 1.1)

And thus preaching through countries and cities, they appointed the first-fruits [of their labors], having first tested them by the Spirit, to be bishops and deacons of those who would afterwards believe.
~ Clement of Rome (c. 96, W), 1.16., Ibid.

1. By the time Paul wrote his letter to the Philippians, the term *deacon* had become a term of official use to refer to Christian leaders who assisted and served in the context of the Messianic community.

2. This text reveals the high position these leaders had in conjunction with the bishops, cf. Phil. 1.1 - Paul and Timothy, servants of Christ Jesus, to all the saints in Christ Jesus who are at Philippi, with the overseers and deacons.

3. Historical development of the concepts

   a. Deacons came to be regarded as *servants and assistants of the community*.

   b. Elders were defined as *leaders and presiders* over the affairs of the community.

   c. Bishops were seen as *guardians and overseers* over the pastors and the assemblies under their care.

You who are deacons, it is your duty to visit all those who stand in need of visitation.
~ Apostolic Constitutions (compiled c. 390, E), 7.432., Ibid.

III. Calling and Criteria for Deacons

Stephen was chosen the first deacon by the apostles.
~ Irenaeus (c. 180, E/W), 1.434., Ibid.

A. The choosing of the Seven, Acts 6.1-8

Acts 6.1-6 - Now in these days when the disciples were increasing in number, a complaint by the Hellenists arose against the Hebrews because their widows were being neglected in the daily distribution. [2] And the twelve summoned the full number of the disciples and said, "It is not right that we should give up preaching the word of God to serve tables. [3] Therefore, brothers, pick out from among you seven men of good repute, full of the Spirit and of wisdom, whom we will appoint to this duty. [4] But we will devote ourselves to prayer and to the ministry of the word." [5] And what they said pleased the whole gathering, and they chose Stephen, a man full of faith and of the Holy Spirit, and Philip, and Prochorus, and Nicanor, and Timon, and Parmenas, and Nicolaus, a proselyte of Antioch. [6] These they set before the apostles, and they prayed and laid their hands on them.

1. The selecting of the Seven may be the historical foreshadowing of a more developed structure later (see Phil. 1.1 and 1 Tim. 3.8-13).

2. Their reason for being: varied and numerous responsibilities emerging in the ever-growing Messianic community, the Church

3. Their authority: the Apostles

    a. The Apostles *authorized* the selection of godly leaders who would be set over the affairs of the just administration of resources in the body.

    b. The congregation *selected* from among their midst seven who would be set before the Apostles.

    c. The Apostles *commissioned these Seven* whom the Church had chosen, prayed for, laid their hands upon, and delegated this important ministry to them.

4. Their burden: assistance to the leaders through the division of labor

    a. The *deacons* gave themselves to the good work of caring for the Hellenist widows.

b.   The *Apostles* gave themselves over to the ministry of the Word and prayer.

B. Calling or position (or both?)

    1.   To be a deacon was an *appointed task* (cf. authorized by the Apostles, chosen by the congregation, Acts 6.6).

    2.   To be a deacon was an *office of the Church* (cf. Phil. 1.1; 1 Tim. 3.8-13).

C. References to the office of *deacons* in the NT

    1.   Phil. 1.1

        a.   The apostolic company saw themselves as "servants of Christ Jesus."

        b.   The deacons were addressed *alongside* the overseers (bishops).

    2.   1 Tim. 3.8-13

        a.   Instructions given as to specific officers within the Church

        b.   Both men and women had to be of sterling character and reputation.

1

c. Those who served well as deacons "gain a good standing for themselves and also great confidence in the faith that is in Christ Jesus," 1 Tim. 3.13.

D. Spiritual stature and maturity

   1. Standards and qualifications coincide with the same standards for bishops.

      a. Truthful

      b. *Monogamous* (husband of one wife)

      c. Not addicted to much wine

      d. If married, a loving husband and responsible steward of his children and household

   2. Standards for women (v. 11): their wives

      a. Dignified

      b. Not slanderers

      c. Sober-minded

      d. Faithful in all things

The deacons should be blameless before the face of His righteousness. They must be the servants of God and Christ, not of men. They must not be slanderers, double-tongued, or lovers of money. Rather, they must be temperate in all things - compassionate, industrious, walking according to the truth of the Lord.
~ Polycarp (c. 135, E), 1.34., Ibid.

Ordain also a deaconess who is faithful and holy for the ministrations towards women. For sometimes the bishop cannot send a deacon (who is a man) to the women, on account of unbelievers. You should therefore send a woman, a deaconness, on account of the imaginations of the bad. For we stand in need of a woman, a deaconness, for many necessities.
~ Apostolic Constitutions (c. 390, E), 7.431., Ibid.

3. Women participated in the work of the diaconate in the early Church, Rom. 16.1-2.

E. Contrast to the role of the bishop

1. No mention of their duty to provide teaching or preaching

2. The position of the *elder* was built upon the Jewish pattern of leadership outlined and practiced in the OT.

   a. The recognition of the *elders* rooted in the selection of the Lord God under Moses, Num. 11.16-17.

   b. Elders were associated with the heads of the tribes functioning as leaders and overseers, Deut. 29.10.

3. The diaconate is based rather on the *example of Messiah Jesus*, the one who came and served and cared compassionately for the needs of the broken and the poor.

   a. Matt. 20.28

   b. Phil. 2.4-8

   c. Isa. 42.1

   d. Rom. 15.8

1

IV. Authority and Functions of the Diaconate (Deacon Office)

A. Deacon as an official office within the Church, Phil. 1.1

B. General ministry of service in the community (what we can infer from Acts 6.1-6)

   1. Charitable works to the neediest members of the Christian assembly

   2. Social service and meeting needs of the body

   3. Monetary and just administration of resources for the benefit of the community, especially those who are most vulnerable

C. The ministry of deacon must be perceived as a spiritual ministry of leadership.

   The office of the deacon must never be understood or limited exclusively to doing works of charity and acts of compassion.

   1. Stephen

      a. Acts 6.5

      b. Acts 6.8-10

      c. A person of spiritual power and stature, did great signs and wonders among the people

There were present there Tertius and Pomponius, the blessed deacons who ministered to us, and who had arranged by means of a gratuity that we might be refreshed by being sent out for a few hours into a more pleasant part of the prison.
~ Passion of Perpetua and Felicitas (c. 205, W), 3.700., Ibid.

2. Philip

    a. Acts 8.5-8

    b. Acts 8.12-13

    c. Acts 21.8

    d. Philip was an evangelist, who worked signs and wonders in his powerful preaching of the good news regarding Christ, and it was he who was selected to serve as a *deacon*.

D. Implications for our understanding of the ministry of deacons

    1. A prominent and honorable position in the Church

    2. Concentrated on providing helps and service within the body

    3. Not merely limited to works of service: were competent to function in a broad range of spiritual care

    4. God gives us deacons, full of the Holy Spirit and faith, who can do the work of service in the spirit and name of Messiah Jesus, the Suffering Servant of Yahweh God.

Conclusion

» The foundations of Christian leadership involve the role of deacons, elders, pastors, and bishops. The term for deacon in the Greek is *diakonoi*.

» The commitment to serving in the Church over time grew to be associated with a specific office in the Church, focused on Christian leadership as compassionate servanthood to the needy and vulnerable in our midst, and as assistants to the Apostles and overseers.

» The ministry of the diaconate (i.e., the ministry of the deacons) is intimately associated with our Lord's own role as servant for us, and the call to care for the practical and spiritual needs of the vulnerable in the body.

Please take as much time as you have available to answer these and other questions that the video brought out. The New Testament understands the nature of Christian leadership through the lens of the life and ministry of Jesus Christ, whose ministry of care and compassion affects every notion of a Christian exercise of authority and care. Leadership is central to every role, including the foundational understanding of the role of deacon, or the *diakonoi*. Your ability to grasp Christ's understanding of the role of service to authentic leadership will be important for all you come to study throughout this module. So take the time to carefully review the key issues and insights contained in this first video teaching segment. Use Scripture to support your arguments and conclusions.

1. What are the various meanings of the term *diakonoi* in the Greek NT, and how do these meanings help us to understand the nature of the role of *deacon* in the early Church?

2. In what way is being a servant of Jesus Christ and others the "hallmark of being a Christian, the normative standard for all disciples of Jesus?" How is it that servanthood is foundational to any authentically *Christian* notion of leading others?

3. How might the concept of the *hazzan* in the Jewish synagogue be a possible precedent for understanding the office of the deacon? In what way did the role of deacon develop historically in the early Church and beyond?

4. In what sense is the record of Acts 6 an important passage to understand the nature of deacons in the early Church? What do we learn from those involved and the incident itself about how deacons functioned and who

Segue 1

Student Questions and Response

page 336 📖 *6*

they were in that setting (i.e., look at both Philip and Stephen to understand *the quality of life* the deacons of the early Church had [cf. chs. 7-8])?

5. In your opinion, is the role of deacon an *appointed task, an office of the Church*, or both? Explain your answer.

6. From the NT, what are the kinds of criteria and qualifications necessary in order to make a person a deacon? How does the *example of Jesus* affect our understanding of the diaconate and their work in the Church?

7. What is the relationship between acts of compassion and charity that deacons are to express and their own spiritual maturity and ability to minister to spiritual needs as well? Explain your answer using Stephen and Philip as examples.

8. Why is aspiring to be a deacon to care for others both a prominent and honorable position in the Church?

The Christian Leader as Deacon (*Diakonoi*)

Segment 2: Models, Equipping, and Practice

Rev. Dr. Don L. Davis

Summary of Segment 2

Three models and images comprise the role of the *deacon* in their ministry in the local assembly. These involve the image of a servant, a steward, and an assistant. Urban congregations especially need godly, available deacons, largely because of the vast number of needy, vulnerable people who make up its membership. The role of the deacon is critical for urban Christian community, both in terms of meeting practical needs as well as dividing the labor amongst the leaders to ensure that the congregation's full priorities are not neglected.

Our objective for this segment, *The Christian Leader as Deacon: Models, Equipping, and Practice*, is to enable you to see that:

- Three models and images comprise the role of the *deacon* in their ministry in the local assembly. These involve the image of a servant, a steward, and an assistant.

- The deacon is one who makes themselves and their resources available to others in order that the needs of the body may be met in every way, both physically and spiritually.

- The deacon is also a servant who has been given the charge to serve the members of the body, distributing and administering resources in a just and compassionate way.

- Finally, a deacon is charged with the role of being an assistant, one called alongside spiritual leaders to support them in the work of the ministry.

- Urban congregations especially need men and women who serve in the diaconate who have proven experience as faithful servants of Christ. Although deacons cannot be used as a substitute for the generous hospitality of the members of the body, urban churches need men and women who can effectively manage the temporal affairs of the church for the benefit of the saints.

- The ministry of *deacon* is one that carries a full assurance of good standing before God and the church, as well as great confidence in the faith. The role of the deacon is critical for the urban congregation, both in terms of meeting practical needs and dividing the labor amongst the leaders to ensure that the congregation's full priorities are not neglected.

I. Models and Analogies for the Diaconate

A. The Deacon is a *Servant*.

The deacon is first and foremost a servant, one who makes themselves and their resources available to others in order that their needs may be met, their person's protected, their situation helped, and their calling fulfilled. A deacon is one who places themselves at the disposal of Christ, the leadership, and the Church in order to meet the concrete needs of the body, and free up the leaders to do what God has called them to do.

Video Segment 2
Outline

If a poor man, or one of low birth, or a stranger, comes upon you—whether he is young or old–and there is no place for him, the deacon must find a place for him.
~ Apostolic Constitutions (compiled c. 390, E), 7.422., Ibid.

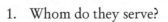

1. Whom do they serve?

    a. The Lord Jesus Christ, 1 Tim. 4.6

    b. The Church of Jesus Christ, Rom. 16.1-2

    c. The leaders of the body, Acts 6.1-6; Phil. 4.2-3

2. How do they serve?

    a. As patrons for those who serve the body, Rom. 16.1-2

    b. As administrators of the body's resources to meet practical needs, Acts 6.1-6

    c. As those who labor side by side with the leaders of the church in ministry, Phil. 4.2-3

        (1) They worked "hard in the Lord," Rom. 16.12.

        (2) They were "patrons" of the members of the body and the leaders: they waited upon the needs of those in the church, cf. Rom. 16.2.

3. What is the result of their service?

    a. 1 Tim. 3.13

    b. Matt. 25.21

1

B. The Deacon is a *Steward*.

The deacon is a steward, one who has been given a specific task to serve on behalf of others, distributing and administering resources in a just and compassionate way in order that all members of the assembly are cared for, nourished, and supplied with God's good supply.

1. Working as an agent on behalf of a master

2. Entrusted with goods and responsibility, Luke 16.10-12

3. A day of reckoning will demonstrate the significance and usefulness of that servant, Luke 19.17.

C. The Deacon is an *Assistant*.

The deacon is an assistant, a side-car helper, one who works alongside the spiritual leaders in order to free them up to do what is of most value in the work of the ministry: the ministry of the Word and prayer.

1. Works side by side with the leaders in the Gospel, Phil. 4.2-3

2. Through division of labor, a deacon's service allows the leaders to focus upon spiritual responsibilities and affairs, Acts 6.1-6

3. Helps to meet the needs of the leaders so they can fulfill God's calling upon their lives, Rom. 16.2

II. Equipping Deacons for Urban Congregations: Critical Issues

A. The kind of deacons we need

1. Urban churches need deacons who possess proven experience of spiritual depth and commitment as faithful servants of Jesus.

a. Matt. 18.4

b. Mark 9.33-35

c. Acts 20.34-35

d. Leadership must be defined in terms of sacrifice and suffering, not in terms of power and personal achievement, 2 Cor. 11.23-27.

2. Urban churches need deacons who can provide godly compassionate service and care to the members of the body.

a. *In practical ministry to the needs of those who are neglected and hurting*

(1) Urban fellowships have a host of practical needs which servants can meet if they follow through on the Lord's assignment, 1 Cor. 3.5.

(2) A deacon is a *co-worker with God* in meeting the real needs of people in their life context (cf. 1 Thess. 3.2 where "deacon" is translated "God's coworker").

b. In *visiting the sick* and those who are *shut-in*, Matt. 25.36

c. In *counseling the bereaved*, and *meeting the real life needs* of our people, (cf. a deacon is charged with meeting the most concrete needs of the assembly on behalf of the church)

    (1) The feeding of widows, Acts 6.1-6

    (2) Demonstration of a living faith in the body, James 2.14-17

d. Deacons are not a substitute for compassionate hospitality and generosity of the members; rather, they are charged with *managing the temporal affairs of the church on behalf of the leaders for the benefit of the saints.*

e. The biblical witness is clear.

    (1) 1 John 3.16-18

    (2) Deut. 15.7

    (3) 2 Cor. 8.9

    (4) Heb. 13.16

3. Urban churches need deacons who will give credible and dignified monetary and administrative help to the affairs of the church.

a. Just distribution of our goods to those who need care

    (1) Prov. 19.17

    (2) Prov. 28.27

    (3) Prov. 22.9

b. Practical counsel and care to our members in their times of need, (in the spirit of the Good Samaritan), Luke 10.29-37

c. Integrity in the affairs of the church which reflects directly on the person and work of our Lord Jesus Christ

       (1) 2 Cor. 4.1-2

       (2) 2 Cor. 2.17

       (3) 1 Thess. 2.3-5

B. How do we find and equip these kind of deacons for our churches?

    1. Pray and ask God to send us servants after his own heart.

    2. Announce opportunities to serve to see who will emerge as servants of the body, Phil. 2.25-30.

    3. Look for those whose lives and ministries display these characteristics, and challenge them to join the work, Phil. 2.19-22.

    4. Challenge qualified individuals to serve as to Christ, John 12.26.

III. Principles and Practice of the Deacon's Office

A. Recognize the importance of the office of deacon: *no church can function effectively without these choice servants of God.*

    1. *No leader can meet everyone's needs:* They meet the practical needs of those whose conditions are ignored because of overburdened leaders.

2. *Spiritual priorities must be kept for a church to remain strong:* The leaders are freed up to concentrate on their spiritual office under God.

B. We should encourage the growing believer to aspire to this office, 1 Tim. 3.13.

   1. Good standing in the church

   2. Great confidence in the faith that is in Christ Jesus

   3. The diaconate is a ministry which resonates with the very person and work of Jesus Christ, Phil. 2.5-8.

C. Equip growing Christians to consider making themselves available for the diaconate.

   1. Challenge them to the dignity and significance of the office.

   2. Set up mechanisms to intern those who are willing to learn how to serve the members of the body.

   3. Put up for candidacy those who show themselves faithful.

D. Only appoint or elect to the diaconate men and women of proven character.

   1. They must be recognized in the body as true servants, cf. Acts 6.3.

2. They must have a record of being faithful stewards, 1 Cor. 4.1-2.

3. They must work well with the elders and pastors as submissive helpers.

E. Honor them in the midst of the community publicly and privately.

IV. The Blessing, Benefit, and Reward of the Christian Leader as Deacon

A. The assurance of doing a significant and critical ministry in the midst of the church, 1 Tim. 3.13

B. A good standing before God, one's leaders, and the Church of Jesus, 1 Tim. 3.13

C. A great confidence in the faith that is in Christ Jesus, 1 Tim. 3.13

D. *A growing conformity to the person and work of Jesus Christ*

1. John 13.4-5

2. Matt. 20.28

3. Luke 22.27

E. The promise of Messiah Jesus to come and serve them, even as they faithfully serve others

1. Luke 12.37

2. John 12.26

Conclusion

» The New Testament outlines the role of the deacon in terms of three interrelated images, the role of a servant, a steward, and an assistant.

» Because of the special needs of the urban church setting, this leadership role is critical for healthy Christian community.

» We must do all we can to recruit godly men and women who can meet practical needs in our communities, while, at the same time, work and cooperate with our other leaders to ensure that our urban congregations are fully protected and established.

The following questions were designed to help you review the material in the second video segment. In this portion of the lesson we covered the three integrated models and images that make up the ministry of *deacons* in the local assembly. The *deacon* functions first and foremost as a servant to the people of God, as a steward of the body's resources for the sake of just and compassionate distribution, and as an assistant to the spiritual leadership of the church. Urban congregations will always require this important office, especially so since the members of the urban community possess a number of tangible needs which will require our ongoing and compassionate attention. Review carefully the teaching in connection to the role of the *deacon* in the urban church, and discuss with your fellow students the ramifications of this important ministry in the city. Refer to the examples in the NT wherever possible.

1. Describe the way in which we may conceive the ministry and function of the *deacon* through the image of a servant. Whom do deacons serve, how do they serve, and what ought to be the result of their service in the church?

Segue 2

Student Questions and Response

2. In what sense can we understand the role of the deacon as a steward of the resources of God for the well being of the members of the body? What are the major issues associated with deacons working as an agent of Christ, being entrusted with goods and responsibility and the wise management of those goods for the sake of the body?

3. What is the relationship of the deacon to the spiritual leaders, and how does the role of assistant help us to better understand it? How is division of labor to function in the local church in order that deacons can learn to support and work side by side with the other spiritual leaders for the well being of its members?

4. Because of the distinctive nature of the challenges and needs of urban communities, what are the kinds of people we should seek to recruit and train to be deacons in our churches? What are some of the kinds of spiritual activities we should expect deacons who serve in urban churches to be capable of?

5. Finish the following statement: "In light of the shortage of godly leaders in the city, the one thing that we can do to find and equip godly deacons for our churches is . . ."

6. Why should we encourage growing believers who are aspiring to care for others to consider the work of the diaconate? Why, however, should we only appoint or elect to the diaconate people of proven character?

7. Describe the kinds of blessings, benefits, and rewards associated with the faithful fulfillment of the office of the deacon? What is the promise of Jesus himself to the one who comes and serves his people with integrity and trustworthiness?

CONNECTION

Summary of Key Concepts

page 336 ☐ 7

This lesson focuses upon our understanding of the foundation of Christian leadership, understood first of all through the lens of the humility and self-sacrifice of our Lord Jesus in his incarnation (i.e., his descent from the realms of glory to live among us). The richness of Christ's example is clearly outlined in the biblical offices and functions of leadership in the Church in the roles of deacon, elder, pastor, and bishop. Listed below are some of the key insights covered in our lesson, with a particular emphasis on the ministry of deacons. Review these truths carefully, especially with an eye to see how the role of deacons is foundational in our understanding of Christian leadership.

- The New Testament underscores the idea of Christian leadership on the foundation of the offices and roles of leaders as they provided care and instruction for the Church. These roles and offices include the position of deacons, elders, pastors, and bishops.

- The fundamental principle of all Christian leadership is servanthood, which is embodied directly in both the terminology and position of the ministry of deacons, or, as it is phrased in the Greek, *diakonoi*. The role of deacon is directly related to the role of offering selfless service to other members of the body of Christ, and it is this meaning that the term *diakonoi* captures in the Greek NT.

- The parallel of the NT ministry of deacons may be traced back to the development of the role of the assistant in the Jewish synagogue, the *hazzan*.

- Historically, the role of the deacon has been established formally in the Church, a ministry which in many traditions is referred to as the diaconate, or ministry of deacons. The NT pastoral epistles provide us with clear criteria and qualifications for both men and women to exercise their responsibility as deacons in the Church of God.

- The primary service of the office of deacon involved charitable works among the believers, supplying the needs of the saints, and administrating resources for the benefit of the community, especially those who were neediest and most vulnerable among them. The office, however, cannot be limited only to doing works of charity and compassion. The deacons of the NT were deeply spiritual individuals who functioned in the whole range of evangelism, teaching, and ministry.

- Three models and images comprise the role of the *deacon* in their ministry in the local assembly. These involve the image of a servant, a steward, and an assistant.

- The deacon is one who makes themself and their resources available to others in order that the needs of the body may be met in every way, both physically and spiritually.

➻ The deacon is also a servant who has been given the charge to serve the members of the body, distributing and administering resources in a just and compassionate way.

➻ Finally, a deacon is charged with the role of being an assistant, one called alongside spiritual leaders to support them in the work of the ministry.

➻ Urban congregations especially need men and women who serve in the diaconate who have proven experience as faithful servants of Christ. Although deacons cannot be used as a substitute for the generous hospitality of the members of the body, urban churches need men and women who can effectively manage the temporal affairs of the church for the benefit of the saints.

➻ The ministry of *deacon* is one that carries a full assurance of good standing before God and the Church, as well as great confidence in the faith. The role of the deacon is critical for the urban congregation, both in terms of meeting practical needs and dividing the labor amongst the leaders to ensure that the congregation's full priorities are not neglected.

Student Application and Implications

page 337 📖 *8*

Now is the time for you to discuss with your fellow students your questions about *The Christian Leader as Deacon (Diakonoi)*. In many ways, the focus of the role of deacon on servanthood is a principle that cuts across the entire spectrum of Christian leadership. Indeed, servanthood is the underlying insight of exercising authority as a Christian. Now is the time for you to explore the ramifications of this principle for your life and ministry in the Church. What are some of the issues and questions that have come to mind as you have meditated on the ministry of the diaconate covered in this lesson? Probe these issues and questions together with your fellow students. The questions below may help you form your own, more specific and critical questions about this important aspect of Christian leadership.

* Why must we pay careful attention to the example of Christ in all so-called inquiries into the principles and practices of Christian leadership? What is the central aspect of Jesus' life and ministry that helps to define its meaning? Explain your answer.

* In what sense do the roles and offices (i.e., deacons, elders, pastors, and bishops) provide us with a ready understanding of the *foundations* of Christian leadership?

* Why do you think the NT in Acts 6 gives us such a tangible picture of the role of deacons in the early Church? Why do all vital churches require this kind of helpful, tangible, supportive leadership?

* Have you ever been in a position to represent the body through your own ministry of serving the tangible needs of the saints, and administrating resources for the benefit of the community? How did it go–was it enjoyable, were you successful, and what did you learn about yourself and others?

* What has been the greatest obstacle in your ministry to caring for the neediest and most vulnerable in your church? How is this ministry perceived by other leaders in your fellowship?

* How is the ministry of the deacons handled in your church? Have you ever been asked to serve in that capacity, or have you volunteered to do so?

* How does your current understanding of the role of the deacon square with the three biblical images covered in our lesson, i.e., the deacon as servant, as steward, and as assistant? Which of these images helps you envision the role in the most clear way?

* Why will planting and growing churches among the poor in the city demand people who can serve in the diaconate who have proven experience as faithful servants of Christ? Do you sense any call to serve in this way? Explain.

* Of all of the excuses one might give for *not serving* as a deacon, which do you believe is the most common, and why? How might we overcome the tendency for selfishness and raise up a new generation of men and women dedicated to meeting the practical, spiritual, and physical needs of the body through the diaconate?

CASE STUDIES

The Board of Deacons and Our Freedom in Christ

In many Baptist churches, the Board of Deacons is the group where the significant issues of the church are considered and decided. From the accountability of the pastor to the disbursements of the budget, the Deacons are invested with the full authority to lead and govern the affairs of the body. While many churches use different names for different positions, some traditions use the Board of Deacons in the same way that others view the Board of Elders. In both cases, the final decisions

page 338 📖 *9*

concerning the physical, social, and economic welfare of the body is handled in their context. In your judgment, based upon what you have studied so far, what are the specific kinds of leadership roles and responsibilities the ministry of deacons should concentrate upon? How does the concept of the Board of Deacons as *authoritative* council square with Scripture? How free are we in our various traditions to pour new meanings into the roles of deacons, elders, pastors, and bishops? Explain your answer.

They Do All the Dirty Work

In many traditions of the Church, the role of deacons has been dramatically underestimated and reduced. Rather than using biblical figures such as Stephen and Philip as models of what the role of deacons ought to be, many have relegated the role to the most lowly position of leadership. In many churches, deacons play no greater role than mere janitors, given virtually no authority to disburse goods for the sake of the needy (as in the case of Acts 6), or allowed to function alongside the spiritual leaders of the body in evangelism and instruction (as in the cases of Acts 7 and 8). Why have so many churches relegated the important role of the ministry of deacons to essentially doing the "dirty work" of leadership? Is there any such thing as "dirty work" in the Church? In what way ought deacons be included in the ongoing decision-making and ministry of the Church today?

A Calling or a Job?

Much of today's ministry is based upon *the desires and inclinations of the volunteer*. Perhaps no era of the Church has been so oriented around the *spare time of available members* for ministry as this one. Most deacons serve only for a limited term, and sometimes they are even forbidden from reapplying for the ministry for a period of time. While this is meant to allow for many to serve in leadership roles in the Church, in urban churches it effectively can make it difficult to have enough qualified leaders to serve. Is the ministry of *deacons* a calling for those who are especially gifted and ambitious to serve, or is it a job that needs to be fulfilled in the Church? Is the ministry of deacons, perhaps, a combination of both, a calling and a formal position? How long should deacons be able to serve in the local church setting? Who is responsible to select and train them?

The Necessary First Step

In many urban churches, the role of the deacon is perceived as the bottom but necessary rung of the spiritual leadership ladder. In other words, those who aspire to lead in more substantive and authoritative roles in the Church are directed, first of all, to the ministry of the diaconate. It is reasoned that if a prospective leader cannot be placed in a position to serve selflessly the members of the body in the most menial and humble tasks, such a person is immediately disqualified from exercising leadership in the body. Many have found this system to be useful and effective in training emerging leaders in how to submit and serve others. Others, on the other hand, have found this process to be demeaning and insulting; it has transformed the ministry of deacons to a kind of "probation for prospective leaders," making it something to "graduate from" rather than to fulfill and receive "a good standing and great confidence in that faith that is in Christ Jesus (cf. 1 Tim. 3.13)." What do you think of utilizing the role of the deacon as a "minister-in-training" capacity? Does this demean or honor the important ministry of deacons in the Church?

The New Testament underscores the foundation of Christian leadership in the life and ministry of Christ, expressed in the Church through the positions of deacons, elders, pastors, and bishops. The fundamental principle of all Christian leadership is servanthood, which is embodied directly in both the terminology and position of the ministry of deacons, or, as it is phrased in the Greek, *diakonoi*. Tracing back to the role of the assistant in the Jewish synagogue, the *hazzan*, the office arose in the Church because of the need for a more formal role of aid in the Church. The NT pastoral epistles provide us with clear criteria and qualifications for both men and women to exercise their responsibility as deacons in the Church of God.

Restatement of the Lesson's Thesis

While the primary service of deacons involved supplying the needs of the saints, and administrating resources for the benefit of the community, they also were deeply spiritual individuals who functioned in the whole range of evangelism, teaching, and ministry. Three models and images comprise the role of the *deacon* in their ministry in the local assembly. These involve the image of a servant, a steward, and an assistant. Urban congregations especially need men and women who serve in the diaconate who have proven experience as faithful servants of Christ. Although deacons cannot be used as a substitute for the generous hospitality of the members of the body, urban churches need men and women who can effectively manage the temporal affairs of the Church for the benefit of the saints.

Resources and Bibliographies

If you are interested in pursuing some of the ideas of *The Christian Leader as Deacon (Diakonoi)*, you might want to give these books a try:

Bilezikian, Gilbert. *Community 101*. Grand Rapids: Zondervan, 1997.

Dresselhaus, Richard. *The Deacon and His Ministry*. Springfield, MO: Gospel Publishing House, 1977.

Getz, Gene A. *The Measure of a Man*. Ventura, CA: Regal Books, 1974.

Strauch, Alexander. *The New Testament Deacon: The Church's Minister of Mercy*. Colorado Springs, CO: Lewis and Roth Publishers, 1992.

------. *The New Testament Deacon Study Guide*. Colorado Springs, CO: Lewis and Roth Publishers, 1992.

Tan, Siang-Yang. *Full Service: Moving from Self-serve Christianity to Total Servanthood*. Baker Books, 2006.

Webb, Henry. *Deacons: Servant Models in the Church*. 2nd ed. Nashville: Broadman and Holman Publishers, 2001.

Ministry Connections

Whether or not you have been called to the specific ministry of the diaconate, Christ desires that we learn what it means to be a servant, to be willing to take the lowest role in order that others may be blessed, encouraged, and equipped. What is certain is that your ministry in Christ, however he leads you, will demand this same level of selfless sacrifice and effort. This is the part of the lesson designed to give you an opportunity to seek to make practical connection of the truths you have just learned to your own walk and ministry. Of all the principles you have learned in this lesson, which one seems to stay with you, which one is the Holy Spirit leading you to both ponder and apply throughout this upcoming week? Furthermore, what particular questions come to mind as you think about your understanding of Christ's example, and how that should impact your own leadership and ministry? Spend time this week prayerfully meditating upon these questions, and respond promptly to the Spirit's leading as he reveals to you his will.

Counseling and Prayer

The role of the Holy Spirit in learning the mind and wisdom of God is central in all theological investigation. Every student of Scripture needs the illumination and filling of the Spirit in order to understand God's will (cf. 1 Cor. 2.9-1). During each lesson, therefore, you will be encouraged to pray about the things you are learning, and for your fellow students and instructor. As you learn and apply these insights in a spirit of dependence and prayer upon the Holy Spirit, God will grant you the wisdom and courage you need to make these truths not merely bits of information you remember, but living truth that you embody and obey (James 1.5). Pray that the Holy Spirit will give you insight into the meaning and expression of living as Christ's servant, and that he will lead you regarding your understanding and practice of the role of the deacon in the body. God will grant you insight as you apply these truths in dependence upon the Holy Spirit.

ASSIGNMENTS

1

Mark 9.35-37

Scripture Memory

To prepare for class, please visit *www.tumi.org/books* to find next week's reading assignment, or ask your mentor.

Reading Assignment

An important element of your study of this module involves your own personal study and fulfillment of the assignments included lesson by lesson in each module. Starting in your next class session, you will be given a *quiz* on the content of the materials covered on the video segment and outline. The purpose of this test is neither to intimidate nor embarrass you; rather, its purpose is to encourage you to *remember the critical insights covered in the lesson*. In order to do well on the quiz, you will need to make certain that you spend adequate study time covering your notes from this lesson, especially focusing on the main ideas included in the teaching outline.

Other Assignments

page 338 📖 *10*

Also, please ensure that you read the assigned textbook pages, and then summarize your reading with no more than a paragraph or two for each. In this summary please give your best understanding of what you think the main point was in each of the readings. Do not be overly concerned about giving detail; simply write out what you consider to be the main point discussed in that section of the book. Please bring these summaries to class next week. (Please see the *Reading Completion Sheet* at the end of this lesson.)

Looking Forward to the Next Lesson

Our lesson underscored the foundation of Christian leadership in the life and ministry of Christ, expressed in the Church through the positions of deacons, elders, pastors, and bishops. We concentrated on the first foundation of Christian leadership of servanthood, that role which is embodied directly in both the terminology and position of the ministry of deacons, or, as it is phrased in the Greek, *diakonoi*. As servants, stewards, and assistants, the deacons are not only involved in supplying the needs of the saints, and administrating resources for the benefit of the community, but they also contribute to the work of evangelism, teaching, and ministry.

In our next lesson we will explore "The Christian Leader as Elder (*Presbyteroi*)," tracing the notion of *elder* from its OT root in the tribal system and synagogue, to the Sanhedrin and then to the NT Church. We will consider the calling and criteria of the role of elder, as well as its function as an overseer, a father or parent, a colleague or team member, and finally a representative. Like deacons, we will see the significance of the role of elders in leading and feeding the body of Christ in the heart of our urban neighborhoods.

1

Name _____

Date _____

For each assigned reading, write a brief summary (one or two paragraphs) of the author's main point. (For additional readings, use the back of this sheet.)

Reading 1

Title and Author: _____ Pages _____

Reading 2

Title and Author: _____ Pages _____

The Christian Leader as Elder
Presbyteroi

page 341 📖 *1*

Lesson Objectives

Welcome in the strong name of Jesus Christ! After your reading, study, discussion, and application of the materials in this lesson, you will be able to:

* Recite the meaning of the Greek term *presbyteros* as the translated term for elder in the NT.

* Narrate the evolution of the concept *elder* from its OT roots in the tribal system of Israel, the development of the concept in the synagogue, to its usage as an official position in the Sanhedrin, and finally to the NT Church.

* Provide a clear record of the elements involved in the calling of NT elders, as well as the biblical qualifications associated with becoming an elder in the Church.

* Lay out critically the biblical authority and responsibilities connected with the faithful fulfillment of the office of serving as an elder in the body, and speak of the implications of this authority and responsibility in the affairs of Christian community today.

* Recreate from memory the key analogies given in Scripture of the *Christian Leader as Elder (Presbyter)*: the Christian elder is imaged as an overseer of the affairs of the community, a father or parent who heads the spiritual family of the Lord, a colleague or team member who contributes to the council of elders in their role as leaders of the congregation, and finally as a representative both of the Lord and the people in the community.

* Articulate the major assumptions and issues needed to understand the significance of elders for urban congregations, and suggest practical ways in which we can both select and equip elders for our churches in the city.

Devotion

Elders Called to Shepherd

page 343 📖 *2*

1 Pet. 5.1-4 - So I exhort the elders among you, as a fellow elder and a witness of the sufferings of Christ, as well as a partaker in the glory that is going to be revealed: [2] shepherd the flock of God that is among you, exercising oversight, not under compulsion, but willingly, as God would have you; not for shameful gain, but eagerly; [3] not domineering over those in your charge, but being examples to the flock. [4] And when the chief Shepherd appears, you will receive the unfading crown of glory.

In this text, the Apostle Peter addresses his exhortation to the elders among the believers, those who were charged with the responsibility to care for the people of God. He exhorts the elders as a "fellow elder and a witness of the sufferings of Christ," i.e., one who was personally called by the Lord himself to "feed his sheep" and thus show in his actions that his love for the risen Savior was authentic (cf. John 21.15-17). For the Christian leader, the demonstration of their deep love for Jesus is shown concretely in their ability to care with compassion and wisdom for the little sheep of Christ. Peter also anchors his exhortation on the fact that he, too, is a "partaker in the glory that is going to be revealed." His testimony is solid and sure, based on his identity in Christ and the calling he has to both lead God's people and inherit the coming glory of the Kingdom. What is the word for elder that invokes such a rich and solemn introduction?

The answer is simple and clear. Elders are to "shepherd the flock of God that is among them." Here is a clear example of the overlap of the terminology of Christian leadership that is recognized by so many scholars. Elders are called to *shepherd the flock*, to be pastoral, guarding and protecting, leading and feeding, caring for and nurturing these dear saints who belong to Christ. To be God's leader is to have a relationship with him *through his people*. To put this another way, Christian leadership is bound to *the context of community*; God's flock is the concern that Christian leaders attend and address. The livelihood of the people of God is the sole concern of Christian leadership.

This connecting of Christian leadership to the context of the people of God ought to radically change our perspective of the nature of authentic Christian leadership. Leadership through the Christian grid can never be construed to be extraordinary personal achievement, project accomplishment, or acquiring goods or fame. The context of Christian leadership is the body of Christ, and superb leadership is to exercise oversight over them for their edification, not because you are compelled to by outward accountability, but willingly even as God would have us do. This care and oversight is not motivated by greed or for the purpose of shameful gain, but to be done with an eager spirit. This oversight neither dominates nor domineers, but leads those under its charge by the power of personal example and modeling. This rule, according to Peter, represents the heart and soul of what it means to shepherd God's people, even as our Lord functions as the Great Shepherd. For, as Peter affirms in 1 Peter 2.25, "you were straying like sheep, but have now returned to the Shepherd and Overseer of your souls." We emulate our Lord, even in our shepherding.

And what is the promise given to those elders who fulfill their task in the manner prescribed by God? Peter ends our passage with the amazing claim: "And when the Chief Shepherd appears, you will receive the unfading crown of glory." For those elders who serve Christ faithfully by shepherding his flock, to them, when the *Chief Shepherd*, our Lord Jesus himself, appears, then from him (by implication) will the faithful elders receive the "*unfading crown of glory.*" What an amazing statement: Jesus himself, the Chief Shepherd will confer on his faithful elders the unfading crown for cherishing his little ones. Could there be a better, more higher, or more glorious motive for serving the people of God from the heart, according to the standard laid out by the great apostle Peter, our fellow elder in shepherding the people of God?

In a day when leadership is seen as extraordinary giftedness for personal success, can we recapture the vision of Christian leadership as selfless sacrifice on behalf of the people of God, as shepherding the flock of God? This is our challenge, and our privilege–"shepherd the flock of God that is among you." May God grant us the heart of a true elder, one whose whole life is spent protecting and caring for the little ones of Christ.

Nicene Creed and Prayer

After reciting and/or singing the Nicene Creed (located in the Appendix), pray the following prayer:

Almighty Father, give to these your servants grace and power to fulfill their ministry. Make them faithful to serve, ready to teach, constant in advancing your gospel; and grant that, always having full assurance of faith, abounding in hope, and being rooted and grounded in love, they may continue strong and steadfast in your Son Jesus Christ our Lord; to whom, with you and your Holy Spirit, belong glory and honor, worship and praise, now and for ever.

~ George Appleton, ed. **The Oxford Book of Prayer**.
Oxford/New York: Oxford University Press, 1988. p. 218

Put away your notes, gather up your thoughts and reflections, and take the quiz for Lesson 1, *The Christian Leader as Deacon (Diakonoi)*.

Quiz

. . . .

Review with a partner, write out and/or recite the text for last class session's assigned memory verse: Mark 9.35-37.

Scripture Memorization Review

. . . .

Turn in your summary of the reading assignment for last week, that is, your brief response and explanation of the main points that the authors were seeking to make in the assigned reading (Reading Completion Sheet).

Assignments Due

. . . .

CONTACT

Led by Elders - a Lost Reality?

Because of the breakdown of so many families, we have generations of people who have never seen or witnessed the reality of leadership in their families by *elders*, or even by the elderly. In a day when so many have grown up with virtually no input from anyone in their family who is older, and who have been trained to see their grandparents as "old people," the elderly are not perceived by them as useful, wise, and resourceful *let alone* authoritative leaders exercising oversight over their lives. For many even the thought of being led by *elders* is *distasteful* and seen as both interference and a form of unnecessary complication in their lives. How are we to communicate biblical concepts such as leadership by elders when whole generations of people today have no tangible or concrete experience with being led at all, by elders or anyone else?

Young People Rule the World

What is immediately noticeable in the world today, most visibly seen in the marketing strategies of worldwide commerce, is that young people rule the world. In many endeavors, youth is the defining symbol of life, vitality, and excitement, whereas age is associated with the old, the discarded, and the unnecessary. While many non-Western cultures still prize the role of elders in their society and family, most Western cultures still unfortunately associate the elderly or aged with weakness, fragility, and even senility. Christian cultures have fallen prey to the same kind of unbiblical thinking; dynamism and growth are all too often associated with the young, hip, and contemporary generation, whereas those who are older can easily be seen as "those who have had their day," those who should move aside and let the next generation "take over." How are we in our Christian communities to answer the uncritical baptism of all things young as good, vital, and dynamic?

Your Day is Past and Gone

 Perhaps no greater sign of the confused thinking of our day is more evident than in the phenomena of the nursing home in modern American society. Like clockwork, nearly without notice or statement, when family members reach a certain age, when they can no longer be conveniently cared for in the home, we place our elderly in nursing homes for the duration of their lives and care. Make no mistake; millions in such care need the kind of daily, even hourly attention that adequate care homes provide, and thousands upon thousands of families who would be ill-equipped to care for their aging parents and grandparents have found these homes to be a blessing from God. This fact is to be cherished by all, and this discussion excludes these situations altogether. What is being addressed, however, is the idea that with the elderly and elders in general, unless they are extraordinary, they are easily discarded, isolated, and ignored. With the entire biblical ethic of leadership development rooted and biased in a dependence on *elders,* what are some of the issues that we as 21st century disciples must struggle with in order to overcome these harmful tendencies to ignore and overlook the asset of the elders in our midst?

 CONTENT

The Christian Leader as Elder (*Presbyteroi*)

Segment 1: Definition and Overview

Rev. Dr. Don L. Davis

Summary of Segment 1

The term translated *elder* in our NT is the Greek term *presbyteros*, meaning "overseer" or "elder." The Greek words for leadership in the NT, *presbyteros* and *episkopos*, are virtually synonymous. The NT concept of elder evolved from its OT usage, seen in the tribal system of Israel, the practices of the Jewish synagogue, the positions in the Sanhedrin, and finally to the NT Church. The NT provides clear records of the calling of elders, who were either appointed by the apostles or their representatives, or commissioned within the Christian community. The Pastoral epistles lay out clear spiritual qualifications for elders, including being spiritually mature leaders able to preach and teach, charged with the responsibility to guard and shepherd God's flock.

Our objective for this segment, *The Christian Leader as Elder: Definition and Overview*, is to enable you to see that:

- The term translated *elder* in our NT is the Greek term *presbyteros*, meaning "overseer" or "elder."

- Many scholars contend that the Greek words for leadership in the NT *presbyteros* and *episkopos* refer to the same office in the NT Church, with the main difference being that *episkopos* is used only in the Gentile church.

- The NT concept of *elder* can be seen to have evolved and been built upon the concept of elder in the OT, with its roots in the tribal system of Israel, which developed further in the practices of the Jewish synagogue, as well as its usage as an official position in the Sanhedrin, and finally to the NT Church.

- The NT provides clear records of the calling of elders, who were either appointed by the apostles or their representatives, or commissioned within the Christian community. The Pastoral epistles lay out clear spiritual qualifications for elders, including being spiritually mature leaders able to preach and teach, charging them with the responsibility to guard and shepherd God's flock.

- According to the injunctions of the NT, elders presided over the spiritual and social affairs of the Church, gave pastoral care to its members, and served as role models for the disciples gathered in community.

- Elders must be people of recognized spiritual maturity and gifting, providing oversight to the doctrine, affairs, and governance of the Church.

Video Segment 1
Outline

Bishop and
Presbyter are Used
Interchangeably
by Church Fathers
*Our sin will not be
small if we eject from
oversight [or, from
the episcopate]
those who have
blamelessly and holily
fulfilled its duties.
Blessed are those
presbyters who have
obtained a fruitful
and perfect
departure, having
finished their course
before now.*
~ Clement of Rome
(c. 96, W), 1.17.,
David W. Bercot, ed.
*A Dictionary of Early
Christian Beliefs*.
Peabody, MA:
Hendrickson
Publishers, 1998.
p. 157.

I. New Testament Meanings of the Term *Presbyteros* ("Elder"; plural *presbyteroi*)

A. Word meanings for *presbyteros* (many scholars contend that the Greek words for leadership *presbyteros* and *episkopos* refer to the same office in the NT Church, with the only difference being that *episkopos* is only used in Gentile churches)

1. "Elder" (i.e., one of prominence and maturity)

2. "Overseer" (i.e., one charged with rulership)

3. "Ruler," (i.e., one who presides)

B. Relationship to other NT leadership terms

1. Virtually synonymous in the early Church with "bishops"

   a. Acts 20.17, 28

   b. Overseers to the flock

2. Also resonates with NT notion of shepherding and pastoring

   a. 1 Pet. 5.1-4, Peter refers to himself both as *elder* and *shepherd*.

   b. 1 Pet. 2.25, Peter refers to Jesus as both *Shepherd* and *Bishop* of our souls.

II. Origins and Development of the Office of Elder

Person who, by virtue of position in the family, clan, or tribe; or by reason of personality, prowess, stature, or influence; or through a process of appointment and ordination, exercised leadership and judicial functions in both religious and secular spheres in the ancient world, both among biblical and nonbiblical peoples. The roots of the development of the presbytery (group of elders) in the NT and post-apostolic church originate in Judaism in the OT, though the figure of the elder or groups of elders can also be found in the world surrounding ancient Israel and in the Greco-Roman world of the NT period.

~ **Tyndale Bible Dictionary**. Wheaton, IL: Tyndale House Publishers, 2001., p. 414.

A. Elders prominent in the Jewish political tribal system

1. The elder concept has a Jewish precedent: tribal system.

   a. Tribes made up of clans, and these clans consisted of large, extended family units

   b. The age and prominence of the ruler of a clan, with its family units, headed in a patriarchal culture by a man who functioned as the ruler or father of the clan.

   c. Appointment associated with wisdom, maturity, and headship

2. Elder in the OT era

   a. One considered by both God and the community to be a leader among and on behalf of Yahweh's people

Paul himself has laid the foundation, that is, the foundation of the church. And he has put us in trust of the law–ordaining deacons, presbyters, and bishops.
~ Disputation of Archelaus and Manes (c. 320, E), 6.229., Ibid., p. 156.

b. An administrator of justice: handled local affairs and judged matters of relationship and societal action

c. Had spiritual importance

(1) It was the elders that Moses instructed concerning the keeping of the first Passover, Exod. 12.21-22.

(2) Chosen as representatives to administer justice when Moses divided up his labor, Exod. 18.13-23

(3) God commanded Moses to select 70 men from among the elders of the people of Israel to help him lead the people, Num. 11.16-17.

(4) Num. 11.24

3. Criteria for Jewish elders

a. Usually a person of advanced years

b. A person of prominence and reputation within his representative clan

c. A person who functions as a colleague and partner with other leaders

d. A person of significant authority to represent and rule within the community: to act as judges who applied the law of God at the gate, the place where disputes and trials were settled

(1) Deut. 19.12

(2) Deut. 21.19

(3) Deut. 22.15

(4) Deut. 25.7-10

B. Church as the New Israel: elder as continuance of leader concept

1. The early Church was regarded as the "new Israel."

   a. Matt. 21.43

   b. Gal. 6.16

   c. 1 Pet. 2.9

   d. Gal. 3.29

2. Connected to the council of elders that function locally in the synagogue and nationally in the Jewish Sanhedrin (cf. Acts 11.30; 15.2-6, 22-23; 16.4; 21.18)

   a. Based in Jerusalem

   b. Made decisions for the Messianic community everywhere (cf. The Jerusalem Council, Acts 15)

3. NT view of elders resonates and is founded upon the historic Jewish view of leadership of the tribes

III. Calling and Criteria for Elders

A. Calling: elders were selected either by *appointment* or *ordination from within the community.*

   1. Appointed by *Apostles and their representatives*

      a. Paul and Barnabas received famine relief from the Antioch church to give to the elders of the Judean churches, Acts 11.27-30.

      b. On their first journey, Paul and Barnabas appointed elders in every city, Acts 14.23.

   2. Elected from within the communities themselves

      a. While we are not told how the elders in Jerusalem were elected, we can probably be confident that they were appointed according to Jewish precedent.

      b. Their age, place in the community, and maturity probably were the key factors.

      c. The culture maintained a deep respect for age: "presbyter" (elder) was taken from its use by the Jews to represent their leadership.

2

3. Implications

    a. The Jewish precedent of the tribal and synagogue system informed Christian use of the idea of elder.

    b. In this understanding, there can be no sense of self-appointment to eldership: it is a position of the *head of a family*, recognized as such among the various families making up the clan.

    c. Recognized and proven character and leadership

B. Spiritual qualifications of spiritual eldership

    1. 1 Tim. 5.17-19

        a. Are worthy of double honor, especially those who preach and teach

        b. Should be honored *spiritually* and *with resources*

        c. No arbitrary rejection of the elders can be allowed.

    2. Titus 1.5-9 - This is why I left you in Crete, so that you might put what remained into order, and *appoint elders in every town as I directed you*— [6] if anyone is above reproach, the husband of one wife, and his children are believers and not open to the charge of debauchery or insubordination. [7] For an overseer, as God's steward, must be above reproach. He must not be arrogant or quick-tempered or a drunkard or

You will tell those who preside over the church to direct their ways in righteousness, so that they will receive in full the promises with great glory.
~ Hermas (c. 150, W), 2.14., Ibid.

violent or greedy for gain, [8] but hospitable, a lover of good, self-controlled, upright, holy, and disciplined. [9] He must hold firm to the trustworthy word as taught, so that he may be able to give instruction in sound doctrine and also to rebuke those who contradict it.

a. Appointed on the basis of *apostolic authority*

b. Had to be persons of *sterling character and reputation*

c. Place as *elder* is made *synonymous with "overseer,"* (compare verse 5 with verse 7)

3. Acts 20.17, 28

a. Were called as elders to *guard the flock* (synonymous with the pastoral role)

b. The Holy Spirit *made them overseers* to care for the Church.

c. This Church has been *purchased with the very blood of God*, Jesus Christ.

C. Implications for the elder's role in the body

2

How Old Was an Elder?

page 344 📖 *3*

"Elders" were highly respected in Greek gymnasia and exercised a ruling function in synagogues and churches, as they had in communities in the Old Testament. Because Timothy joined Paul before A.D. 50 (Acts 16.1–3; men entered adulthood around puberty, so Timothy may have been in his midteens) and Paul is writing in the early sixties, Timothy is at least in his mid-twenties and could well be in his early or mid-thirties; this term for "youth" (KJV) could apply up to the age of forty, although it usually applied especially to someone under twenty-nine. But those who were not elders were often considered inappropriate for leadership positions (cf. 1 Sam 17.33), and many offices even in Judaism became available only at age forty. Most stories about the appointment of young men were made up later to extol prodigies (postbiblical stories about Daniel, Solomon or several rabbis); Timothy's appointment was thus a rare privilege in his culture. But even though Timothy is younger than the elders he is advising, he is to take the role of the mature leader and act as an example for the community. Teachers normally asked disciples to imitate them, and in so doing took the role of father figures.

~ Craig S. Keener. **The IVP Bible Background Commentary: New Testament** (1 Tim. 4.12). (electronic ed.). Downers Grove, IL: InterVarsity Press, 1993.

1. The concept developed in sync with OT understanding.

    a. They were persons of *mature age*.

    b. They were recognized as *spiritually mature*.

    c. They functioned *together as a unit*, and held *equal respect and authority* as individuals.

2. They were known as *representatives* of the community.

3. Theirs was a *distinctly local oversight* (i.e., the synagogue council).

4. *Invested with authority* to lead, speak on behalf of, and manage the affairs of the community.

IV. Authority and Functions of the Elder

A. Elders presided over the spiritual and social affairs of the community.

1. The Apostles referred to themselves as elders of the Church.

   a. John, 2 John 1.1

   b. Peter, 1 Pet. 5.1

2. Elders gave rule over the general affairs of the community, 1 Tim. 5.17.

3. Some elders labored especially in preaching and teaching, (cf. 1 Tim. 5.17, with 1 Thess. 5.12-13).

   a. Elders provided oversight, i.e., those who "labor among you and are over you in the Lord and admonish you" (elders functions as *ruling elders*).

   b. Were worthy of the esteem and love of those whom they led.

We exhort those who are mighty in word and of blameless life to rule over churches. We reject those who are ambitious to rule. . . . And if those who govern in the church . . . rule well, they rule in accordance with the divine commands and never allow themselves to be led astray by worldly policy.
~ Origen (c. 248, E), 4.668., Ibid., p. 159.

2

c.   Elders instructed the community in the Word and will of the Lord (elders functioned as *teaching elders*).

4.   Worked alongside the deacons, Phil. 1.1

5.   No accusation was to be entertained against them without sufficient witnesses and evidence, 1 Tim. 5.19.

B.   Elders gave pastoral care to the members of the community.

1.   They were charged with tending the flock, 1 Pet. 5.1-3.

2.   They exercised pastoral care and counseling.

    a.   They are charged with the task of feeding the flock of God through preaching and teaching, 1 Tim. 5.17.

    b.   They were to take the lead in healing ministry (i.e., anointing the sick and praying for their restoration and healing), James 5.14.

    c.   They were charged with nurturing the flock as an example to the believers, 1 Pet. 5.1-4.

C.   Elders were charged with serving as a role model for the members of the community.

1.   They were invested with apostolic sanction and authority, Titus 1.5.

In the meanwhile, let those certain [presbyters] among you who are rash, incautious, and boastful . . . be suspended from offering [the Eucharist].
~ Cyprian (c. 250, W), 5.290., Ibid.

2. Elders were to serve as an example in five critical areas, 1 Tim. 4.12.

   a. In speech

   b. In conduct

   c. In love toward others

   d. In faith

   e. In purity before God

3. Elders in all respects were to be a model of good works and in their teaching showing both integrity and dignity, Titus 2.7.

D. Implications for our understanding of the role of elders in the Church.

   1. The concept grows out of a historic understanding of the role of elders within the rulers of the Jewish tribal system of government.

   2. Elders are persons of recognized spiritual maturity.

   3. As a general rule elders were persons of years, but could be younger by virtue of gifting and spiritual appointment, 1 Tim. 4.

   4. Provided oversight to the affairs of the community

2

Conclusion

» The term translated *elder* in our NT is the Greek term *presbyteros*, meaning "overseer" or "elder."

» The NT concept of *elder* can be traced to and is built upon its OT root in the tribal system of Israel, the practices of the Jewish synagogue, and the governance of the Sanhedrin.

» The apostolic understanding of elder, built upon its Jewish roots, defines itself as godly rulership and administration of spiritual justice among the people of God, guarding and protecting the flock.

Please take as much time as you have available to answer these and other questions that the video brought out. In our video segment we learned that the term translated *elder* in our NT is the Greek term *presbyteros*, meaning "overseer" or "elder." The concept evolved from its OT usage, seen in the tribal system of Israel, the practices of the Jewish synagogue, the positions in the Sanhedrin, and finally to the NT Church. As a foundational principle of Christian leadership in the NT, the calling and criteria for elders shapes much of what we know God demands for those exercising authority over his people in the Church. Review some of these foundational insights by answering the questions together below.

1. What is the meaning of the term translated elder in our NT? What is the relationship between the meaning of the Greek term *presbyteros*, and its related term *episkopos*? What is the major difference between the use of these terms in reference to Christian leadership in the NT?

2. Explain the evolution of the NT concept of elder in its various phases: its roots in the OT through the tribal system of Israel, through the various practices of the Jewish synagogue, and the governance within in the Sanhedrin. How did the apostles expand and fill out this concept for the NT Church?

3. How were elders called in the experience of the apostles, as recorded in Acts and the rest of the NT? In what ways are these appointments and commissionings related to how we ought to select elders to rule in our churches today?

Segue 1

Student Questions and Response

page 344 📖 *4*

4. What criteria did the apostles provide for those who were qualified to be elders in the NT? When taken together, what do these various stipulations suggest about the nature of Christian leaders in the body of Christ?

5. What is the relationship between the qualification for *preaching and teaching the Word* and that of *ruling well in the Church*? Can one be qualified to be an elder if they do not possess both of these qualifications? Explain your answer.

6. How do Peter and Paul help us in 1 Peter 5 and Acts 20 to understand the relationship between being an *elder* to *shepherding the flock of God*? Can one still maintain the position of an elder if they refuse to shepherd God's people? If so, under what situation would this be possible?

7. The pastoral epistles place special emphasis on the need for elders to *preside over* the spiritual and social affairs of the Church. Is the role of elder, therefore, a *political position in the church*? Explain your answer.

8. In what ways are elders to serve as examples and role models for the disciples gathered in community? In light of this, what might this suggest as to the *age* of elders? Does this have any implications as to the *gender* of elders? Explain your answer.

9. What does it mean that we must select elders who are "people of recognized spiritual maturity and gifting?" What ought we to do if *we cannot find anyone in our church who meets these qualifications*? Be thorough in your answer.

The Christian Leader as Elder (*Presbyteroi*)

Segment 2: Models, Training, and Practice

Rev. Dr. Don L. Davis

Summary of Segment 2

The NT provides us with key analogies of the Christian Leader as *elder* or *presbyter*: the Christian *elder* is seen as *an overseer,* providing oversight of the various spiritual affairs of the community, as *a father or parent* who leads and heads the Church as the Lord's household, as *a colleague or team member* who contributes as a member to the *council of elders* as they give oversight to the congregation, and finally as *a representative* both of the Lord and the people of God to those who are outsiders. Urban churches desperately need to affirm the role of such leaders for their congregations and discover practical, effective ways to identify and equip such leaders for believers in the city.

Our objective for this segment, *The Christian Leader as Elder: Models, Training, and Practice*, is to enable you to see that:

- The NT provides us with key analogies of the Christian Leader as *elder* or *presbyter*. These analogies fill out for us the various dimensions of the faithful fulfillment of the role of elder in the NT Church.

- The Christian leader as elder is *an overseer,* charged with the solemn responsibility to oversee the various affairs of the Church for its well-being, edification, and overall benefit.

- Furthermore, the elder is *a father or parent*, a person of significance, prominence, and maturity in the Christian assembly and therefore able to provide instruction, protection, and guidance as a spiritual parent.

- An elder is *one among many*, that is an elder is *a colleague and team member* who makes their gifts and resources available to the council of elders for the benefit of the council and for the sake of the body.

- The elder is also *a representative*, one who stands with fidelity for the interests and purposes of the Lord and the body, and serves as an agent on behalf of the community and the faith to those who are outside.

- Elders are not to be selected on the basis of social place, wealth, academic achievement, or prominence, but on the basis of their spiritual maturity and personal integrity.

- We are not to place novices (immature believers) into positions of authority and oversight in the Church. Rather, we are to seek to create structures and processes that allow for spiritually mature and available members to exercise servant leadership in the body.

- Urban congregations especially need godly elders in leadership, due to the prevalence of broken families, moral compromise, and social upheaval.

- The blessings, benefits, and rewards of faithful service as an elder are enormous, the greatest of which is the promise of personal reward from the Lord Jesus himself with the "unfading crown of glory."

**Video Segment 2
Outline**

Let everyone reverence the deacons as an appointment of Jesus Christ; and the bishop as of Jesus Christ, who is the Son of the Father; and the presbyters as the Sanhedrin of God and assembly of the apostles. Apart from these there is no church.
~ Ignatius (c. 105, E), 1.67., Ibid., p. 158.

I. Models and Analogies for Eldership

A. The elder is an overseer (i.e., one who presides over the affairs of the community), Acts 20.28.

The elder is an overseer, one charged with the responsibility to oversee the various affairs of the Church for its well being, edification, and overall benefit.

1. This oversight involves *critical assessment of the state of its members.*

2. This oversight means that elders must *be informed about* the various dimensions of the church's life and ministry.

3. The oversight is *continuous*; it is compared to being on guard or paying careful attention.

B. The elder is a *father*, 1 Tim 5.17.

The elder is a person of significance, prominence, and maturity in the Christian assembly, and therefore is to lead and provide instruction, protection, and insight like a father.

1. As one who exercises authority, this must not be understood as a lording over the members, but in terms of *parental care and oversight.*

2. The elders exercised authority in the way a responsible parent would care for the needs of his household: with care for their needs, with deep affection, and an unlimited willingness to sacrifice for them (cf. praying for the sick, James 5.14).

C. The elder is a *colleague*, Phil. 1.1.

The elder is one among many. Whatever the system of government we might hold to within our church tradition, an elder was surrounded by others with whom they worked as a team together to address the concerns of the Church.

1. The elders are mentioned *in the plural* in the Scriptures in a number of examples.

    a. Acts 20.17 - Now from Miletus he sent to Ephesus and *called the elders of the church* to come to him.

    b. 1 Tim. 5.17 - Let the *elders who rule* well be considered worthy of double honor, especially those who labor in preaching and teaching.

    c. Titus 1.5 - This is why I left you in Crete, so that you might put what remained into order, and *appoint elders* in every town as I directed you.

    d. James 5.14 - Is anyone among you sick? Let him call for *the elders of the church*, and let them pray over him, anointing him with oil in the name of the Lord.

    e. 1 Pet. 5.1 - So I exhort *the elders* among you, as a fellow elder and a witness of the sufferings of Christ, as well as a partaker in the glory that is going to be revealed.

2. This implies *cooperation and collaboration*: the ability to support one another and build each other up as they led others together.

3. *Mutual submission* is critical for a responsible eldership.

    a.   Phil. 2.3

    b.   Eph. 5.21

D. The elder is a *representative*, 1 Pet. 5.1-3.

The elder is one who represents the interests of the Lord and of the Church, serving as an agent on behalf of the community and the faith to which God has called them.

1. Elders do not exercise their authority arbitrarily; they are to be obeyed and submitted to because God has placed them in a position to guard and care for his flock (cf. Acts 20.28).

2. This does not mean that elders are to be given unqualified obedience; saints have the duty and privilege to weigh all things against God's biblical standard, and follow accordingly.

3. The attitude toward elders should, therefore, be of supreme esteem; love and respect for their important work among the members of the body.

    a.   1 Thess. 5.12-13

    b.   Heb. 13.7

    c.   Heb. 13.17

2

II. Equipping Elders for Urban Congregations

A. Traditional forms of equipping elders

In many settings, selection for the position of elder is not based on maturity and spiritual power, but rather on social place and prominence in the business and/or secular community.

1. Persons of prominence in business and community ("successful people")

2. Well known or influential people within the corridors of power in our city

3. Academically credentialed persons (i.e., those who have been formally prepared within a college, seminary, or other kind of accredited institution)

4. While none of these things are a problem for a selection criteria, in the end they ought not determine what it means to be a leader in the Church: sharing in the death of Christ so one can be free to serve others, 2 Cor. 4.7-12.

   a. Leaders are *bondslaves of Jesus Christ*.

   b. Leaders are *servants for the well-being* of the members of the Church.

   c. Leaders *die to themselves* in order that the *life of Christ* might be poured into others!

Beloved, we know that the bishop and all the clergy should be an example in all good works to the people.
~ Malchion (c. 270, E), 5.379., Ibid., p. 160.

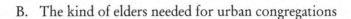

B. The kind of elders needed for urban congregations

1. Persons of credible character and proven ability to lead: we need individuals of *integrity and dignity*.

2. *Team players*: we need individuals willing to cooperate and work alongside others.

3. Experienced individuals: we need individuals whose walk with Christ is *rich enough and long enough* that they can rule matters in the life of the body.

4. Those possessing *the ability to spiritually nurture and give pastoral care* to the members of the community

5. Those who can serve as *examples and models of authentic Christian discipleship* in the midst of the challenges of urban life

C. How do we find and equip elders of this kind for our congregations?

1. Pray for them.

2. Clearly define in our congregations the need for distinctive leaders who can provide oversight to our assemblies (i.e., every congregation must have clearly defined structures of governance: who is in charge, and what are their bounds of authority and responsibility, cf. Acts 15.2).

2

3. Provide opportunities for service: internships and projects (we can train leaders through apprenticeship and discipleship).

   a. 2 Tim. 2.2

   b. 2 Tim. 1.13

   c. 2 Tim. 3.10

   d. 2 Tim. 3.14

4. Place emphasis upon faithfulness to represent God and his biblical truth, not societal status and socio-economic background.

   a. Num. 12.7

   b. Luke 12.42

   c. Luke 16.10-12

   d. 1 Cor. 4.2

   e. 1 Tim. 1.12

5. Create an affordable, culturally sensitive, and biblical means to equip men and women in your church for the ministry.

If we are priests of God and of Christ, I do not know anyone whom we ought rather to follow than God and Christ.
~ Cyprian (c. 250, W), 5.363., Ibid., p. 162.

III. Principles and Practice for the Eldership

A. Do not place novices (immature believers) into positions of authority and oversight in the Church, 1 Tim. 3.6.

    1. Novices are *easily influenced by external* persons, situations, and conditions.

        a. Rom. 16.17-18

        b. Col. 2.8

        c. 2 Thess. 2.2

    2. Novices are *not grounded in the truth* well enough to help others become what God wants them to be and do, Eph. 4.11-15.

    3. Novices *need to be established first* before they are placed into situations requiring experience, wisdom, and biblical skill.

        a. 1 Cor. 3.1

        b. Heb. 5.12-13

        c. 1 Pet. 2.2

2

B. Create structures and processes that allow for the spiritually mature to exercise leadership in the body.

    1. Show no partiality (employ fair standards responsibly in selecting and appointing elders).

        a. James 2.1-7

        b. Lev. 19.15

        c. Deut. 1.17

        d. Prov. 28.21

        e. 1 Tim. 5.21

    2. Place no restrictions upon candidates that the Scriptures do not demand.

    3. Take the biblical criteria seriously however you appoint elders in your community.

        a. By election of the elder board

        b. By selection of the congregation

c. By appointment of the bishop or church superintendent

C. Provide opportunities to give support and training to emerging elders.

1. Train them to *lead*.

2. Train them to *pastor others*.

3. Train them to *preach and teach*.

4. Train them to *work with others as a team*.

IV. Particular Issues for Urban Churches and Selection of Elders

A. *The presence of broken families*: elders as surrogate fathers

1. The standards regarding strong families are critical for urban ministry.

2. In the midst of a community torn by broken families, we must insist on leaders who are solid, responsible spouses and strong parents.

3. We should expect the power of God to be shown in these areas in the midst of our communities.

a. Matt. 19.26

b. Mark 9.23

c. Eph. 3.20-21

B. *Teaching people godly submission*: teaching authority and scope of the elders.

1. We must teach urban saints the importance of the principle of obedience in Christian discipleship.

    a. The Great Commission involves obeying all that Christ has commanded us, Matt. 28.19.

    b. Those who hear Jesus' words and obey them are like a wise person who builds their house on solid ground, Matt. 7.24-27.

    c. It is only in training urban Christians to submit to solid biblical teaching that they will be protected from the various pitfalls and prey that are out to destroy them.

        (1) Heb. 13.17

        (2) Heb. 13.7

        (3) 1 Thess. 5.12-13

        (4) 2 Thess. 3.14

C. *The presence of moral compromise*: the issue of church discipline

1. We are bound to encounter situations where urban disciples will need to be restored in Christ, James 5.16.

2. We are to do this with meekness and fear, a task to be done by those who are spiritual, Gal. 6.1-2.

D. *Rebuking an elder*: restoring the fallen leader, 1 Tim. 5.19 Do not admit a charge against an elder except on the evidence of two or three witnesses.

E. Women as elders: ongoing debates and issues

V. The Benefits, Blessing, and Reward of the Elder

1 Pet. 5.1-4 - So I exhort the elders among you, as a fellow elder and a witness of the sufferings of Christ, as well as a partaker in the glory that is going to be revealed: [2] shepherd the flock of God that is among you, exercising oversight, not under compulsion, but willingly, as God would have you; not for shameful gain, but eagerly; [3] not domineering over those in your charge, but being examples to the flock. [4] And when the chief Shepherd appears, you will receive the unfading crown of glory.

A. The charge: shepherd the flock of God.

1. Exercise oversight.

2. Exercise it willingly.

3. Not for shameful gain

4. Do it eagerly.

2

5. Not dominating those under one's charge

6. Live as an example to the flock.

B. The reward: the recognition of the Chief Shepherd

1. The Chief Shepherd will appear.

2. The Chief Shepherd will crown the faithful elder with the unfading crown of glory.

3. The personal acknowledgment, thanksgiving, and reward from the Savior himself!

Conclusion

» The office of elder consists of fulfilling the role of *overseer* that provides oversight for the affairs of the community and a *parent* that supplies affectionate attention to the needs of all the family members in the community.

» Moreover, an elder is both a *team member* and a *representative* who works with others elders in council, and seeks to shepherd the flock of God in humility and godliness.

» God's Church in the city needs solid godly elders to protect and feed God's people.

Segue 2

Student Questions and Response

The following questions were designed to help you review the material in the second video segment. In this lesson we saw how the NT provides us with key analogies of the Christian leader as elder. The Christian *elder* is seen as an overseer, a father or parent, a colleague or team member, and a representative both of the Lord and the people of God. In some ways, to comprehend the role of elder is to gain insight into the very heart of what it means to be a leader in the Church, and a Christian leader in society. In light of this, pay careful attention to your answers to the review questions below, concentrating on being as clear and concise in your answers as possible, and using Scripture to support your conclusions.

1. What is the role of images and analogies in helping us understand the nature and the character of leadership in the NT? Why are these analogies important in communicating the nature of leadership to those in the Church?

2. What does statement mean that "the Christian leader as elder is *an overseer*?" What are the limits of authority and rulership given to elders in the various affairs of the local church?

3. In what sense is the faithful service of an elder like the work of *a father or parent*? How does this image help us understand the role of providing instruction and protection as well as demonstrating affection and care in Christian leadership?

4. What is the relationship between the role of an elder as a personally mature individual as well as the elder as "*one among many*, and as a colleague and team member? How does the OT help us understand the role of an elder not as an individual position but as one who exists as part of a council, a plurality of leaders?

5. In what ways ought an elder *represent* both the interests and purposes of the Lord and those of the body? What implications does this hold for elders to serve as agents on behalf of the community and the faith to *those who are outside*?

6. Why is it important to never select elders merely on the basis of social place, wealth, academic achievement, or prominence? According to the NT, what are the criteria for which elders ought to be elected and commissioned to service in the body?

7. On a related issue, why is it necessary to avoid placing *novices* (i.e., *spiritually immature* believers) into positions of authority and oversight in the church? Does this apply to them even if they have been successful and prominent in areas of business or society? Explain.

8. What are the particular challenges and needs that make godly elders a special need for urban congregations?

9. List out some of the blessings, benefits, and rewards of faithful service as an elder. What would you say are the prices that need to be paid and the burdens that will need to be borne in order to fulfill this call?

CONNECTION

This lesson focuses upon meaning and practice of eldership in the NT Church. The Greek words for leadership in the NT, *presbyteros* and *episkopos*, are virtually synonymous. Elders are called to give oversight over the affairs of the Church in a way that glorifies God, edifies the Church, and testifies to the world. The concepts below summarize the critical concepts related to this important office in the Church of Christ.

Summary of Key Concepts

page 344 📖 *5*

➥ The meaning for term translated *elder* in our NT is the Greek term *presbyteros*, meaning "overseer" or "elder." The Greek words for leadership in the NT *presbyteros* and *episkopos* refer to the same office in the NT Church, with the main difference being that *episkopos* is used only in the Gentile church.

➥ The NT concept of *elder* evolved from its OT roots in the tribal system of Israel, which developed further in the practices of the Jewish synagogue, as well as its usage as an official position in the Sanhedrin, and finally to the NT Church.

➥ According to the NT, elders were either appointed by the apostles or their representatives, or commissioned within the Christian community. The pastoral epistles lay out clear spiritual qualifications for elders, who must be of recognized spiritual maturity and gifting, providing oversight to the doctrine, affairs, and governance of the Church, and serve as role models for the disciples gathered in community.

➥ Four analogies fill out for us the various dimensions of the faithful fulfillment of the role of elder in the NT Church. As *overseer*, elders oversee the various affairs of the Church for its well-being, edification, and overall benefit. As *fathers and parents*, elders are mature and respected members who protect and instruct the assembly. As *colleagues and team members*, elders function in a plurality of leadership to guide the Church. Finally, as *representatives*, elders stand with fidelity for the interests of the Lord and the body as agents on behalf of the community.

- Elders are not to be selected on the basis of social place, wealth, academic achievement, or prominence, but on the basis of their spiritual maturity and personal integrity.

- We are not to place novices (immature believers) into positions of authority and oversight in the church. Rather, we are to seek to create structures and processes that allow for spiritually mature and available members to exercise servant leadership in the body.

- Urban congregations especially need godly elders in leadership, due to the prevalence of broken families, moral compromise, and social upheaval.

- The blessings, benefits, and rewards of faithful service as an elder are enormous, the greatest of which is the promise of personal reward from the Lord Jesus himself with the "unfading crown of glory."

Student Application and Implications

Now is the time for you to discuss with your fellow students your questions about the importance of the role of elders in the NT. Whether or not God has called you to *serve in the role of elder*, it is nonetheless highly important for you to understand and apply the rich supply of principles this teaching has on the subject of Christian leadership. Possibly in your searching out of the key nuggets of truth associated with this theme you have identified some problems or issues that require further clarification. Bring these to the surface now, and share them with your fellow students, and seek to get at the heart of these as you discuss them together. Perhaps the questions below may trigger some of your own specific questions on the content of this lesson on the role of elders in the Church.

* To what extent ought elders to take their cues or imitate the rules of business in either establishing or running their councils of elders? Explain.

* What is a church, which has a shortage of leaders who match the biblical criteria, to do in terms of finding elders to rule well?

*   Can women be elders of the church? What if there are women who match the biblical qualifications for spiritual maturity but no men who correspond to the standard–are we to place the men in positions, even if they are not spiritually qualified to lead?

*   How old must a person be in order to become a candidate for elder? Is there an age minimum that should be recognized in this process?

*   How would you know if God is calling you to such a position? Paul seems to give a sense in 1 Timothy 3.1 that one may *aspire to the office*: "The saying is trustworthy: If anyone aspires to the office of overseer, he desires a noble task." What place does spiritual ambition to serve play in the selection of qualified elders for leadership?

*   In your view, how young in Christ is simply *too young* to be considered for a place on the council or board of elders? Explain your answer.

*   Read 1 Timothy 5.17: "Let the elders who rule well be considered worthy of double honor, especially those who labor in preaching and teaching." What does this text teach about both the *willingness* and *ability* of elders to preach and teach in order to be an elder in the church? Explain your answer.

Sisters in the Gate

CASE STUDIES

1

The OT image of elders consulting "in the gate," a symbolic phrase for exercising judgment regarding the affairs of the city and/or village, is a common image in the narratives of the Hebrew Bible. In deep contrast today, many urban neighborhoods are virtually matriarchal in structure and authority. In the wake of the near complete collapse of many urban families, and the dramatic absence of men to rule and lead the children and families that remain, women have necessarily assumed the position of heads of households, bread winners, and leaders of their homes and neighborhoods. Furthermore, often the most reliable and competent leaders in urban neighborhoods are women who have hesitantly but boldly stepped in to be "sisters in the gates." Under the conditions of the absence of men and the corresponding raising up of competent, godly women in a community, what are the biblical prohibitions against women in positions of Christian leadership? Does Paul's injunction in 1 Timothy 2.12 "I do not permit a woman to teach or to exercise authority over a man; rather, she is to remain quiet" make it practically impossible for a woman to serve on a council of elders?

I've Never Seen One

What seems impossible to fathom has now actually become something of a normal standard in many urban settings. Whereas a generation ago one could find a good number of solid, effective, and credible male leaders in urban neighborhoods, the absence of such symbols and role models make it increasingly difficult for many post-modern urban dwellers to comprehend the plain meaning of the text of Scripture. For those who have not grown up in a home with a solid male father figure, the texts in the NT are hard to imagine, let alone apply. How do you comprehend the meaning of an image when you have never actually *seen an elder who was male, godly, selfless, and committed to protecting and leading the community?* How are we to equip men for the ministry of such oversight if, in their entire life experience, they have never known even a single example of such a person *in their family or neighborhood?* Be specific in your answer as to how we address such a situation.

Older Is Not Necessarily Better

Sometimes, questions of *age* enter into the mix of elder selection, even as *gender* does. Sometimes, as the adage goes it is "easier to build a boy than to remake a man." Such a doctrine, taken without biblical critique, can easily call into question the saving and transforming power of the Gospel, and the indwelling and filling of the Holy Spirit in the life of those with a checkered or spotted background. Nevertheless, many younger people (early twenties and thirties) may in their actual spiritual maturity and leadership ability be in a better position to actually lead in church settings than their older brothers and sisters. Do we have any biblical clues as to what, if any, *age minimum* may exist for the placing of a young adult in a position of elder leadership? What precedent do we have to take young adults from Bible colleges and seminaries and to put them into immediate positions of spiritual maturity? How long ought we to wait before we begin to cultivate young people for leadership at the elders council level?

Over-committed Leadership?

In an actual case of a church seeking to rediscover its charge to "let the elders rule well" in the context of their church, some members of an urban church gave the right to court and marry over to the council of elders. What began as a edifying attempt to protect the younger sisters in the body from predatory males seeking to exploit them sexually, over time turned into a near-Inquisition like inquiry into virtually every romance and dating match in the congregation. While some were deeply appalled at even the thought that the elders would go so far as to "mix" and "match" partners of potential dating couples in the church, many also welcomed this kind of "protection" for the beautiful yet vulnerable young women in the church. In your opinion, as elders contemplate what it means to provide protection and guardianship over the members of the church, what are the limits of elders' leadership in the body? What areas, if any, should be "off limits" to the scope of the elders making decisions regarding the lives of the members? How does our submission to the elders relate to the amazing freedom that Christ won for us on Calvary, a freedom to be a slave of Christ and not to be enslaved by others (cf. Gal. 5.1)? Explain your answer.

2

The term translated *elder* in our NT is the Greek term *presbyteros*, meaning "overseer" or "elder." The Greek words for leadership in the NT, *presbyteros* and *episkopos*, are virtually synonymous. The NT concept of *elder* evolved from its OT usage, seen in the tribal system of Israel, the practices of the Jewish synagogue, the positions in the Sanhedrin, and finally to the NT Church. The NT provides clear records of the calling of elders, who were either appointed by the apostles or their representatives, or commissioned within the Christian community. The pastoral epistles lay out clear spiritual qualifications for elders, including being spiritually mature leaders able to preach and teach, charging them with the responsibility to guard and shepherd God's flock.

The NT provides us with key analogies of the Christian leader as elder or presbyter: the Christian *elder* is seen as an *overseer*, providing oversight of the various spiritual affairs of the community, as a *father or parent* who leads and heads the Church as the Lord's household, as a *colleague or team member* who contributes as a member to the council of elders as they give oversight to the congregation, and finally as a *representative* both of the Lord and the people of God to those who are outsiders. Urban churches desperately need to affirm the role of such leaders for their congregations, and discover practical, effective ways to identify and equip such leaders for the maturity of the believers in the city.

Restatement of the Lesson's Thesis

Resources and Bibliographies

If you are interested in pursuing some of the ideas of *The Christian Leader as Elder (Presbyteroi)*, you might want to give these books a try:

Bilezikian, Gilbert. *Beyond Sex Roles*. Grand Rapids: Baker Books, 1985.

Getz, Gene. *The Measure of a Church*. Ventura, CA: Regal Books, 2002.

Kreider, Larry, and Ron Myer, Steve Prokopchak. *The Biblical Role of Elders for Today's Church: New Testament Leadership Principles for Equipping Elders*. Lititz, PA: House to House Publications, 2003.

Strauch, Alexander. *Biblical Eldership: Restoring the Eldership to Its Rightful Place in Church*. Colorado Springs, CO: Lewis and Roth Publishers, 1997.

------, and Richard. Swartley. *The Mentor's Guide to Biblical Eldership: Twelve Lessons for Mentoring Men to Eldership*. Colorado Springs, CO: Lewis and Roth Publishers, 1997.

------. *Biblical Eldership: An Urgent Call to Restore Biblical Church Leadership*. rev. expanded ed. Colorado Springs, CO: Lewis and Roth Publishers, 1995.

Ministry Connections

However the Lord may call you to serve, the wisdom derived from understanding the principles of biblical eldership can dramatically impact and shape your life and ministry. In this section your aim must be to make the mental transfer from a focus on *getting the concepts clear* to *making the truth real in your life*. Begin to ponder the various facets and angles of truth you discovered on the nature of being an elder of the Lord, and seek the Spirit's aid to help you make a personal and practical life and ministry connection, one which you can take and make a matter of prayer and application throughout the next week. Ask the Holy Spirit for the specific connections that he would like you to make in regard to your own role of leading others, whether in your home, on the job, or in the body. Ask God to give you insight into particular situations in which you need to apply the truths that he has given you in your own study, and in discussion with your instructor and fellow students. Be open to the Lord and he will provide you with these kinds of insights for your own application and edification (Ps. 139.23-24).

Counseling and Prayer

One of the great blessings of the Lord is to be led by the Spirit of God as you lead others. Ask the Lord to give you insight and opportunity into practical and meaningful ways your own life and ministry can become more healing and helpful

page 346 6

as you provide oversight, give counsel, or live as a model for others around you. Ask for the intercessory help of your fellow students and instructor as you seek God's leading and filling. Also, if you find that you require counsel to deal with a particular situation, make an appointment to see your immediate ministry supervisor, Bible study leader, pastor, or whomever you submit to in your tradition, and seek their aid and counsel. Remember, the soundness of the advice given to us in Proverbs on the nature and importance of godly counsel:

> Prov. 11.14 - Where there is no guidance, a people falls, but in an abundance of counselors there is safety.

> Prov. 15.22 - Without counsel plans fail, but with many advisers they succeed.

> Prov. 24.6 - For by wise guidance you can wage your war, and in abundance of counselors there is victory.

Seek out the advice and counsel of your godly leaders, and solicit their prayers and help on your behalf.

2

ASSIGNMENTS

1 Peter 5.1-4

Scripture Memory

To prepare for class, please visit *www.tumi.org/books* to find next week's reading assignment, or ask your mentor.

Reading Assignment

As always, your between-class work plays a significant role in your ability to be prepared for every phase of our in-class discussion and dialogue. Please read carefully the assignments above, and as last week, write a brief summary for them and bring these summaries to class next week (please see the "Reading Completion Sheet" at the end of this lesson). Also, now is the time to begin to think about the character of your ministry project, as well as decide what passage of Scripture you will select for your exegetical project. Do not delay in determining either your ministry or exegetical project. The sooner you select, the more time you will have to prepare!

Other Assignments

Also, remember to take good time to review the various major insights of this lesson in preparation for your quiz next class session, and make certain that you set aside much time to memorize your new texts, as well as review the memory verses from last week. Practice does not make perfect; *correct practice* makes perfect!

....

Looking Forward to the Next Lesson

In today's lesson we explored the meaning and application of the role and office of elder in the Church, whose Greek rendering is *presbyteros*, meaning "overseer" or "elder." We saw how the NT concept of elder evolved from its OT usage, seen in the tribal system of Israel, the practices of the Jewish synagogue, the positions in the Sanhedrin, and finally to the NT Church. We also discovered some of the key analogies for an elder in the Church, as an overseer, a father or parent, a colleague or team member, and as a representative both of the Lord and the people of God to those who are outsiders.

In our next lesson, we will continue to research the foundations of Christian leadership by considering the important role of the Christian leader as *pastor*, or *poimen* in the Greek NT. We will outline the biblical context of the idea of the pastorate, and highlight both the calling and the criteria for godly pastoral ministry in the Church. We will see that pastors are *undershepherds of the flock of God*, called to serve the body as its nurturers, protectors, and leaders.

2

Name _____

Date _____

For each assigned reading, write a brief summary (one or two paragraphs) of the author's main point. (For additional readings, use the back of this sheet.)

Reading 1

Title and Author: _____ Pages _____

Reading 2

Title and Author: _____ Pages _____

LESSON 3

The Christian Leader as Pastor
Poimenes

page 347 📖 *1*

Lesson Objectives

Welcome in the strong name of Jesus Christ! After your reading, study, discussion, and application of the materials in this lesson, you will be able to:

* Define and outline the meaning of the pastor, rehearsing both the OT and NT contexts of the idea of the pastorate, moving to the definition of the Greek term for pastoring, and tracing historically the development of the idea of a formal office of the pastorate.

* Detail both the calling of individuals to the pastorate, and highlight the criteria for representing God as an undershepherd of the flock.

* Lay out the NT contours of the authority and role of the pastor viewed through the lens of the various forms of church government (episcopal, monarchical, and congregational).

* Recite the functions of the godly biblical pastor as outlined in the NT and Church history.

* Elaborate the three biblical models and analogies of what a pastor does in relationship to the flock of God, i.e., the pastor as nurturer and care giver, as protector and guardian, and as leader of the flock of God.

* Give evidence of the particular perils and promise for fulfilling the pastoral role in the inner city, as well as the specific ways we may equip urban pastors for their important duty.

* Discuss some of the more important principles in the practice of pastoring the urban congregation, as well as the wonderful promises associated with the pastoring of the flock of God.

Devotion

An Unusual Occupation

page 348 📖 *2*

John 10.10-18 - The thief comes only to steal and kill and destroy. I came that they may have life and have it abundantly. [11] I am the good shepherd. The good shepherd lays down his life for the sheep. [12] He who is a hired hand and not a shepherd, who does not own the sheep, sees the wolf coming and leaves the sheep and flees, and the wolf snatches them and scatters them. [13] He flees because he is a hired hand and cares nothing for the sheep. [14] I am the good shepherd. I know my own and my own know me, [15] just as the Father knows me and I know the Father; and I lay down my life for the sheep. [16] And I have other sheep that are not of this fold. I must bring them also, and they will listen to my voice. So there will be one flock, one shepherd. [17] For this reason the Father loves me, because I lay down my life that I may take it up again. [18] No one takes it from me, but I lay it down of my own accord. I have authority to lay it down, and I have authority to take it up again. This charge I have received from my Father.

Jesus used vivid metaphors and images to communicate his understanding of caring for his people, and one of his most cherished was the image of the shepherd. He addressed himself as the "Good Shepherd," the one who would, in obedience to his Father's command, gladly give his life for the sheep, his redeemed company. Throughout every dimension of his life and ministry our Lord stands out as one who offered care to those who were in need, whatever their lot, situation, or position. Whether spending time with one of the rulers in Israel in dialogue (Nicodemus) or befriending a lonely, spurned Samaritan woman, our Lord provided clear evidence of his caring heart, of the nature of true pastoral care.

Our Lord was neither biased nor bigoted, and never seemed to berate or belittle the individuals that he encountered and cared for. He met each particular individual in the moment and at the point of their specific need. In all of the representative examples of his rich ministry provided in the NT, our Lord respected the dignity and worth of each one, whether, child, woman, or man. Our Lord did not believe that "one size fits all" in terms of caring for the people he encountered in his ministry. Rather, he was careful to honor the individuality and uniqueness of each person's situation, and tailored his own particular response to that person's need, lack, and burden. This kind of specific, particular, and contextualized care is the heart and soul of the pastoral ministry, and is also why the art of pastoring is so little practiced today.

At a time when many pastors envision the role of the senior pastor as a religious CEO who does not "dirty his hands" in the details of people's lives, we desperately need a new (or rather, a truly old) kind of pastoral leadership. A great need exists to rediscover the nature of biblical caring, a kind of ministry which is focused on meeting the needs of individual persons, particular families, and specific neighborhoods and communities. Look again at the remarkable care of our Lord to *specific individuals*-the widow of Nain, the blind Bartemeus, Zacchaeus the publican, and the demoniac of the Gadarenes. In each case it is the same Lord loving, caring, comforting, but also in each case his *grace and care* are given in a particular way. Our Lord did not love from afar nor even at arm's length. He got close enough to touch the ones he ministered to, and as a result of his specific and particular love for each and every sheep in their own life context, he transformed their lives.

What kind of motivations and incentives will enable us to find individuals willing to give this kind of taxing, exhausting, and costly care to those who so desperately need spiritual shepherding? Ephesians 4 suggests that it is *God alone* who provides pastors to his people, gifted, available persons who like our Lord are willing to lay down their lives for the sheep. God alone can provide the kind of Christian leadership that his people need, care givers that will follow our Lord's example and become the kind of sacrificing shepherds that he was, which culminated with his remarkable act of dying on our behalf.

In light of the shortage of godly pastors for our cities, we need to fervently and continuously ask God to give to us what he promised his people of Israel so many centuries ago: "And I will give you shepherds after my own heart, who will feed you with knowledge and understanding" (Jer. 3.15). How we desperately need pastors who, like our dear Lord, will lay down their lives for the sheep.

R. Robert Cueni has given a funny, fine, and factual summary of the odyssey of care giving as a pastor: Being a pastor is . . .

- Spending three years studying systematic theology only to discover that the most scholarly comment that people respond to is "God loves you."

- Never having enough money to pay one's bills and enough time to count one's blessings.

- Receiving two anonymous letters in the same week—one correcting the grammar in last Sunday's sermon and the other containing money to be given to a family experiencing difficulty.

- Seldom living near relatives but always near friends.

- Trying not to laugh when asked to say a blessing at the dedication of the town's new sewage treatment plant.

- Always working overtime but seldom feeling the need to watch the clock.

- Uniting with God's children at all of the turning points of life.

- Sharing the joys of the wedding, the birth of the child, the baptism of the believer, and tears in the hospital and the funeral home.

3

- Pushing the button of hope for those who have hit bottom.

May God give all of us, whether he calls us to the pastorate or not, to be care givers like our Lord, and be willing to lay down our lives for our brothers and sisters, for the glory of God through Christ.

After reciting and/or singing the Nicene Creed (located in the Appendix), pray the following prayer:

A prayer for pastors . . .

O God, Father of our Lord Jesus Christ, who sent Thy Son not to be ministered unto but to minister, and who made him the great Head of the Church, set apart and consecrate this thy servant for the work of the ministry. Give him thy wisdom, and in counsel may he deal wisely as one who has the mind of Christ. Grant him thy spirit of compassion for human needs and fill him with love that he may tenderly care for every soul whom thou dost so graciously love. Strengthen and nourish his faith in thee and in the values of thy Church, that he may increase the faith of his fellow Christians. Cause his study to be meaningful and his work in thy Church fruitful. And give grace unto us all that working together, seeking to know thy will, we may advance thy cause in this place and throughout the world; to the glory of him who preached good news to the captives, even Christ our Lord. Amen.

~ John E. Skoglund. **A Manual of Worship**. Valley Forge, PA: Judson Press, 1968. p. 256

Put away your notes, gather up your thoughts and reflections, and take the quiz for Lesson 2, *The Christian Leader as Elder (Presbyteroi).*

Review with a partner, write out and/or recite the text for last class session's assigned memory verse: 1 Peter 5.1-4.

Turn in your summary of the reading assignment for last week, that is, your brief response and explanation of the main points that the authors were seeking to make in the assigned reading (Reading Completion Sheet).

3

Nicene Creed and Prayer

Quiz

Scripture Memorization Review

Assignments Due

A Non-pastoral Pastor

1 It has now become fashionable in the culture of the mega-church for many senior pastors to delegate the responsibility for pastoral care to "staff" who do the menial work of counseling the depressed and bereaved, visiting the sick, and nurturing the individuals and families which make up the membership of the church. The role of the senior pastor is to be the "up front" person, the "public face" of the church, the one who teaches in the prime time of the congregation's public ministry, whether on television, radio, or the internet. This kind of phenomena has created the reality of the "non-pastoral Pastor," a person who is called the "pastor" of the church, but in fact, does virtually no pastoral ministry with actual families or individuals. What do you think of these kinds of trends in the church? Is the nature of the pastoral call to ministry to *specific individuals and families* or can you in fact pastor a congregation of 3,000, 5,000, or even 10,000 members? It is legitimate to delegate virtually all pastoral responsibility to others, while retaining the title of "pastor"?

Brother X on Television Is My Pastor

2 In a corresponding way, many now associate their spiritual authority and pastoral oversight to presenters on various religious broadcasts on television or radio. It is not uncommon today to meet believers who claim that their primary spiritual input and authority comes from this, that, or the other television preacher. They purchase their materials, religiously "attend" their presentations on the radio and television, and identify with their emphases, perspectives, and initiatives. They give to their ministries, and associate with their fellow followers. Is it possible or desirable to claim that a person who teaches on radio, television, or on the web *is your spiritual authority, and to see that person as your pastor*?

A Lost Art

3 An entire generation of urban pastors who were mentored in the art of offering care for the poor and the oppressed is about to be lost. We are speaking here of those faithful shepherds who have given themselves selflessly on behalf of little, anonymous congregations who needed the faithful guidance of a spiritually mature servant who was willing to pour out their lives for the sake of Christ's little ones in the city. Many of these dear pastors never received any formal theological training, yet served small urban congregations for little or no remuneration, and usually were forced to work another job in order to pastor their flocks. Still, in spite of hardship and sacrifice, these servants poured out their lives for others. What is interesting to note is that most of these pastors who served in this ways were *mentored* in this role, that is, they learned this art from others who had given the same kind of service for the poor. It is becoming increasingly rare to find those willing to give themselves with this level of selflessness and sacrifice, especially on behalf of congregations who can offer little in terms of financial support. How do we recover this "lost art" of equipping pastors who will care selflessly for congregations which will never be able to afford their full salary, benefits, and perks known in larger churches?

The Christian Leader as Pastor (*Poimenes*)

Segment 1: Definition and Overview

Rev. Dr. Don L. Davis

In both the OT and NT, the image of shepherding is given for the leader of God's people, *roeh* in Hebrew and *poimen* in koine Greek, with both meaning "shepherd," "to shepherd," and to "provide pastoral care." The Lord God, rulers and kings, and the coming Messiah are all perceived as shepherds of God's people. The concept of *pastor* developed throughout the Church, from the care that all Christians provided until eventually it became a formal role for those individuals who would care for God's flock. Jesus himself is the prototype for the pastoral ministry, and God call's and gifts particular individuals to provide this care for the Church. Depending on the government structure of the church, the pastor exercises his care giving responsibility in different ways, but all through the functions of a *shepherd*, i.e., one who teaches and preaches the Word, administers the sacraments, comforts the bereaved, performs marriages, and equips the body for the work of the ministry.

Our objective for this segment, *The Christian Leader as Pastor: Definition and Overview*, is to enable you to see that:

- In both the OT and NT, the image of shepherding is given for the leader of God's people, *roeh* in Hebrew and *poimen* in koine Greek, with both meaning "shepherd," "to shepherd," and to "provide pastoral care."

- The Lord God, rulers and kings, and the coming Messiah are all perceived as shepherds of God's people.

CONTENT

Summary of Segment 1

page 349 📖 *3*

3

- The concept of *pastor* can be traced historically from the apostolic admonitions to provide care to one another as members of God's people in the Church, to the more formal notions of this care being delegated to specific individuals charged with shepherding the body as members of the clergy, or the formal office of the pastorate.

- Jesus himself is the prototype for the pastoral ministry, whose life demonstrates the character of the kind of feeding, love, and care God's flock requires. The Father himself calls and endows his pastors with special authority and gifts to provide this care for the Church.

- Depending on the government structure of the church, the pastor exercises his care giving responsibility in different ways, those including the episcopal, presbyterian, and congregational forms of church government.

- Regardless of the form of government, the pastor functions in the body as a *shepherd*, i.e., one who teaches and preaches the Word, administers the sacraments, comforts the bereaved, performs marriages, and equips the body for the work of the ministry.

3

Video Segment 1 Outline

Our Lord Jesus Christ is the Savior of our souls, the Governor of our bodies, and the Shepherd of the catholic church throughout the world.
~ Martyrdom of Polycarp (c. 135, E), 1.39., David W. Bercot, ed. A Dictionary of Early Christian Beliefs. Peabody, MA: Hendrickson, 1998. p. 146.

I. New Testament Meaning of the Term: *Poimen*

A. Word meanings for *poimen*

1. Shepherd, to shepherd, to provide pastoral care

2. Used in both OT and NT in general sense as to rulership and providing *leadership* over God's people

B. Twelve times in NT is synonymous with the concept of "leaders"

1. Shepherd is a verb: to shepherd

2. A kind of care and personal attention given to the flock of God

   a. Acts 20.28

   b. 1 Pet. 5.2-3

3. God employs the metaphor of *spiritual shepherding* to communicate the nature of the pastorate.

   a. God's intent for his flock is to provide godly shepherds who will feed the flock, and not feed upon them, Jer. 3.15.

   b. False teachers are conceived as ravenous wolves, who won't spare the tender, young lambs of the flock, Acts 20.29.

   c. God's people are conceived as a "little flock," Luke 12.32.

   d. Godly leadership is directly connected with one's treatment of and provision for the flock of God, John 21.17.

II. Origins and Development of the Concept of Pastor

A. Shepherding was a rich, often-used image for leading God's people.

   1. The Lord God relates to his own people as a shepherd tends to and leads his sheep.

He who does anything apart from the bishop, the presbyters, and the deacons, such a man is not pure in his conscience.
~ Ignatius (c. 105, E), 1.67., Ibid., p. 158.

a. Ps. 23.1-2

b. Ps. 79.13

c. Ps. 80.1

d. Isa. 40.11

B. The kings and rulers over God's people are referred to as shepherds.

1. Jer. 23.3-4

2. Ezek. 34.23

3. Ps. 78.70-72

C. Messiah is himself conceived of as a shepherd who will ultimately lead God's people into God's perfect will.

1. Ezek. 34.23

2. Mic. 5.2-4

3. Jesus of Nazareth as the Messiah fulfills the shepherd motif of the OT.

3

a. John 10.11

b. John 10.14

c. Heb. 13.20-21

d. 1 Pet. 2.25

e. 1 Pet. 5.4

D. Pastors and teachers: the equipping ministry

Eph. 4.11-16 - And he gave the apostles, the prophets, the evangelists, the pastors and teachers, [12] to equip the saints for the work of ministry, for building up the body of Christ, [13] until we all attain to the unity of the faith and of the knowledge of the Son of God, to mature manhood, to the measure of the stature of the fullness of Christ, [14] so that we may no longer be children, tossed to and fro by the waves and carried about by every wind of doctrine, by human cunning, by craftiness in deceitful schemes. [15] Rather, speaking the truth in love, we are to grow up in every way into him who is the head, into Christ, [16] from whom the whole body, joined and held together by every joint with which it is equipped, when each part is working properly, makes the body grow so that it builds itself up in love.

1. Pastors and teachers are a part of a *team of equippers*.

2. The pastor-teacher gifts *complement and work together with* the gifts of the apostles, prophets, and evangelists.

3. The purpose of these gifts is to *equip God's people for the work of the ministry.*

4. This work results in spiritual maturity and reproduction.

5. Fluidity in the terms regarding spiritual leadership in the NT

a. Notion of pastor synonymous with "elder" and "bishop," but places the focus on *intimate personal loving care* for the needs of the sheep

b. Jesus referred to as "Shepherd and Bishop" of our souls, 1 Pet. 2.25

c. Peter exhorts elders to shepherd the flock of God in the same way that Jesus the Chief Shepherd does, who will reward their faithfulness, 1 Pet. 5.1-4.

E. Development of the pastoral concept in Church history

1. A casual sketch of the NT reveals that the Apostles expected all Christians, in one way or another, to be involved in pastoral care for one another.

2. All of the requirements of pastoral ministry are given, in varying degrees, to disciples of Jesus as they live in the Christian community (i.e., the "one anothers" in the NT).

a. We are to love one another deeply, from the heart, 1 Pet. 1.22.

Innumerable commands like these are written in the Holy Scriptures, pertaining to chosen persons: some to presbyters, some to bishops, and some to deacons.
~ Clement of Alexandria (c. 195, E), 2.294., Ibid., p. 156.

b. We are to bear with and forgive one another, Col. 3.13.

c. We are called to serve one another in love, Gal. 5.13.

d. Every believer receives the comfort of God in their trials in order that they may comfort others who encounter trouble with the *very comfort that we ourselves received from the Lord*, 2 Cor. 1.4.

e. Christians were called upon to care for others in need, to teach one another, and to use our gifts for the sake of one another.

3. Pastoral care evolved with the expansion of the Church and the growing responsibilities of the twelve.

a. The calling of the Seven introduces the need for specific assistants to the Apostles in the care of the newly formed Messianic community, Acts 6.1-6.

b. The appointing of elders in every city was done to conserve fruit and lay a foundation for *ongoing care and ministry for the Church*, Acts 14.23.

4. The Pastoral Epistles represent a distinct apostolic move to provide instruction for church leaders who would care for the newly formed churches after they would pass on.

5. What started in the Pastoral Epistles grows to be the key idea of ministry in the second and third centuries.

a. A shift from mere Christian "one anothers" to a focused responsibility of pastoral care

b. Two reasons emerge for this focus during the time of the 2nd and 3rd centuries.

    (1) The abuse of power by some who acted as if they were legitimate leaders of the flock but who fleeced them instead

    (2) The need for an orderly approach to ministry to exercise church discipline

6. Thomas C. Oden, *Constitutions of the Holy Apostles*, Cyprian, Origen, Ignatius of Antioch and John Chrysostom (Oden, pp. 41-53)

    a. By the fourth century: pastoral care evolves to be the specific responsibility of those holding pastoral offices, to the exclusion of the ministry of the whole people of God.

    b. Church division between the Eastern and Western understandings of the faith reinforced the principle that pastoral care was the responsibility and ministry of those holding a pastoral or priestly office.

    c. This focus on pastoral care as the exclusive domain of a distinct class wasn't challenged or broadened again in a strong way until the 16th century, which reintroduced the idea of including all Christians as care givers in the Church.

III. Calling and Criteria for Pastors

A. Pastors are called and gifted by God for their work of service in the Church.

1. Pastors are the gift of God to the Church, Eph. 4.11.

   a. They are *equipped with God's own heart for the people*, Jer. 3.15.

   b. They are given spiritual gifts which allow them *to nurture and nourish God's people*, Rom. 12.7.

2. The Holy Spirit himself selects the undershepherds who tend the flock of God, Acts 20.28.

3. These undershepherds respond to the flock under the direct charge of Jesus Christ to care for his flock: *the pastorate emerges from a call from Christ to protect and care for his own*, John 21.16 - He said to him a second time, "Simon, son of John, do you love me?" He said to him, "Yes, Lord; you know that I love you." He said to him, "Tend my sheep."

4. This tending is to be done with tender loving care and wisdom.

   a. Acts 20.28: with special care and attention

   b. 1 Pet. 5.4: willing, eager loving care not for monetary gain or to dominate over God's people

Those square white stones which fitted exactly into each other, are apostles, bishops, teachers, and deacons, who have lived in godly purity, and have acted as bishops, teachers, and deacons chastely and reverently.
~ Hermas (c. 150, W), 12.14, Ibid., p. 158.

5. God will personally reward pastors for their faithful service in tending his flock, 1 Pet. 5.4.

B. Jesus as prototype of the pastoral ministry: following the Good Shepherd, John 10

1. He goes before them, leading them personally and not by proxy: *personal leadership over the flock.*

2. He leads them out by name: *intimate knowledge of each sheep.*

3. He leads them into spiritual nourishment, health, and abundance: *feeds the sheep well.*

4. He lays his life down for the sheep: *willing to make the extreme sacrifice for their benefit.*

5. He does not abandon them in times of need: *is not a hireling ("only in it for the fringe benefits").*

6. He knows his own and they know him: *possesses a personal knowledge of each member of his flock.*

C. The fundamental criteria of pastoral care: *personal care and attention to the safety and well being of the flock.*

John 21.15 - When they had finished breakfast, Jesus said to Simon Peter, "Simon, son of John, do you love me more than these?" He said to him, "Yes, Lord; you know that I love you." He said to him, *"Feed my lambs."*

3

Pastoral care has to do with doing all that one can in one's power to see that each tender lamb is fed, protected, and cared for, enabling it to grow, reproduce, and flourish.

1. Not a matter of seminary training or effort

2. Not a matter of management skill or administrative ability

3. Pastoring is a matter of tending the sheep, of shepherding the flock of the Lord.

    a. Presence *among* them

    b. Love *for* them

    c. Protection *around* them

    d. Leading *before* them

    e. Standing *by* them

IV. Authority and Functions of the Pastoral Ministry

The pastor functions to strengthen and build up the flock of God in all the various areas of their lives, in order that they may grow to maturity and be fruitful in the salvation that they have in Christ Jesus.

It is necessary to abstain from all of these things, being subject to the presbyters and deacons, as unto God and Christ.
~ Polycarp (c. 135, E), 1.34., Ibid.

A. The pastorate is universally recognized as a necessary office of the Church.

B. Churches organize their forms of government in different ways.

    1. Problem of defining how to "pastor" a church

        a. No prescription in the NT for just how to organize

        b. Much variation in the NT as to what was involved in the government of the churches

    2. Different churches govern themselves in different ways, and the pastor's authority varies based on each system.

        a. *Episcopal* form of church government

            (1) Authority resides with the bishop.

            (2) The number and scope of the bishops may vary from church to church.

            (3) Different levels of ministry and degrees of authority

                (a) Level one: *ordinary minister* (or priest)

                (b) Level two: level of the *bishop*

        b. *Presbyterian* form of church government

            (1) Authority placed upon bodies and groups which represent the churches and exercise the authority

            (2) Elders chosen by the congregation who are selected as qualified to oversee the affairs of the church

3

c.   *Congregational* form of church government

        (1) The church is self-governing (autonomous).

        (2) The church functions by democratic processes (voting).

    d.   Non-governmental: stress upon the Holy Spirit working through the members of the body

C. Pastoral authority varies greatly depending on the governmental structure of the church.

    1. In episcopal forms, the authority of the pastor conforms to the authority allowed for at *his level of ministry function*.

    2. In presbyterian forms, the authority of the pastor is determined by his or her role as *a teaching elder* (no higher levels of ministry exist [such as a bishop]).

    3. In congregational forms, the authority of the pastor may vary from *strong, independent, authoritative leader* to one who serves at *the beck-and-call of the congregation*.

    4. In non-governmental forms, the authority of the pastor is based on *the individual group's definition of the pastoral role* as it reads the NT.

D. Implications for our understanding of the pastoral ministry

    1. Virtually all forms of church government recognize the significance of the pastoral ministry.

2. God gives to his Church the shepherds she needs to see her members grow unto maturity in Christ.

3. The pastoral ministry grows directly out of an understanding of the Lord's shepherding role of his people, and Jesus's identity as the Good Shepherd.

4. Pastoral ministry is largely a matter of competent, compassionate nourishment and care for disciples, not formal training or governmental structure.

E. The pastor is a *shepherd*: the general functions of the pastoral ministry

1. To *teach and preach the Word of God*, 1 Thess. 5.12-13

2. *To lead the pastoral team* as they counsel and care for the members of the flock

3. To administer the *sacraments*, 1 Cor. 11.23-26

4. To *comfort the bereaved* during the death of loved ones (officiate at funerals), Rom. 12.15

5. To *make ready those who are preparing for marriage* (i.e., officiate at marriages), Heb. 13.4

6. To *equip and disciple* for the work of the ministry, Eph. 4.11-12

Conclusion

» The role of the pastor, or *poimen* in the NT can be historically tied to the development of the pastorate, or that class of individuals who are charged with shepherding of the flock of God.

» While functionally the term pastor deals with the same subject matter as the Scriptures' teaching on elders and bishops, the nuance of *poimen* or shepherding helps us understand what it means to lead a flock of God.

» The pastor is a shepherd, called to tend, protect, and feed the lambs of God.

Please take as much time as you have available to answer these and other questions that the video brought out. As mentioned before, there is a great need to reclaim the majestic office of the pastorate as *caring*, i.e., that kind of ministry which focuses upon meeting the needs of individual persons, particular families, and specific neighborhoods and communities in the context of the church and beyond. A cursory look at the life and ministry of our Lord reveals his shepherding heart and ministry, and it is this same level of loving, caring and comforting that all leaders must aspire to. As you review the insights into the pastoral ministry given in this segment, concentrate on the roots of the pastoral ministry, and how these roots can be rediscovered in our ministries today.

1. Explain the meaning of the metaphor of *shepherding* in both the OT and NT analogies of a leader. In what sense does the *image of shepherding* stand for and fill out the biblical understanding of providing care and oversight for God's people?

2. What is the meaning of the term *roeh* in Hebrew and *poimen* in koine Greek, and how do they both point to the same reality of "shepherding God's flock?"

3. How was the image of shepherding God's people applied in the OT, specifically to the oversight of the Lord God of his people, the ministry of the rulers and kings of Israel, and the prophecies regarding the coming Messiah?

4. Briefly give the high points in the history of the evolution of the concept of *pastor* from its original settings in the apostolic teaching of the NT to the more formal notions of this care being delegated to specific individuals

Segue 1

Student Questions and Response

page 350 📖 *4*

3

charged with shepherding the body as members of the clergy, or the formal office of the pastorate.

5. How and in what specific ways is our Lord Jesus himself the prototype for the pastoral ministry–how did his life, teaching, ministry, and death reveal the character of the kind of feeding, love, and care God's flock requires?

6. Are pastors called by God, and endowed by him in their roles, authority, and gifts to provide this care for the church, or are they also equipped for ministry by others? Explain your answer.

7. What are the three kinds of government structures of the church that today's pastors exercise in their pastoral roles today. Based on what you know of these structures, which seems to fit best with the role of pastoral care of a congregation's members? Explain your answer.

8. List out some of the major functions that a godly pastor must accomplish in order to shepherd a local congregation. Of these various functions and duties, which do you believe are the most important for the pastorate?

The Christian Leader as Pastor (*Poimenes*)

Segment 2: Models, Training, and Practice

Rev. Dr. Don L. Davis

Summary of Segment 2

The Word of God provides three clear models and analogies of what a pastor does as care giver to the people of God as his flock. The pastor is a nurturer who ensures that God's people receive proper nourishment, feeding, tending, and care. Furthermore, the pastor is a protector and guardian who guards the people of God against any predators or situations which would seek to harm or destroy them. Finally, the pastor is a leader called to go before the people of God and lead them into the fullness of the will of God for their individual and corporate lives. More than ever before the urban church needs pastors who will nourish, protect, and lead urban disciples of Christ to mature in Christ and give witness to the Kingdom of God in the city. God makes unequivocal promises to those who faithfully fulfill their work of shepherding the flock of God–they will receive the unfading crown of glory when the Chief Shepherd appears at the Second Coming.

Our objective for this segment, *The Christian Leader as Pastor: Models, Training, and Practice*, is to enable you to see that:

- The Word of God provides three clear models and analogies of what a pastor does as care giver to the people of God as his flock: the pastor as nurturer, as protector, and as leader.

- The pastor is a nurturer who ensures that God's people receive proper nourishment, feeding, tending, and care.

- In addition, the pastor is a protector and guardian who guards the people of God against any predators or situations which would seek to harm or destroy them.

- Finally, the pastor is a leader called to go before the people of God and lead them into the fullness of the will of God for their individual and corporate lives.

- Because of the unique problems and challenges of urban communities, more than ever before the urban church needs pastors who will nourish, protect, and lead urban disciples of Christ to mature in Christ and give witness to the Kingdom of God in the city.

- God makes unequivocal promises to those who faithfully fulfill their work of shepherding the flock of God–they will receive the unfading crown of glory when the Chief Shepherd appears at the Second Coming.

I. Models and Analogies of the Pastorate

Video Segment 2
Outline

A. The pastor is a *nurturer*.

The pastor is a nurturer, one who ensures that the flock of God receives its proper nourishment and feeding, tending and care.

1. As the Shepherd of Israel, God's distinct role was to provide his people with feeding and nourishment that would cause them to grow, to be strengthened, and experience the abundance of his leading.

a. Isa. 40.11

b. Jer. 23.4

c. Ezek. 34.23

2. A pastor is a nurturing shepherd; you can't shepherd if you don't have a flock.

3. A pastor will not tend a flock if he does not have a heart for them, Jer. 3.15 .

4. A pastor is a nurturer not one who dominates or intimidates, 1 Pet. 5.3.

5. A pastor nurtures in a number of ways.

a. By supplying *a godly example* of what it means to live as a disciple of Christ.

   (1) Titus 2.7

   (2) 1 Tim. 4.12

   (3) 2 Thess. 3.9

b. By *teaching sound doctrine* and preaching the Word of God.

   (1) 1 Thess. 5.12-13

   (2) 1 Tim. 4.6

   (3) 1 Tim. 5.17

   (4) Acts 20.32

3

c. By providing tender, loving, care on the journey as God leads the flock, John 21.16.

B. The pastor is a *protector and guardian*.

    1. A hireling flees at the first sign of danger of an approaching predator on the flock, John 10.12-13.

    2. The abandonment of a flock will certainly result in some of the lambs being eaten, others scattered, John 10.12.

    3. A pastor is a guardian, who like Messiah Jesus guarded and protected his sheep by dying for us on the cross.

        a. Christ never forsook us, but laid his life down for the sheep, John 10.11.

        b. Christ's pastoral sacrifice for us is the standard by which we measure all other forms of caring for the flock, Heb. 13.20.

    4. As guardians of the flock, our responsibility is to pay careful attention to their needs and guard them against those things that would seek to harm or destroy them.

        a. Jesus warned that wolves would in fact come within his flock.

           (1) Matt. 7.15

           (2) Matt. 10.16

3

b. Fierce wolves will arise among the flock, Acts 20.28-31.

c. Destructive heresies are certain to abound, 2 Pet. 2.1-3.

5. The nature of our guardianship as pastors

a. *Extreme*: not willing to lose a single lamb, Luke 15.4

b. *Critical*: no flock will survive if the shepherd is destroyed or abandons his flock, Mark 14.27.

c. *Radical*: we may have to give up our very lives for the survival and abundance of our flocks, John 10.11.

d. Rallying cry: a shepherd guards by leading the sheep in the right direction, away from those things which may cause them to stray or be destroyed, 1 Pet. 2.25.

C. The pastor is a *leader*.

1. Jesus, as the Chief and Good Shepherd, leads us into the way and the pastures that are beneficial to us.

a. Ps. 23.1-2

b. John 10.4

3

c.   John 10.16

d.   John 10.26-27

e.   John 10.3-5

2.   The godly pastor leads the flock into the will of God through the Word of God: he will not lead the flock astray, Jer. 50.6.

3.   As the godly pastor follows Christ as a disciple, he challenges members of the flock to follow his lead.

a.   1 Cor. 11.1

b.   1 Cor. 4.16

c.   1 Cor. 10.33

d.   Phil. 3.17

e.   1 Thess. 1.6

f.   2 Thess. 3.9

4.   The pastor *is the message*, as well as the one who gives messages, Titus 2.7.

5. The youth of the pastor is not an issue; *godly modeling is*, 1 Tim. 4.12.

II. Equipping Pastors for Urban Congregations: Critical Issues

A. The domination of management models among evangelical pastors

   1. The *do-everything myself* pastor: the pastor as Jack of all trades (the super charismatic Christian)

   2. The *managerial pastor*: the pastor as CEO of the Christian corporation

   3. The *aloof pastor*: the pastor who brackets the various tasks he does, virtually isolating himself from the flock

B. The need for solid urban pastors

   1. *A vulnerable, unsafe environment*: the primacy of the shepherding role of pastoral care

   2. *Vicious predators*: those who would prey upon urban Christians

   3. *Proneness to wander*: the inclination of sheep toward distraction and departure from the flock

   4. *Dry, parched ground for grazing*: the increased amount of spiritual materials and doctrines in urban areas

3

5. *Hirelings abound*: many who feast upon the flock rather than protect it

C. Where do we find and how do we equip solid pastors for urban churches?

1. Pray for them: God said that he would provide them for us! Cf. Eph. 4.11-12.

2. Change our ways of producing them: many of our modern ways of training pastors are simply inadequate.

   a. They take too long.

   b. They focus on academic systems and structures.

   c. They are too expensive.

   d. They don't equip urban pastors to care for disciples in urban contexts.

   e. They don't give the training in the urban church setting.

3. Concentrate again on *biblical criteria* for leadership in the local church.

   a. Watch over the flock of God, (we're looking for people who never sleep when it comes to the well-being of the flock).

      (1) Acts 20.28

      (2) Heb. 13.7

b.   Counter false teaching and their heresies by nourishing the saints on the Word of God, Acts 20.29-32.

    c.   Equip the saints for the work of ministry (training pastors who are skilled in the art of making disciples and disciple makers, 2 Tim. 2.2).

4.   Simplify the process of recruiting, training, and commissioning pastors.

    2 Tim. 3.16-17 - All Scripture is breathed out by God and profitable for teaching, for reproof, for correction, and for training in righteousness, [17] that the man of God may be competent, equipped for every good work.

    a.   The Gospel of Jesus Christ

    b.   The Kingdom of God

    c.   The Nicene Creed

    d.   The Sacraments

    e.   Teaching and preaching the Word of God

5.   Let's rediscover the elegant simplicity of the early Church to equip undershepherds for the urban flocks around us.

    a.   Authentic courage from *compassionate servants*

3

b. Defenders of the apostolic tradition: *the Nicene Creed*

c. Concentration on the essentials: *laying one's life down for the sheep*, John 10.11

6. Place calling and gifting before credential and education.

a. God has raised up pastors for the body, Eph. 4.11-12.

b. A single true call of God is worth 10,000 lesser endorsements, Rom. 11.29.

III. Principles and Practice of the Pastoral Ministry

A. Recognize the importance of the pastoral office.

1. No pastor, the sheep will be scattered and feasted upon, John 10.10-13.

2. No pastor, fierce predators will devour the sheep, 1 Pet. 5.8-9.

3. No pastor, no flock at all!

B. Recruit workers to the pastoral ministry.

1. Appeal to their love for Jesus Christ, John 21.16.

Do not receive any stranger–whether bishop, presbyter, or deacon–without commendatory letters. And when such are offered, let them be examined.
~ Apostolic Constitutions (compiled c. 390, E), 7.502., Ibid., p. 157.

2. Appeal to their desire for a growing healthy church, Col. 1.25-28.

3. Appeal to their passion to equip others for ministry, Eph. 4.11-12.

C. Emphasize biblical standards and criteria (i.e., the Word of God is sufficient to equip the man or woman of God for every good work), 2 Tim. 3.15-17.

1. It never fails, Isa. 55.8-11.

2. It nurtures the soul and spirit, 1 Pet. 2.2.

3. It brings to maturity, Heb. 5.11-14.

D. Redefine the pastorate in terms of care-giving, nurturing, and tending the lambs, not administrating the corporation.

E. Embrace styles and methods of training conducive to urban disciples.

1. Become all things to all people in order to save and edify them, 1 Cor. 9.19-23.

2. Emphasize your freedom in Christ for the sake of loving others.

a. Gal. 5.1

b. Gal. 5.13

3

3. Ground believers in Christ, not in the plaque of Christian tradition, Col. 2.6-10.

F. Place the focus on helping to multiply ministry by equipping the saints, Eph. 4.11-16.

IV. The Blessing, Benefit, and Reward of the Christian Leader as Pastor

The same promise to elders is the very same reward promised to the godly shepherd who serves the Lord by willingly, eagerly, and carefully tending the flock of God on behalf of the Chief Shepherd.

1 Pet. 5.1-4 - So I exhort the elders among you, as a fellow elder and a witness of the sufferings of Christ, as well as a partaker in the glory that is going to be revealed: [2] shepherd the flock of God that is among you, exercising oversight, not under compulsion, but willingly, as God would have you; not for shameful gain, but eagerly; [3] not domineering over those in your charge, but being examples to the flock. [4] And when the Chief Shepherd appears, you will receive the unfading crown of glory.

A. The charge: *shepherd the flock of God that is among you.*

B. The reward: *when the Chief Shepherd appears, you will receive the unfading crown of glory.*

Conclusion

» The Word of God articulates three key images of the pastorate.

» A pastor is a nurturer and care giver, a protector and guardian, and a leader of the flock of God.

» The Word of God is able to equip the worker of God with all they need in order to fulfill their calling in leading God's flock.

» We must joyously flesh out the freedom that Christ has won for us in order to discover new, innovative ways to meet the deep needs of the lambs God has given to us to equip.

Therefore, appoint for yourselves bishops and deacons worthy of the Lord.
~ Didache (c. 80-140, E), 7.381., Ibid., p. 158.

3

Segue 2

Student Questions and Response

The following questions were designed to help you review the material in the second video segment. This segment discussed Scripture's vision of the kinds of roles that a pastor offers the people of God in his function as shepherd of the body. The pastor is a nurturer who ensures that God's people receive proper nourishment, feeding, tending, and care, a protector who guards the people of God against any harm or damage, and a leader called to go before the people of God and lead them into the fullness of the will of God for their individual and corporate lives. As those called to exercise leadership for the church in the city, it is critical that we understand these dimensions and roles with care and exactness. As you review the questions below, please concentrate on how these roles will need to be fleshed out in the urban community, and look to apply the Scriptures with an eye toward the urban scene and needs.

1. In looking at the examples of shepherding in the Word of God, what are three clear models and analogies given to us of what kind of *persona* (i.e., identity) a pastor ought to adopt as he cares for the people of God?

2. Explain the role of the pastor as a nurturer of the people of God. What does this role involve, and how does one prepare for this kind of ministry in the church? How can you tell if one is fulfilling this role in a local congregation to the maturity and well-being of the members of the body?

3. Lay out the various dimensions of the pastor as protector or guardian of the people of God. What are some of the things that a pastor may have to protect God's people from? What kind of training or input do you need in order to be able to fulfill this ministry in the church? How can you tell if someone is doing a good job at protecting a local congregation from predators and other things that may want to harm them?

4. What are the different kinds of things involved in providing overall leadership and direction for a local congregation? In what way should a pastor lead a congregation, and what kinds of things are emphasized in that leadership? What is the best way to help pastors learn how to lead others in the church? How can you tell if a pastor is not fulfilling this crucial role in the body?

5. Name three unique challenges of the urban community that makes nurturing, protecting, and leading an important ministry for Christian leaders in the city? How can urban churches identify, train, and release pastors who will nourish, protect, and lead urban disciples of Christ to mature in Christ and give witness to the Kingdom of God in the city?

3

6. How have modern views and models of management deeply impacted the way in which many churches have come to understand the pastoral ministry? Have these changes been healthy for the Church? Why or why not?

7. According to 1 Peter 5.1-4, what are the specific duties God requires for elders who are called to shepherd God's flock? How may these instructions be applied today specifically to shepherding small, poor congregations in the city?

8. What are the specific promises given to those who fulfill the high calling of shepherding the flock of God with integrity and excellence?

CONNECTION

Summary of Key Concepts

This lesson focuses upon the nature and meaning of the pastorate, that duty to shepherd the flock of God. The need for godly, dedicated, and well-equipped pastors is as great today as any time in the past, and perhaps even more necessary in urban communities which, for whatever reason, do not attract many who are willing to come and nurture, protect, and lead the people of God there. Review these foundational truths, making certain that you have a good grasp of the content of the statements, as well as their biblical support.

- In both the OT and NT, the image of shepherding is given for the leader of God's people, *roeh* in Hebrew and *poimen* in koine Greek, with both meaning "shepherd," "to shepherd," and to "provide pastoral care."

- The Lord God, rulers and kings, and the coming Messiah are all perceived as shepherds of God's people.

- The concept of *pastor* can be traced historically from the apostolic admonitions to provide care to one another as members of God's people in the Church, to the more formal notions of this care being delegated to specific individuals charged with shepherding the body as members of the clergy, or the formal office of the *pastorate*.

- Jesus himself is the prototype for the pastoral ministry, whose life demonstrated the character of the kind of feeding, love, and care God's flock requires. The Father himself calls and endows his pastors with special authority and gifts to provide this care for the Church.

- Depending on the government structure of the church, the pastor exercises his care giving responsibility in different ways, those including the episcopal, presbyterian, and congregational forms of church government.

- Regardless of the form of government, the pastor functions in the body as a *shepherd*, i.e., one who teaches and preaches the Word, administers the sacraments, comforts the bereaved, performs marriages, and equips the body for the work of the ministry.

- The Word of God provides three clear models and analogies of what a pastor does as care giver to the people of God as his flock: the pastor as nurturer, as protector, and as leader.

- The pastor is a nurturer who ensures that God's people receive proper nourishment, feeding, tending, and care.

- In addition, the pastor is a protector and guardian who guards the people of God against any predators or situations which would seek to harm or destroy them.

- Finally, the pastor is a leader called to go before the people of God and lead them into the fullness of the will of God for their individual and corporate lives.

- Because of the unique problems and challenges of urban communities, more than ever before the urban church needs pastors who will nourish, protect, and lead urban disciples of Christ to mature in Christ and give witness to the Kingdom of God in the city.

- God makes unequivocal promises to those who faithfully fulfill their work of shepherding the flock of God–they will receive the unfading crown of glory when the Chief Shepherd appears at the Second Coming.

Student Application and Implications

Now is the time for you to discuss with your fellow students your questions about the calling, criteria, and character of the pastoral ministry. Whether or not God has called you to be the *pastor* of a church or congregation, it is clear that, in some sense, God is calling all Christian leaders to be *pastoral* in their need to be nurturing, protecting, and guiding figures for those whom they mentor and lead. Now, list out your own particular questions about the nature of the pastorate that this lesson has unearthed for you, and address specifically any unresolved issues that remain for you on the nature of the pastoral ministry. The questions below are meant to spur your own questions about this important ministry.

* Is it possible to be called to the pastorate even when in fact you don't want to be a pastor? Explain your answer.

* How specifically would you know that God wanted you to join the pastorate? Must this come from one's own sense of calling, from your leader's sense of your own gifting and ministry, or a combination of both?

* Are women allowed to be in the pastorate? What are we to make of the many denominations which recognize pastoral authority for godly, mature women today?

* Should there be only *one senior pastor* or should we always seek a plurality of pastors in charge of the church?

* How much of a church's operations (i.e., administration, finances, facilities, etc.) should be under the control and oversight of the pastor? Should a pastor's responsibility be limited to the *spiritual responsibilities* associated with leading the people of God, and the more mundane items be turned over to others? Why or why not?

* How long should the term of pastor, elder, or deacon be? Ought we to place any limits in regards to term limits for any Christian leaders in the church?

* How confidential must a pastor be in the various kinds of dealings that they have with the different members of the church? Do any circumstances exist where a pastor might have to break confidence, both for the good of the individuals and of the congregation. Site examples.

* Can a pastor function properly if they do not also have an *authority structure* that they must report and answer to? What are the implications of this for the kind of church government that churches ought to establish for their own and their pastor's benefit?

* What are the qualifications that we ought to use for identifying and selecting pastoral candidates for the ministry? How important ought things like salary, housing, insurance, and similar items be in selecting a congregation to lead? Explain your answer.

CASE STUDIES

Not Until You Fix It Up

1 (Based on a true story). In a denomination where the bishop appoints pastors to care for congregations in his district annually, an appointment was made of a pastor who refused to move into the parsonage. Although the parsonage (i.e., the pastor's residence) was included in the financial package provided to the pastor, upon his arrival to the city and his first inspection of the parsonage, he decided that it was in too rundown of a condition for him to move his family into it. He refused to move into the parsonage until the leaders of the church funded its renovation. Staying at a local motel, the pastor of this poor urban church argued that asking your pastor, any pastor, to move into substandard housing was neither spiritually advisable nor fiscally desirable. The church had very few financial resources but, in obedience to their new pastor, renovated the inside of the parsonage, and after some weeks the pastor and his family moved into the newly decorated home. The actual tenure of the pastor at the church was both fruitful and cordial. What do you think of this pastor's insistence that the congregation provide for its leaders in an acceptable manner–did he go too far in his leadership here?

I Can't Submit to a Woman

2 A rift is beginning to occur among the members and leaders of a socially progressive evangelical church in a needy urban neighborhood. This congregation has become known around the city for its staunch stance against racism and sexism in any form. At its annual business meeting, the head elder announced the retirement of the church's current pastor, and in his place, the elders are recommending a godly, mature woman to pastor the church. Seminary trained, a gifted teacher, and deeply spiritual individual, this sister is liked by the entire congregation, whom she has served in various capacities over the last ten years. Some of the male members, however, struggle with this candidacy, not because she is not qualified spiritually, but because she is a woman. This has sparked a strong debate among the members, some of which feel so deeply that they have promised to leave the church if she is voted in. How ought the church approach and handle this issue of women and the pastorate?

3

No Wiggle Room to Maneuver

Many churches do not allow their pastor to be involved in the everyday decisions of administration, finance, personnel, or facilities. Arguing from the position of Acts 6, those who refuse this kind of participation for their pastors suggest that the role of the pastor is *spiritual* not *administrative* or *technical*. Issues of finance and administration are the province of others; the pastor ought to concentrate on issues surrounding the Word of God, prayer, and equipping the saints for ministry. Because of these restrictions, however, many pastors have little or no input into many things that affect the church's future, including their own salaries and benefits. What is the proper role for pastoral leadership in the ongoing operations of a church? Should they concentrate solely on spiritual matters, or should they be included in all decisions affecting the church. Make your case with Scripture, if possible.

In both the OT and NT, the image of shepherding is given for the leader of God's people, *roeh* in Hebrew and *poimen* in koine Greek, with both meaning "shepherd," "to shepherd," and to "provide pastoral care." The Lord God, rulers and kings, and the coming Messiah are all perceived as shepherds of God's people. The concept of pastor developed throughout the Church, from the care that all Christians provided to eventually a formal role for those individuals who would care for God's flock. Jesus himself is the prototype for the pastoral ministry, and God call's and gifts particular individuals to provide this care for the Church. Depending on the government structure of the church, the pastor exercises his care giving responsibility in different ways, but all through the functions of a *shepherd*, i.e., one who teaches and preaches the Word, administers the sacraments, comforts the bereaved, performs marriages, and equips the body for the work of the ministry.

Restatement of the Lesson's Thesis

The Word of God provides three clear models and analogies of what a pastor does as care giver to the people of God as his flock. The pastor is a nurturer who ensures that God's people receive proper nourishment, feeding, tending, and care. Furthermore, the pastor is a protector and guardian who guards the people of God against any predators or situations which would seek to harm or destroy them. Finally, the pastor is a leader called to go before the people of God and lead them into the fullness of the will of God for their individual and corporate lives. More than ever before the urban church needs pastors who will nourish, protect, and lead urban disciples of Christ to mature in Christ and give witness to the Kingdom of God in the city. God makes unequivocal promises to those who faithfully fulfill their work of shepherding the flock of God–they will receive the unfading crown of glory when the Chief Shepherd appears at the Second Coming.

Resources and Bibliographies

If you are interested in pursuing some of the ideas of *The Christian Leader as Pastor (Poimenes)*, you might want to give these books a try:

Dawn, Marva, and Eugene H. Peterson, Peter Santucci, eds. *The Unnecessary Pastor: Rediscovering the Call*. Grand Rapids: Eerdmans, 2000.

Hansen, David. *The Art of Pastoring: Ministering without All the Answers*. Downers Grove: InterVarsity Press, 1994.

Oden, Thomas C. *Pastoral Theology: Essentials of Ministry*. New York: HarperCollins Publishers, 1983.

Willimon, William H. *Pastor: The Theology and Practice of Ordained Ministry*. Nashville: Abingdon Press, 2002.

Ministry Connections

page 351 📖 *5*

Whether or not God has called you to the pastorate, your understanding of this vital role of Christian leadership will affect every area of your own life and ministry through your church. You are called to be *pastoral* in terms of offering care and love to those to whom you minister, and through your own application of these truths, God may desire to change and/or alter your ministry approach. How has the Holy Spirit been influencing your own judgments about the pastorate as you studied this material? Have you sensed any calling from the Lord regarding your own appointment to this high ministry? What do you believe the Lord is specifically calling you to do right now, if anything, about these truths? Set aside good time this week to review these truths, and rethink your own understanding of the pastoral ministry. Also, as you consider your ministry project for this module, you can possibly use it to connect to these truths in a practical way. Seek the face of God for insight, and come back next week ready to share your insights with the other learners in your class.

Counseling and Prayer

If for any reason you need spiritual direction for unanswered questions and/or unresolved issues in this lesson, seek the Lord's guidance about getting with your own pastor, spiritual supervisor, or leader to get further clarification. Also, be open to ask your fellow students to lift up your particular requests to God. Of course, know that your instructor is extremely open to discussing related questions to Christian leadership, the pastorate, or related questions with you, whatever they are related to the materials in this lesson. The more open you are to the Lord's counsel

3

through his people the better you will be led to discover his particular insights and will for you. Be open to God and allow him to lead you as he determines.

Acts 20.26-28

Scripture Memory

To prepare for class, please visit *www.tumi.org/books* to find next week's reading assignment, or ask your mentor.

Reading Assignment

As usual you ought to come with your reading assignment sheet containing your summary of the reading material for the week. Also, you must have selected the text for your exegetical project, and turn in your proposal for your ministry project.

Other Assignments

page 351 📖 *6*

In this lesson we considered the significant role of the pastor in ministry. In both its Old and New Testament contexts, the image of shepherding was given to help us understand the nature of pastoral oversight and care. This imagery is applied to many who shepherded the people of God, including the Lord himself, appointed rulers and kings of Israel, and the coming Messiah, fulfilled in the person of Jesus of Nazareth. The Word of God pictures forth this shepherding ministry in the images of nurturer, protector, and leader. In our next and final lesson on foundations of Christian leadership we will consider the dynamic concept of bishop or overseer. We will examine its NT meanings, trace its probable context in the council of elders in Jewish rulership, and its continued development through the Church, considering its historical calling and criteria. We will also examine this role of leader through the images of supervisor, apostle, and spiritual director. Understanding this broad and important role, we will seek to show how the very nature of Christian leadership and Christian community demands oversight and relationship which goes beyond just the local body itself.

Looking Forward to the Next Lesson

3

For each assigned reading, write a brief summary (one or two paragraphs) of the author's main point. (For additional readings, use the back of this sheet.)

Reading 1

Title and Author: _____ Pages _____

Reading 2

Title and Author: _____ Pages _____

The Christian Leader as Bishop
Episkopoi

LESSON 4

page 353 📖 *1*

Lesson Objectives

Welcome in the strong name of Jesus Christ! After your reading, study, discussion, and application of the materials in this lesson, you will be able to:

- Recite the meanings of the term *episkopos* (i.e., bishop) with the Septuagint, its usages in the classic Greek, and within the New Testament itself.

- Articulate how and in what ways the terms for "pastor," "elder," and "bishop" all refer to the same office, with emphases on different roles and responsibilities of Christian leadership in the Church.

- Outline possible origins and the development of the office of the bishop through the council of elders in Jewish rulership where an elder could be recognized as one to speak on behalf of and represent the entire council of elders.

- Elaborate how in the history of the Church the office of the bishop expanded to mean an appointed or elected individual given charge over a number of pastors or groups of congregations in a given context.

- Define both the calling and criteria of the bishop, from the biblical qualifications in 1 Timothy 3 and Titus 1, as well as the example of Jesus.

- Detail how bishops were selected, and then provide the nature of the bishop's authority and function to give oversight, including the bishop's expanded authority as "pastor of pastors," as well as one given the responsibility to oversee *all the churches* within his area of responsibility.

- Lay out how all traditions have some version of the *function* of a bishop even though they may not have any *nomenclature* (language, categories) of the bishop. All churches require ongoing oversight and supervision.

- Reproduce the three biblical images of the role of the bishop: as supervisor, as apostle, and as spiritual director.

- Show how the bishop as supervisor functions as a superintendent, coordinating and organizing the outreach, personnel, and resources of churches under his/her care to make maximum impact for the Church's edification and the Kingdom's advancement.

- Specify the ways in which a bishop functions as an apostle, charged with the ongoing care of new churches and their leaders, doing all they can to ensure the protection, edification and development of them.

- Give evidence how the bishop functions as a spiritual director, providing challenge and encouragement to budding ministries and churches as they mature in Christ.

- Sketch out carefully the importance of pastoral and church association, both as it relates *regionally* through the locale church, and through affinity and shared identity.

- Argue for the role of the bishop-level oversight being given to urban churches in association with each other, and how that ministry might flesh itself out among urban congregations.

- Review the blessing, benefit, and reward of faithful obedience to the call of the Christian leader as bishop, with the prospect of exercising authority in the Kingdom of God.

Filling Up What Is Lacking for the Church

Devotion

page 354 📖 2

Col. 1.24-29 - Now I rejoice in my sufferings for your sake, and in my flesh I am filling up what is lacking in Christ's afflictions for the sake of his body, that is, the church, [25] of which I became a minister according to the stewardship from God that was given to me for you, to make the word of God fully known, [26] the mystery hidden for ages and generations but now revealed to his saints. [27] To them God chose to make known how great among the Gentiles are the riches of the glory of this mystery, which is Christ in you, the hope of glory. [28] Him we proclaim, warning everyone and teaching everyone with all wisdom, that we may present everyone mature in Christ. [29] For this I toil, struggling with all his energy that he powerfully works within me.

Paul's zeal for the Church is one of the most noticeable features of his remarkable apostolic career. No commentator on the great apostle can possibly miss his unusual zeal for Christ, for the Gospel, and for his desire to fulfill his ministry. He counts all things as loss for the supremacy of the knowledge of Christ (cf. Phil. 3.4-7), and he counts his life as nothing so he can fulfill his course with joy, and the ministry that he received of the Lord Jesus. His own testimony makes this zeal visible to all: "But I do not account my life of any value nor as precious to myself, if only I may finish my course and the ministry that I received from the Lord Jesus, to testify to the gospel of the grace of God" (Acts 20.24). Paul was intensely and continuously committed to his ends, all of which involved his own calling to help advance the Kingdom of God through his faithful testifying of Jesus of Nazareth as both Lord and Christ.

If we look even more specifically at this zeal, it was extraordinarily focused on the people of God, and providing the Church with the requisite care and love needed to bring her to full maturity in Christ. Along these lines, Paul could reveal that God provided apostles like himself and the others in order to equip the saints for the work of the ministry in order that the Church might be built up both in terms of maturity in Christ and fullness of number (Eph. 4.9-16). Undoubtedly, Paul had an affinity with the Church of God that determined all that he did and desired.

This great burden for the well-being and nourishing of the body of Christ is spoken of Colossians 1 in a striking and even peculiar way. Paul suggests that his sufferings on behalf of the Church in some mysterious way was a completion, a kind of filling up in his own flesh (through the beatings, fastings, struggles, nakedness, and tortures) "what is lacking in Christ's afflictions for the sake of his body, that is, the church." This language is both unique and remarkable. In some mysterious way, God has assigned his leaders both the privilege and responsibility to enter into the very sufferings of Christ for his body, the Church. Paul makes plain that this is neither simply the result of his own sincere choice or effort; God himself through his stewardship of grace had made him a minister in order that he might make the word of God's mystery fully known among the Gentiles. This great mystery had not been known for ages and generations (cf. Rom. 16.25-27; Eph. 3.4-8) but now was revealed to God's saints through the prophets and the apostles. What is this remarkable mystery? God has chosen to reveal the riches of his grace among the Gentiles, which is Christ in them, the very hope of glory.

Those who serve the mysteries of God are intimately connected to God's people. The ministry exists for them. Paul puts this ministry in a number of different ways, all of which speak of the remarkable honor we have as we serve the Church of God:

> 2 Cor. 11.2 - I feel a divine jealousy for you, for I betrothed you to one husband, to present you as a pure virgin to Christ.

> Col. 1.28 - Him we proclaim, warning everyone and teaching everyone with all wisdom, that we may present everyone mature in Christ.

4

Eph. 3.7-8 - Of this gospel I was made a minister according to the gift of God's grace, which was given me by the working of his power. [8] To me, though I am the very least of all the saints, this grace was given, to preach to the Gentiles the unsearchable riches of Christ

What an unbelievable privilege to actually sacrifice and suffer on behalf of Christ's very own body, the Church, and mysteriously through our sufferings to actually "fill up that which is lacking" of Christ's afflictions for his people. Truly, this is a privilege, an honor, and a great blessing to stand for the Lord Jesus in such a way that he himself is honored through our sufferings on behalf of his people. This is the challenge of all who sacrifice on behalf of the people of God.

Regardless of the kinds of things we will endure as we care for the well-being of other believers, let us embrace these sufferings as somehow related to our Lord's own sufferings on behalf of his people. And truly, may our dear Lord provide us who lead the church with the same kind of spiritual dynamism and vision displayed when the apostles were first dishonored on behalf of the Gospel and the Church.

Acts 5.41-42 - Then they left the presence of the council, rejoicing that they were counted worthy to suffer dishonor for the name. [42] And every day, in the temple and from house to house, they did not cease teaching and preaching Jesus as the Christ.

4

After reciting and/or singing the Nicene Creed (located in the Appendix), pray the following prayer:

A prayer for the bishop . . .

To you, O Father, all hearts are open; fill, we pray, the heart of this your servant whom you have chosen to be a bishop in your Church, with such love of you and of all the people, that he may feed and tend the flock of Christ, and exercise without reproach the high priesthood to which you have called him, serving before you day and night in the ministry of reconciliation, declaring pardon in your Name, offering the holy gifts, and wisely overseeing the life and work of the Church. In all things may he present before you the acceptable offering of a pure, and gentle, and holy life; through Jesus Christ your Son, to whom, with you and the Holy Spirit, be honor and power and glory in the Church, now and for ever.

~ Episcopal Church. **The Book of Common Prayer and Administrations of the Sacraments and Other Rites and Ceremonies of the Church, Together with the Psalter or Psalms of David**. New York: The Church Hymnal Corporation, 1979. p. 521.

Nicene Creed and Prayer

Quiz

Put away your notes, gather up your thoughts and reflections, and take the quiz for Lesson 3, *The Christian Leader as Pastor (Poimenes).*

....

Scripture Memorization Review

Review with a partner, write out and/or recite the text for last class session's assigned memory verse: Acts 20.26-28.

....

Assignments Due

Turn in your summary of the reading assignment for last week, that is, your brief response and explanation of the main points that the authors were seeking to make in the assigned reading (Reading Completion Sheet).

....

Independent Is Not Heretical

1 ▸ Many churches today count themselves as "unaffiliated," "non-denominational," or "independent." This trend has led to a steady increase in the number of churches which proudly and gladly affirm no formal connection with any organized tradition or church association. Some see this trend not to formally affiliate with other churches as a bold reaffirmation of the voluntary and apparently natural affinity of the NT churches. Others, however, see this trend as a further sign of the Western church's lack of understanding and appreciation of tradition. What do you think both of the *fact* of so many churches functioning as non-denominational and independent churches, as well as the *trend* of so many congregations electing not to formally associate with other congregations?

An Impulse to Become a Sect

2 ▸ Many who argue that churches need connection without formal association argue persuasively that often when churches associate too closely that they can become ingrown and sectarian. One need not do much research to find examples of a number of church movements that splintered from the mainstream of faith and practice because they were adversely affected by a person who was both highly charismatic and yet cultic in orientation. Because of the tendency for movements to lose their own identity to the influential thoughts of a single individual, many congregations organize around strictly congregational structure. Many ministries today were formed on the basis of the dominance of a single personality whose

4

impact and authority touches every phase of the work. One only needs to look at the tragedies of Jim Baker and Jimmy Swaggart to see the power of one person to influence a movement. How would you answer the criticism that denominations tend to be too influenced by the dominant personality of individuals rather than the will of the people to lead the movement in a godly way?

A Highly Efficient Structure

Another trend among many evangelicals today is the move to traditions which are led with strong episcopal authority. Plainly stated, many Bible-believing Christians are leaving the independent movement and are going to high church traditions. In other words, at the same time that there has been a marked increase in the number of independent congregations, you also see many evangelical leaders going to traditions which are known for their strong centralized leadership structures. They argue that these traditions have a deep sense of history, a keen identity as churches, and a respectful appreciation for tradition. Many are entering traditions like the Orthodox and Anglican churches, which are governed by episcopal structures which allow for strong, efficient leadership of the whole. Such structures are administratively efficient, and tend to reduce the possibility of renegade or maverick leaders or congregations to gain ground. What do you make of this trend, that so many Bible-believing Christians in the West are moving to more traditional, historical, and episcopal kinds of church and spirituality?

The Christian Leader as Bishop (*Episkopoi*)

Segment 1: Definition and Overview

Rev. Dr. Don L. Davis

The NT Greek term *episkopos* ("bishop") can be interpreted as overseer; the term has a history that originated with the *Septuagint* (i.e., the Greek OT), various usages of the term in the classical Greek tradition, and finally in its use by the apostles in the New Testament itself. In one sense the terms for "pastor," "elder," and "bishop" all refer to the same office, with emphases on different roles and responsibilities of Christian leadership in the church. The use of the concept of *elder as overseer* may have some resonance with council of elders in Jewish rulership where an elder could

CONTENT

Summary of Segment 1

page 356 📖 *3*

be recognized as one to speak on behalf of and represent the entire council of elders. The concept in the Church has been expanded through history to refer to the office of the bishop appointed or elected to oversee a number of pastors or groups of congregations in a given context. The standards of bishop are articulated in 1 Timothy 3 and Titus 1, as well as the example of Jesus. As a "pastor of pastors," bishops have historically come to represent the leaders of large areas and numbers of churches within his area of responsibility. While some traditions may reject the *nomenclature* (i.e., language) of the bishop, most groups have supervisors who assume the *function* of a bishop, i.e., ongoing oversight and supervision of churches in association together.

Our objective for this segment, *The Christian Leader as Bishop: Definition and Overview*, is to enable you to see that:

- The Greek NT term *episkopos* refers to the office of the "bishop," and can be translated "overseer." This term and its meaning can be traced through its usages in the *Septuagint*, in the classical Greek tradition, and finally within the New Testament itself.

- The terms for "pastor," "elder," and "bishop" are virtually synonymous, and probably refer to the same office, with emphases on different roles and responsibilities of Christian leadership in the church.

- The origins and the development of the office of the bishop may probably be connected to the council of elders in Jewish rulership where an elder could be recognized as one to speak on behalf of and represent the entire council of elders.

- Through church history, the office of the bishop has expanded to refer to those individuals who have been either appointed or elected to a position of oversight over a number of pastors or groups of congregations in a given context.

- The qualifications for bishop are clearly outlined in the New Testament, including extended passages in 1 Timothy 3 and Titus 1, and concretely demonstrated in the example of Jesus, referred to as the "Shepherd and Bishop of our souls," 1 Pet. 2.23.

- Bishops have been selected in various ways through the history of the Church, and once installed, have been given substantive authority to oversee pastors and churches for their edification and growth. As "pastor of

4

pastors," bishops provide concrete answerability to all pastors and churches under their charge.

- While some traditions may reject the *nomenclature* (i.e., language) of the bishop, most groups have supervisors who assume the *function* of a bishop, i.e., ongoing oversight and supervision of churches in association together.

I. New Testament Meanings of the Term *Episkopos* (pl. *Episkopoi*)

Video Segment 1
Outline

A. Word meanings for *episkopos*: in the Septuagint and the Classic Greek context

1. The Greek version of the OT (*Septuagint*)

   a. Provides the meaning for *episkopos* as "to superintend," "to give oversight," "searching" in matters of the army, the people of God, and the state government

   b. Num. 4.16 - And Eleazar the son of Aaron the priest shall have charge of the oil for the light, the fragrant incense, the regular grain offering, and the anointing oil, with the *oversight* of the whole tabernacle and all that is in it, of the sanctuary and its vessels.

   c. Num. 31.14 - And Moses was angry with the officers of the army, the *commanders* of thousands and the *commanders* of hundreds, who had come from service in the war.

   d. 2 Kings 12.11 - Then they would give the money that was weighed out into the hands of the workmen who had the *oversight* of the house of the Lord. And they paid it out to the carpenters and the builders who worked on the house of the Lord.

**Ignatius,
Bishop of Antioch**
I do not issue orders to you, as though I were some great person. . . . For now I begin to be a disciple, and I speak to you as fellow disciples with me.
~ Ignatius (c. 105, E), 1.50., David W. Bercot, ed. A Dictionary of Early Christian Beliefs. Peabody, MA: Hendrickson, 1998. p. 70.

4

e. 2 Chron. 34.17 - They have emptied out the money that was found in the house of the Lord and have given it into the hand of the *overseers* and the workmen.

2. The word *episkopos* was used in classical Greek speaking contexts (Homer applied it to the gods as overseers, and in Athens, the governors of conquered states were called *episkopoi*).

3. The meaning of "guardian," "overseer," or "superintendent" corresponds to *episkopos*.

B. The NT uses words in a fluid way when it comes to defining Christian leaders in the Church.

1. Paul often uses this term in his letters and epistles; Peter uses it in regards to Christ and to elders.

a. Acts 20.28 - Pay careful attention to yourselves and to all the flock, in which the Holy Spirit has made you *overseers*, to care for the church of God, which he obtained with his own blood.

b. Rom. 12.8 - . . . the one who exhorts, in his exhortation; the one who contributes, in generosity; the one who *leads*, with zeal; the one who does acts of mercy, with cheerfulness.

c. Phil. 1.1 - Paul and Timothy, servants of Christ Jesus, to all the saints in Christ Jesus who are at Philippi, with the *overseers* and deacons.

4

d. 1 Tim. 3.1 - The saying is trustworthy: If anyone aspires to the office of *overseer*, he desires a noble task.

e. 1 Tim. 5.17 - Let *the elders who rule* well be considered worthy of double honor, especially those who labor in preaching and teaching.

f. Titus 1.7 - For an *overseer*, as God's steward, must be above reproach. He must not be arrogant or quick-tempered or a drunkard or violent or greedy for gain.

g. 1 Pet. 2.25 - For you were straying like sheep, but have now returned to the Shepherd and *Overseer* of your souls.

h. 1 Pet. 5.2 - Shepherd the flock of God that is among you, exercising *oversight*, not under compulsion, but willingly, as God would have you; not for shameful gain, but eagerly.

2. Greek word for bishop (*episkopos*) often is translated "overseer," "leader," "elder," or "guardian."

3. "Bishop" and "elder" refer to the same person.

a. Titus 1.5 and Titus 1.7 refer to the *same person* (referred to as *elder* on the one hand and *overseer* on the other).

(1) Titus 1.5

(2) Titus 1.7

b.   The elders of Acts 20.17 are referred to as *overseers* in Acts 20.28.

        (1) Acts 20.17

        (2) Acts 20.28

4.   The idea of a bishop as an elder who gave oversight resonates with the NT usage of the terms: traditional senses of elder leadership.

    a.   *Ruling elders*: those elders (i.e., bishops) whose responsibility focused on presiding over the affairs of the Christian community

    b.   *Teaching elders*: those elders whose primary responsibility focused on laboring as teachers and preachers within the Christian community

5.   Why the difference between elder and bishop?

    a.   The term "presbyter" (*elder*), a term familiar to the Jews, signifies their place and age within the Church community.

    b.   The term "bishop" (*overseer*), a term used more in Gentile settings, refers to *their office and authority.*

    c.   *Whatever the case, bishop and elder refer to the same person.*

4

II. Origins and Development of the Office of the Bishop

A. The Council of the Elders in Jewish governance

    1. The council of elders = those leaders who served as leaders over the various tribes of Israel, and who together exercised authority for its protection and growth

    2. Elders were equal in status; governed through dialogue and consensus reached on issues together.

B. Notion of the Bishop

    1. Probably emerged in relation to the concept of oversight within the Council of the Elders

    2. A bishop = an elder recognized by the other members of the council as an overseer to speak on behalf of and represent the entire council of elders

        a. Rooted in Jewish precedents

        b. Informed by secular systems of governance

C. Definitions of leadership in great transition during NT era

    1. Phil. 1.1 and Acts 20 show that the definitions between the various terms (i.e., pastor, elder, and bishop) are in a period of transition.

Our apostles also knew, through our Lord Jesus Christ, that there would be strife on account of the office of oversight. For this reason, therefore, inasmuch as they had obtained a perfect foreknowledge of this, they appointed those already mentioned. Afterwards, they gave instructions, that when those men should fall asleep, other approved men should succeed them in their ministry. We are of opinion, therefore, that those appointed by the apostles or afterwards by other eminent men, with the consent of the whole church, and who have blamelessly served the flock of Christ in a humble, peaceable, and disinterested spirit, and have for a long time possessed the good opinion of all, cannot be justly dismissed from the ministry.
~ Clement of Rome (c. 96, W), 1.17., Ibid.

4

2. Best to conceive of the various terms in light of the *primary function* which the concept highlights

    a. The term *pastor* highlights the *shepherding role* of the Christian leader in the congregation.

    b. The term *elder* highlights the *place, position, and prominence* of the Christian leader in the congregation.

    c. The term *bishop* highlights the role of providing *broad oversight authority* of the Christian leader in the congregation.

D. In the history of the Church, the office of *bishop* was expanded to represent an appointed or elected individual who was *given charge over a number of pastors or groups of congregations.*

    1. This definition corresponds to *the apostolic office* of giving oversight to the churches (the Apostle to the Gentiles, Rom. 15.16).

    2. Paul's responsibility included all the congregations, 2 Cor. 11.28.

    3. His journeys were motivated by his desire to care for all the churches where they had planted them, Acts 15.36.

    4. His ongoing work was to strengthen all the churches in his circuit.

        a. Acts 15.40-41

    b.   Acts 18.23

   5.   Paul as apostle showed great concern, even for those congregations which had never seen him face to face, Col. 2.1.

E.   The concept of bishop embraced this apostolic responsibility for leadership in the Church and expanded the meaning of the original context (the idea corresponding to exercising authority and oversight) to *all churches in a given context.*

   1.   The meaning was applied not merely to ruling and leading an individual congregation, but *a group of them*, Rom. 12.8.

   2.   Expanded to mean not merely overseeing affairs in a congregation, but *in many of them*

      (1)   Acts 20.28

      (2)   1 Pet. 5.2

   3.   Broadened to not only exercising authority in the context of a group of elders in a church, but among *a group of churches*, cf. Phil. 1.1, see 1 Tim. 4.14

F.   This idea of *bishop* oversight touches all traditions, even those who would reject this as an explicit form of church government.

   1.   This sense of oversight is oftentimes associated with the founder of the movement.

a.   The churches are inspired by their *personage*.

b.   The churches are informed by their *teachings*.

c.   The churches are committed to follow their *organizational structures*.

d.   The churches associate themselves explicitly with their *emphases and vision*.

2.   Regardless of the organizational form of government, most Christian movements have recognized this broader form of church oversight.

a.   Martin Luther and the *Lutheran Church*

b.   John Calvin and the *Reformed Church*

c.   John Wesley and the *Methodist Church*

d.   John Wimber and the *Vineyard Church*

e.   George Fox and the *Quaker Church*

f.   Richard Allen and the *African Methodist Episcopal Church*

G. The history of the Church demonstrates the need for pastors and churches to congregate, not merely as individual congregations, but in association with others.

1. For fellowship and like-minded identity

2. For support and financial aid

3. For outreach and mission efforts

III. Calling and Criteria for the Bishop Office

A. The biblical qualifications for a bishop, 1 Tim. 3.2-7; Titus 1.6-9

1. Spiritual qualifications

2. Family qualifications

3. Character qualifications

B. Jesus as the standard for exercising oversight: the Shepherd and Bishop of our souls, 1 Pet. 2.25

Jesus is the standard by which we understand the exercising of oversight and authority. It is not done on the basis of coercion and domination, but willing, eager, and loving oversight for the sake of protection, provision, and peace.

But deacons should remember that the Lord chose apostles– that is, bishops and overseers. But apostles appointed for themselves deacons after the ascension of the Lord into heaven, as ministers of their episcopacy and of the church.
~ Cyprian (c. 250, E), 5.366., Ibid., p. 72.

4

1. Whatever term we employ regarding the Christian leader (*diakonos*, *poimen*, *presbyteros*, or *episkopos*), Jesus' life and ministry fills out the details for the *meaning* of Christian leadership in the Church.

2. He is our *Servant* (*diakonia*), Rom. 15.8 - For I tell you that Christ became *a servant* to the circumcised to show God's truthfulness, in order to confirm the promises given to the patriarchs.

3. He is our *Elder Brother*, Rom. 8.29 - For those whom he foreknew he also predestined to be conformed to the image of his Son, in order that he might be *the firstborn among many brothers*.

4. He is our *Chief Shepherd*, 1 Pet. 5.4 - And when the *chief Shepherd* appears, you will receive the unfading crown of glory.

5. He is the *Bishop of our souls*, 1 Pet. 2.25 - For you were straying like sheep, but have now returned to the *Shepherd and Overseer of your souls*.

6. The standard of Christian leadership, then, is the exhortation of others to follow us *as we follow Christ*.

    a. 1 Cor. 11.1

    b. Phil. 2.5

    c. Matt. 20.26-28

    d. John 13.14

     e. Eph. 5.2

     f. 1 Pet. 2.21

C. Selection of bishops

    1. In conjunction with an *appointment from recognized spiritual authority*

    2. Through the *election from a group of pastors or churches endowed with the authority to select its guardians*

D. Nature of bishop's oversight: the historical development of the bishop's expanded authority

In modern times, the role of bishop has been expanded to include not just oversight of the spiritual affairs of a particular congregation or parish, but all of those congregations and their pastors within a particular jurisdiction.

In this sense, the modern day bishop functions much the same way as an apostle functioned in the early Church environment. (Cf. Paul's care and anxiety for all the churches, 2 Cor. 11.28 - And, apart from other things, there is the daily pressure on me of my anxiety for all the churches.)

    1. Protector of the faith and *defender of the apostolic doctrine*, 2 Cor. 11.12-15

    2. *Superintend the churches and missionaries* of pastors under their care in a jurisdiction or area, Phil. 2.19-24

    3. Provide oversight for the health and growth of the churches within their appointed area of responsibility, Titus 1.4-5

4. Appoint pastors and other officials in an area to ensure the healthy growth and functioning of the churches under their care, Acts 14.21-23

5. Connect with other churches, denominations, or agencies whose practices correspond to the purpose and mission of the church the bishop represents, 1 Thess. 2.13-14

IV. Authority and Functions of the Bishop

A. Authority of the bishop

   The biblical notion of bishop is synonymous with the biblical idea of elder and/or pastor.

   1. Bishops are elders who provide both pastoral and ruling oversight usually over a number of pastors and churches.

   2. Bishops derive their authority of actually being "one from among them" (i.e., pastors, elders) who has been granted authority to nurture and give oversight to them.

      a. A "pastor of pastors"

      b. A "first among equals"

      c. A "shepherd of the shepherds"

   3. *Bishops (like apostles) provide oversight and leadership over groups of pastors and churches for their well being and growth, Acts 20.28.*

B. Functions of the bishop

The modern-day understanding of the bishop arises from the very biblical notion of the need for pastors and churches to be given solid pastoral oversight if they are to remain healthy and reproduce.

1. Bishop has historically been understood as both a legitimate and necessary office of the Church.

2. While it may be difficult to pin down the *fluid nature* of the concept as a NT office, the *function* of a bishop has been recognized in all of the life of the Church through its history.

3. Bishops pastor *pastors.*

    a. Pastors need pastoring.

    b. The Pastoral Epistles reveal that developing leaders require teaching, training, and encouragement.

    c. Regardless of the church government style, churches have historically recognized the need for pastors to receive *ongoing support, fellowship, and input from godly overseers.*

4. Bishops oversee *churches* (not just a single congregation).

    a. Churches function best in association with other like-minded congregations.

b. Bishops functioned in the early Church as those who provided support and health not just for the congregations where they pastored, but for the entire cluster of churches in their area which they led.

5. The function of guardianship and oversight for pastors and churches is the heart of the apostolic church planter's responsibility.

C. Implication for our understanding of the bishop office.

1. A prominent and important office in the Church of Jesus Christ.

2. While the person of elder and bishop may be the same, the function may be highlighted in different contexts to emphasize different understandings of the office.

3. Although many traditions of the church would not accept the role of bishop as a form of church government, it is virtually impossible to conceive of any church group functioning well without a living concept of the role of bishop as overseeing the group of churches affairs and serving its assembly.

Conclusion

» The notion of *episkopos* or "bishop" or "overseer" was developed through its usage in the Septuagint, in the classical Greek tradition, and its use within the NT church.

» God has established overseers who exercise godly authority over the affairs of the Church to strengthen and advance his kingdom cause through the Church.

Please take as much time as you have available to answer these and other questions that the video brought out. In this last segment we saw how the NT concept of *episkopos* ("bishop") was affected by its usage, not only in the *Septuagint* (i.e., the Greek OT), but also in its various usages of the term in the classical Greek tradition. The importance of this concept can hardly be overstated. As it has developed, it has outgrown its more biblical sense as a synonym for "pastor," "elder," and has come to refer to that office of offering oversight to a number of pastors or groups of congregations in a given context. It is more than merely a concept of church governance, but of *spiritual direction and godly oversight* of an entire constellation of pastors and churches. While denominations differ greatly in the role of oversight, virtually all traditions have individuals who function as supervisors or overseers; they reject the *nomenclature* (i.e., language) but they embrace the *function* of a bishop. As a emerging Christian leader, it is important for you to be conversant with these concepts, so review the material in this segment carefully.

Segue 1

Student Questions and Response

page 358 4

1. What is the meaning of the Greek NT term *episkopos*? Trace the various uses of this term in its usages in the *Septuagint* and in the classical Greek tradition. How were these meanings adopted or changed in the Apostles' use of the term in the New Testament?

2. What is the relationship of the various biblical terms "pastor," "elder," and "bishop"– in what ways are they different and the same? How do the various terms help us look at particular facets of the role of Christian leadership?

3. How might the use of the term *episkopos* relate to the expressing of leadership in the council of elders in Jewish rulership? Since *episkopos* was generally a secular term, what kinds of differences do you suspect were noted between the idea of a Jewish elder and a Roman *episkopos*?

4. How did the notion of the bishop develop from the NT to its more expanded use as a term to refer to individuals appointed or elected to a position to give oversight over a number of pastors or groups of congregations in a given context?

5. What are some of the key qualifications for bishops as given in such passages as 1 Timothy 3 and Titus 1? How can the example of Jesus and his ministry of oversight (i.e., as the "Shepherd and Bishop of our souls," 1 Pet. 2.23) inform our own understanding of what an *episkopos* ought to be and to do?

6. List out some of the ways that historically bishops have been selected to serve. Once installed in their roles as bishops, what have been the historic roles and responsibilities of these leaders of the Church? Explain how today many bishops function as a "pastor of pastors."

7. Why should we not be surprised that virtually all denominations have some role of supervisory leadership that functions very much in the historical vein of *bishop as overseer of pastors and congregations*?

The Christian Leader as Bishop (*Episkopoi*)

Segment 2: Models, Training, and Practice

Rev. Dr. Don L. Davis

Summary of Segment 2

The Word of God and church tradition provides us with several key images to understand the role and function of the office of the bishop: the bishop as overseer of pastors and churches functions as supervisor, apostle, and as spiritual director. As *supervisor* the bishop functions as a superintendent, coordinating and organizing the outreach, personnel, and resources of churches under his/her care to make maximum impact for the Church's edification and the Kingdom's advancement. As an *apostle*, the bishop functions as one charged with the ongoing care of new churches and their leaders, doing all they can to ensure the protection, edification and development of them. Finally, as a *spiritual director* the bishop provides challenge and encouragement to budding ministries and churches as they mature in Christ. The notion of bishop relates to the idea of how churches associate with one another, either *regionally* through the locale church, or through affinity and shared identity. Urban churches need both the godly association of other fellowships as well as the oversight that godly bishops can provide them. The Scriptures are clear that the faithful bishop will experience God's full blessing and reward at the Second Coming of Christ, who personally will give them the unfading crown of glory.

Our objective for this segment, *The Christian Leader as Bishop: Models, Training, and Practice*, is to enable you to see that:

- The Word of God and church tradition provides us with several key images to understand the role and function of the office of the bishop: the bishop as overseer of pastors and churches functions as supervisor, apostle, and as spiritual director.

- As *supervisor* the bishop functions as a superintendent, coordinating and organizing the outreach, personnel, and resources of churches under his/her care to make maximum impact for the Church's edification and the Kingdom's advancement.

- As an *apostle*, the bishop functions as one charged with the ongoing care of new churches and their leaders, doing all they can to ensure the protection, edification and development of them.

- The bishop as a *spiritual director* provides challenge and encouragement to budding ministries and churches as they mature in Christ.

- The authority and ministry of the bishop closely relates to and depends upon the association that churches and pastors maintain, either *regionally* through the locale church, or through affinity and shared identity of denomination or tradition.

- Congregations in the city desperately require the benefits and blessings of godly association with other like-minded fellowships, as well as the continuous godly oversight that bishops can provide.

- The Scriptures are clear that the faithful bishop will experience God's full blessing and reward at the Second Coming of Christ, who personally will give them the unfading crown of glory.

I. Models and Analogies for the Episcopate

A. The bishop as *supervisor*

The bishop, as one exercising oversight over the flock of God, is a superintendent, a supervisor, coordinating and organizing outreach, personnel, and resources to make maximum impact for the edification of the Church and advance of the Kingdom.

Video Segment 2 Outline

As therefore the Lord did nothing without the Father, being united to Him, . . . so neither should you do anything without the bishop and presbyters.
~ Ignatius (c. 105, E), 1.66, 67., Ibid., p. 70.

1. Bishops superintend the outreach and efforts of various ministers and their congregations as they seek to strengthen church life and outreach in a given locale, Phil. 2.25-26.

2. A bishop provides oversight and answerability to those ministers and churches under their care.

    a. Col. 4.17

    b. 2 Tim. 4.5

    c. Col. 4.7-9

    d. 1 Cor. 4.17

    e. 2 Cor. 12.18

    f. Eph. 6.22

    g. Phil. 2.28

    h. 1 Thess. 3.5

3. As a superintendent, a bishop challenges those ministers and churches under his care to deepen in their faith walk and attain to the goals which they have committed themselves to.

4

4. The bishop has oversight authority not merely influence: they direct ministers and churches to act, and exercise decision making authority in all the affairs of the church, coordinating the efforts of personnel for the sake of edifying the churches and expanding the kingdom outreach.

   a. 1 Cor. 4.18-21

   b. 2 Cor. 10.6

   c. 2 Cor. 12.20-21

   d. 2 Cor. 13.2

B. The bishop as *apostle*

The bishop functions like an apostle, as one who is burdened with an ongoing anxiety and care for the well-being of new churches and their leaders, and does all s/he can to ensure the protection, edification, and development of the churches and their emerging leaders.

   1. S/he has a deep passion and concern for the ongoing well-being of the churches.

      a. 2 Cor. 11.28

      b. Acts 15.36

      c. Acts 15.40-41

Appoint, therefore, for yourselves, bishops and deacons worthy of the Lord: men who are meek, not lovers of money, truthful, and tested; for they also render to you the service of prophets and teachers. Do not despise them, therefore, for they are your honored ones, together with the prophets and teachers.
~ Didache (c. 80-140, E), 7.381., Ibid.

d.   Acts 18.23

2. S/he visits the churches and ministers with an eye to build them up and edify them.

    a.   Rom. 1.11-12

    b.   Rom. 15.23

    c.   Rom. 15.32

3. The bishop appoints elders (pastors, ministers) for believers in new areas, commissioning them to their work, Acts 14.23.

4. S/he rebukes, exhorts, and reproves with all authority and confidence in order to protect, strengthen, and build upon all the work that has been done thus far.

    a.   Acts 20.28

    b.   Titus 1.5

5. S/he is committed to seeing new churches planted while simultaneously upbuilding those which have already begun, by multiplying laborers and new ministries.

    a.   Rom. 15.20-22

4

      b. 2 Tim. 2.2

      c. Rom. 1.14-16

      d. 2 Tim. 2.10

C. The bishop as *spiritual director*

The bishop is a spiritual director, providing spiritual challenge and encouragement to budding ministers and churches as they proceed on their faith journeys, daring them to expand their ministries and impact as they conform more and more to the death of Christ that his life might be seen in them.

    1. S/he provides spiritual counsel and support to ministers under his charge.

      a. 1 Tim. 4.16

      b. 1 Tim. 6.11-14

    2. S/he communicates and corresponds to those churches under his charge for their uplifting and challenge (this includes believers, his fellow bishops [elders and pastors], and deacons).

      a. 2 Tim. 1.6

      b. 1 Tim. 4.6

c. 1 Tim. 5.21

    d. Phil. 1.27-28

3. S/he uses his own example and experience as a touchstone for challenge and learning.

    a. 2 Tim. 1.13

    b. Phil. 4.9

    c. Phil. 3.17

    d. 1 Thess. 1.6

    e. 1 Thess. 2.9-12

    f. 1 Thess. 2.14

    g. 1 Thess. 4.1

4. S/he exhorts and charges with full spiritual authority.

    a. 2 Tim. 4.1-2

    b. 1 Tim. 4.14

5. S/he reminds ministers and churches of their original commitments and vision, and provokes them to think in new ways regarding their future.

    a. 1 Tim. 6.20

    b. 2 Tim. 1.14

    c. 2 Tim. 4.5

II. The Concept of Pastoral and Church Association: the Locale Church

A. The importance of a fluid understanding of church: the locale church

We can think of church in a number of closely connected and yet broadly defined concepts of church as an assembly, an association or affiliation of like-minded congregations which exists to support and build up one another.

1. The concept of two or three gathered together, there Christ is in the midst, Matt. 18.20

2. The concept of a local assembly of believers, (a church in a house)

    a. Prisca and Aquila

        (1) Rom. 16.3-5

        (2) 1 Cor. 16.19

We hold communion with the apostolic churches because our doctrine is in no respect different than theirs. This is our witness of truth.
~ Tertullian (c. 197, W), 3.252, 253., Ibid., p. 148.

4

b.   Nympha, Col. 4.15

c.   Philemon, Philem. 1.2

3.   The idea of a cluster of congregations in a particular local community

a.   Eph. 1.1

b.   Col. 1.2

c.   Rom. 1.7

d.   1 Cor. 1.2

4.   The idea of an association of churches organized regionally, nationally, or internationally

a.   1 Pet. 1.1

b.   Rom. 16.3-4

c.   1 Cor. 16.19

5.   The notion of all the believing churches, 2 Cor. 11.28

B. The concept of the locale church: *an association of like-minded congregations in close affinity (common interests or background) or proximity (location) which offer one another benefits through the connection without overthrowing congregational independence.*

1. An association of like-minded congregations: *faith in Jesus Christ*

2. In close affinity or proximity

   a. 1 Thess. 2.14 - For you, brothers, became imitators of the *churches of God in Christ Jesus that are in Judea.* For you suffered the same things from your own countrymen as they did from the Jews.

   b. Rom. 16.3-4 - Greet Prisca and Aquila, my fellow workers in Christ Jesus, [4] who risked their necks for my life, to whom not only I give thanks but *all the churches of the Gentiles* give thanks as well.

   c. Acts 15.41 - And he went through Syria and Cilicia, *strengthening the churches.*

   d. 2 Cor. 8.1 - We want you to know, brothers, about the grace of God that has been given among *the churches of Macedonia.*

   e. Rev. 1.4 - John to *the seven churches that are in Asia*: Grace to you and peace from him who is and who was and who is to come, and from the seven spirits who are before his throne.

3. Which offer one another benefits through the connection without overthrowing congregational independence

In a company of two is the church. But the church is Christ. When, then, you cast yourself at the brethren's knees, you are handling Christ. You are entreating Christ. In like manner, when they shed tears over you, it is Christ who suffers, Christ who begs the Father for mercy.
~ Tertullian (c. 203, W), 3.664., Ibid.

4

C. The Melvin Hodges paradigm: the "selfs" of church government

Churches require freedom to grow and reproduce.

1. Self-governing: the indigenous church controls its own affairs and direction.

2. Self-supporting: the indigenous church supports its activities and leaders on the basis of its own funding and resources.

3. Self-propagating: the indigenous church produces outreach and mission through its own efforts, evangelizing, discipling, and reproducing daughter churches.

4. The problem of the "selfs" model if viewed by *as self-and-only-ourselves alone*

   a. No church can be fully autonomous (i.e., a law to itself; we are all connected to one another and Jesus Christ), Eph. 4.4-6.

   b. It is unrealistic to expect every church to meet its own needs entirely; the apostles ignored this rule (the Jerusalem famine and the Macedonian offering, 2 Cor. 8-9).

   c. The early Church was a network of churches bound together by their common parentage from the Apostles and common struggles under the Roman rulership, 2 Cor. 11.9.

4

5. The role of bishop arises from this idea of the connectedness of pastors and their congregations to one another in an association or a locale.

    a. *Urban churches need godly oversight*: this enhances their self-governance.

    b. *Urban churches need to share resources*: this expands their base of self-support.

    c. *Urban churches need to partner with other congregations in mission*: this expands the overall impact of their outreach and mission.

D. Why the ministry of bishop is so critical today for urban churches

    1. *Scattered, alienated, and disconnected flocks*: the importance of the unity of the Church in our witness to Christ, John 17.21-23

    2. *Under-supported, financially strapped congregations*: need for inter-connected livelihood and growth of urban congregations

        a. 2 Cor. 8.1-4

        b. Acts 11.27-30

    3. *Poorly coordinated outreach and mission*: the need for coordinated efforts at outreach, evangelism, social service, and mission, Acts 15.22

It is your duty, O bishop, neither to overlook the sins of the people, nor to reject those who are penitent.
~ Apostolic Constitutions (compiled c. 390, E), 7.402., Ibid., p. 73.

4

E. How do we find and equip these kind of bishops (pastoral guardians) for our urban churches?

1. Pray for them (ask God to supply godly overseers for his Church, Acts 20.28).

2. Recognize that the "self-existing" concepts, while sufficient for conceiving life *within* an assembly, are inadequate for authentic body life *between and among congregations and ministers*.

3. Work on understanding the believers and their congregations in your locale.

    a. Do your demographics.

    b. Introduce yourself to the pastors and churches in your area.

    c. Connect at the various unified efforts to connect believers in your neighborhood.

    d. Recruit solid pastors to a vision of strengthening *the church* in our locale.

4. Begin to shift your loyalties from your own affairs to *the church in your area and city*.

5. Share this vision with your own pastor.

4

6. Support the efforts of our local community where we as believers are seeking to strengthen our shared witness and edification.

III. Principles and Practice of the Episcopate Ministry

A. Recognize the truth that all pastors need to be *pastored*.

B. Further acknowledge that, in spite of the self-principles of church governance, all churches need relationships with other churches if they are to mature.

C. Acknowledge how a pastor with a bishop's heart can bring inspiration and refreshment to our church life.

1. Bishops are key to *connecting pastors and churches*.

2. Bishops ensure the *sharing of provision among churches* which cannot meet their full need alone.

3. Bishops establish *some level of self-chosen oversight for pastors* who are accustomed to functioning as lone rangers.

4. Bishops open up the possibility of new outreach and mission by connecting believers of good will around issues and projects which require our attention as *believers in our locale*.

Preaching through countries and cities, the apostles appointed the first-fruits of their labors to be bishops and deacons of those who would believe afterwards. However, they first tested them by the Spirit.
~ Clement of Rome (c. 96, W), 1.16., Ibid., p. 70.

IV. The Blessing, Benefit, and Reward of the Christian Leader as Bishop

1 Pet. 2.25 - For you were straying like sheep, but have now returned to the Shepherd and Overseer of your souls.

A. The charge: *faithfulness in a few things*

Luke 16.10-12 - One who is faithful in a very little is also faithful in much, and one who is dishonest in a very little is also dishonest in much. [11] If then you have not been faithful in the unrighteous wealth, who will entrust to you the true riches? [12] And if you have not been faithful in that which is another's, who will give you that which is your own?

B. The reward: *authority over many things*

Luke 19.17 - And he said to him, "Well done, good servant! Because you have been faithful in a very little, you shall have authority over ten cities."

Rev. 2.26-28 - The one who conquers and who keeps my works until the end, to him I will give authority over the nations, [27] and he will rule them with a rod of iron, as when earthen pots are broken in pieces, even as I myself have received authority from my Father. [28] And I will give him the morning star.

1 Pet. 5.1-4 - So I exhort the elders among you, as a fellow elder and a witness of the sufferings of Christ, as well as a partaker in the glory that is going to be revealed: [2] shepherd the flock of God that is among you, exercising oversight, not under compulsion, but willingly, as God would have you; not for shameful gain, but eagerly; [3] not domineering over those in your charge, but being examples to the flock. [4] And when the chief Shepherd appears, you will receive the unfading crown of glory.

4

Conclusion

» The concept of bishop is rich, involving supervisory, apostolic, and spiritual directing roles over the Church.

» This dynamic concept is also connected to the idea of giving apostolic oversight to the churches in an area or region, and offering support and encouragement to both churches and pastors within them.

» While the term bishop is virtually synonymous with elder and applies to local leadership of individual congregations, we have seen the validity and need for there to be connection and contact amongst and between pastors, and the value of having godly leadership which facilitates our cooperation, growth, and connection.

» May the Lord provide us with godly Christian leaders—deacons, elders, pastors, and bishops-who can enable us to fulfill our calling to advance the Kingdom of Christ until the Chief Shepherd returns again. Amen and amen.

The following questions were designed to help you review the material in the second video segment. In this segment we looked at some of the key functions of the office of Bishop the through the images of supervisor, apostle, and as spiritual director. The idea of the bishop is closely connected to the way in which churches associate with one another, whether that is through regional contact through the locale church, or through doctrinal and spiritual affinity and shared identity. Our ability to be a part of a story larger than ourselves or even our local church is directly connected with our understanding of our place in a larger whole. The concept of bishop relates directly to this more holistic, broad understanding of the Church. Carefully explore these and related issues as you review the materials on the concept of the bishop in the Church.

1. What are the three ways in which church tradition has interpreted the Word of God to make sense of and fill out the concept of bishop? In your view, how do these three images and functions relate to one another?

2. Describe the role of the bishop as *supervisor*. How ought we to understand this role as it relates to the independence of pastors and elders within their own congregations?

Segue 2

Student Questions and Response

4

3. Explain the way in which the modern role of the bishop mirrors the work and responsibility of an apostle? How are they similar? How are they different? What boundaries exist in the bishop's role as an apostle of the Church in terms of authority, spirituality, and status?

4. In what sense does a bishop function as a *spiritual director* for the life of the pastors and churches under their authority? What are the limits of this *spiritual* direction? What kinds of things could bishops do to enhance the spiritual vitality of churches under their charge?

5. In what specific ways does the authority and ministry of the bishop connect to the association that churches and pastors maintain among themselves, either *regionally* through the locale church, or through affinity and shared identity of a denomination or tradition? Could churches that have no association function with a bishop role? Explain.

6. Why do urban churches require close and constant association with other like-minded fellowships and pastors? What is the likelihood that churches and pastors without association or connection with others will prosper and thrive spiritually in the city? Elaborate in your answer.

7. What kinds of blessings and benefits do the Scriptures promise to those bishops who faithfully carry out their responsibility as supervisors, apostles, and spiritual directors? What will Christ himself do for them at his coming?

CONNECTION

4

Summary of Key Concepts

This lesson focuses upon the role and function of bishops as those offering oversight and guidance to both pastors and churches under their charge. If in fact it takes a village to raise a child, it takes a movement to raise a church! Churches require oversight, not just within them but among them as well, and God has given us the role of bishop to supply the kind of holistic oversight and supply that churches in association together require. The following statements lay out these concepts clearly and concisely.

☞ The Greek NT term *episkopos* refers to the office of the "bishop," and can be translated "overseer." This term and its meaning can be traced through its usages in the *Septuagint*, in the classical Greek tradition, and finally within the New Testament itself.

- The terms for "pastor," "elder," and "bishop" are virtually synonymous, and probably refer to the same office, with emphases on different roles and responsibilities of Christian leadership in the Church.

- The origins and the development of the office of the bishop may probably be connected to the council of elders in Jewish rulership where an elder could be recognized as one to speak on behalf of and represent the entire council of elders.

- Through church history, the office of the bishop has expanded to refer to those individuals who have been either appointed or elected to a position of oversight over a number of pastors or groups of congregations in a given context.

- The qualifications for bishop are clearly outlined in the New Testament, including extended passages in 1 Timothy 3 and Titus 1, and concretely demonstrated in the example of Jesus, referred to as the "Shepherd and Bishop of our souls," 1 Pet. 2.23.

- Bishops have been selected in various ways through the history of the Church, and once installed, have been given substantive authority to oversee pastors and churches for their edification and growth. As a "pastor of pastors," bishops provide concrete answerability to all pastors and churches under their charge.

4

- While some traditions may reject the *nomenclature* (i.e., language) of the bishop, most groups have supervisors who assume the *function* of a bishop, i.e., ongoing oversight and supervision of churches in association together.

- The Word of God and church tradition provide us with several key images to understand the role and function of the office of the bishop: the bishop as overseer of pastors and churches functions as supervisor, apostle, and as spiritual director.

- As *supervisor* the bishop functions as a superintendent, coordinating and organizing the outreach, personnel, and resources of churches under his/her care to make maximum impact for the Church's edification and the Kingdom's advancement.

- As an *apostle*, the bishop functions as one charged with the ongoing care of new churches and their leaders, doing all they can to ensure the protection, edification and development of the them.

- The bishop as a *spiritual director* provides challenge and encouragement to budding ministries and churches as they mature in Christ.

- The authority and ministry of the bishop closely relates to and depends upon the association that churches and pastors maintain, either *regionally* through the locale church, or through affinity and shared identity of denomination or tradition.

- Congregations in the city desperately require the benefits and blessings of godly association with other like-minded fellowships, as well as the continuous godly oversight that bishops can provide.

- The Scriptures are clear that the faithful bishop will experience God's full blessing and reward at the Second Coming of Christ, who personally will give them the unfading crown of glory.

Student Application and Implications

Now is the time for you to consider the role of the bishop as it applies to your own life and ministry, and those of your fellow students. The dynamic reality of the bishop is grounded in the fact that *we are not alone*; the Church is one, and we are connected to all other churches and believers, in our region, our district, our nation, and our world. Perhaps you are not a part of an episcopal district, and do not recognize an official bishop as-such over your pastor or church. Nevertheless, coming to understand who God's appointed "bishops" (leaders of pastors and churches) are for the church in your region will enable you to better understand what God is doing in your area, what are the critical issues the body needs to be mindful of, and how God wants us to collaborate to see his Kingdom advanced where we live. Who are those leaders who are blazing trails for our movement in our locale and region, and what are we to do in connection with them? The questions below may prompt some of your own questions or ideas regarding the role and ministry of supervisors in your locale.

* Who are those who give oversight and supervision to your pastor, elders, and your church? Are you a part of a larger network of assemblies to whom you answer and for whom you serve?

* Is it possible to really mature in Christ as a pastor or church without any oversight from someone outside of the church? How independent can you be as a pastor and congregation and still remain connected to others in a vital way?

4

* What are the kinds of problems that could occur if a group of churches found themselves under the authority of a bishop who failed to meet God's standards of godliness, doctrine, and mission? In such a case, what could a pastor or congregation do to remedy the situation?

* What are the signs that a pastor or church has simply lost touch with others, and are on the verge of becoming sectarian, even cultic in their isolation from others?

* In your opinion, what is the bare minimum contact that churches should have with others in order to keep them connected and integrated with the other believers in an area or region? Explain your answer.

* Many affirm a congregation's near absolute right to govern itself, finance its own initiatives, and control its own missions outreach. Under what conditions would the three selfs of self-government, self-support, and self-propagation be too "self"-ish? What safeguards must any church take to ensure that it does not lose contact with others?

* In your view, how has the mega-church either undermined or strengthened the possibility for connection and oversight between and among churches? Does a church with a membership of 7,000 people *need* to be associated with other congregations for its own health and well-being?

* Can you envision a situation where churches in a region would not want to associate together for the well-being of each other? Describe that situation.

CASE STUDIES

1

The Lord Has Given Me a Vision

A common phrasing with many in ministry today is the idea that they are pursuing a vision that the Lord gave them directly. Often it can be heard that "The Lord told me to begin this initiative" or "The Lord told me to come here and begin this ministry." Unfortunately, the only evidence for these revelations are the statements themselves; with no overarching authority or credible connection to anyone, many of these initiatives do not last. However, often God has in fact directed certain individuals through his Spirit to undertake innovative and exciting new ministries for his Kingdom's advancement, and these new churches and ministries have thrived because the Lord did in fact instruct them to initiate these tasks. What are the criteria and qualifications of an authentically God-ordained, God-directed vision? To what extent should legitimate spiritual authority endorse a vision *before*

page 358 📖 5

we place our stamp of approval upon it? Under what conditions ought we to continue with an initiative even if the so-called legitimate authority rejects the idea out of hand?

We Decline to Participate

2 ▶ There are many churches which fail to participate in any local, regional, or national initiatives by other Christians. Arguing that they are not obligated to march to the drum beat of any other church or organization, some congregations believe deeply in the Holy Spirit's guidance of the leadership *within and only within* the church as an authoritative voice for directing their affairs. Under what circumstances or situations might it be appropriate for a local church to not participate in the activities and emphases of fellow congregations in the area? Is it possible to be a legitimate church and refuse to participate in *any other activities sponsored by other churches in an area*? Can a church decline to participate in all forms of connection and supervision of its affairs by any outside institution or group?

How Do I Join?

3 ▶ Many urban churches are becoming clearer on the necessity for their fellowships to become connected to other traditions and integrated into the life of the church *at the locale, regional, and national, even international* level. However, many traditions demand so much in terms of doctrine, governance, leadership, funding, and other areas that many urban churches would be refused membership within them. Some denominations are neither welcoming to urban congregations, nor capable of integrating them within the life and ministry of the denomination. Some traditions are not diverse, either in terms of fiscal difference (e.g., most of the congregations are wealthy), ethnic diversity, or cultural distinction. If an urban church senses the need to become linked to a larger network of assemblies, how would you propose they go about it–what steps ought they to take in establishing relationships and connections with other churches, or with another like-minded tradition?

The Self-Appointed Bishop

4 ▶ In many of the more public and prominent ministries headed by likeable and persuasive televangelists and preachers today, the title of "bishop" is one of the more

4

popular titles. Often these titles are not to be understood in the classic historical sense of a bishop, i.e., one who commissioned to supervise and oversee a number of churches and pastors in a given area, the title becomes a synonym for the title "pastor" or "reverend." The term "bishop" however, because of its historical breadth and the gravity of the authority and position usually associated with some traditions with that title, is preferred. In looking at the history of the ordination of bishops, however, this is neither a title nor a position that one takes on oneself or without grave sobriety. It is possible, though, to take on this title today in many Protestant settings and to neither be associated with a movement or tradition, to have been commissioned nor appointed by any legitimate church, nor be affiliated with any other spiritual body. What do you make of the uneven application of the term "bishop" among many today, and how might we remedy and reclaim this term in more its biblical and historical meaning? Is a person a bishop *simply because he calls himself one?*

4

The NT Greek term *episkopos* ("bishop") can be interpreted as overseer, the term has a history that originated with the *Septuagint* (i.e., the Greek OT), various usages of the term in the classical Greek tradition, and finally in its use by the apostles in the New Testament itself. In one sense the terms for "pastor," "elder," and "bishop" all refer to the same office, with emphases on different roles and responsibilities of Christian leadership in the Church. The use of the concept of *elder as overseer* may have some resonance with council of elders in Jewish rulership where an elder could be recognized as one to speak on behalf of and represent the entire council of elders. The concept in the Church has been expanded through history to refer to the office of the bishop appointed or elected to oversee a number of pastors or groups of congregations in a given context. The standards of bishop are articulated in 1 Timothy 3 and Titus 1, as well as the example of Jesus. As a "pastor of pastors," bishops have historically come to represent the leaders of large areas and numbers of churches within his area of responsibility. While some traditions may reject the *nomenclature* (i.e., language) of the bishop, most groups have supervisors who assume the *function* of a bishop, i.e., ongoing oversight and supervision of churches in association together.

The Word of God and church tradition provides us with several key images to understand the role and function of the office of the bishop: the bishop as overseer of pastors and churches functions as supervisor, apostle, and as spiritual director. As *supervisor* the bishop functions as a superintendent, coordinating and organizing the outreach, personnel, and resources of churches under his/her care to make

Restatement of the Lesson's Thesis

maximum impact for the Church's edification and the Kingdom's advancement. As an *apostle*, the bishop functions as one charged with the ongoing care of new churches and their leaders, doing all they can to ensure the protection, edification and development of them. Finally, as a *spiritual director* the bishop provides challenge and encouragement to budding ministries and churches as they mature in Christ. The notion of bishop relates to the idea of how churches associate with one another, either *regionally* through the locale church, or through affinity and shared identity. Urban churches need both the godly association of other fellowships as well as the oversight that godly bishops can provide them. The Scriptures are clear that the faithful bishop will experience God's full blessing and reward at the Second Coming of Christ, who personally will give them the unfading crown of glory.

Resources and Bibliographies

If you are interested in pursuing some of the ideas of *The Christian Leader as Bishop (Episkopoi)*, you might want to give these books a try:

Galloway, John T. *Ministry Loves Company: A Survival Guide for Pastors.* Louisville, KY: Westminster John Knox Press, 2003.

Purves, Andrew. *Pastoral Theology in the Classical Tradition.* Louisville, KY: Westminster John Knox Press, 2001.

Wilimon, William H. *Calling and Character: The Virtues of the Ordained Life.* Nashville: Abingdon Press, 2000.

4

Ministry Connections

The principles of Christian leadership covered in this module were designed in order to enable you to secure a solid and defensible understanding of the various principles and roles of leadership in the Church of Jesus Christ. Hopefully, your own study, meditation, and investigation, along with your fellow students, has given you a solid foundation of Christian leadership. Now, it is time for you to explore ways in which you may apply the insights of this module's key insights in a practicum that you and your mentor agree to. The ramifications of these insights are clear; Christian leadership, in the end, is not something that one simply studies or ponders, but a calling to serve Christ by laying down one's life and goods for the sake of others, especially those in the body of Christ. Your ability to follow through on these insights will show your understanding of them. The truth of Christ in Christian leadership must become a part of who you are–how you pray, how you live at home and on the job, your response to other members at church, and your own submission to your leaders. The ministry project is your opportunity to select a place in your own life situation where you can correlate this teaching in your life, work, and ministry. In the next days you will have the opportunity to share these insights in real-life, actual ministry environments. Pray that God will give you insight into his ways as you share your insights in your projects.

Coming upon the end of such a challenging study, undoubtedly the Holy Spirit wants you to go deeper in your experience of these truths. Perhaps as you have considered the various dimensions of Christian leadership revealed in the role of deacon, elder, pastor, and bishop certain issues, persons, situations, or opportunities have emerged that have grabbed your attention, and that you now need to address. Are there any particular issues or people that God has laid upon your heart that require focused supplication and prayer for through this lesson? Ask the Lord for insight and his leading, and do not hesitate to seek the necessary support in counsel and prayer for what the Spirit has shown you.

Counseling and Prayer

ASSIGNMENTS

No assignment due.

Scripture Memory

No assignment due.

Reading Assignment

At this point in the course you should have decided all pertinent issues associated with your ministry and exegetical project. These both should now be outlined, determined, and accepted by your instructor. *If you have not done so, do not wait a minute longer to determine these assignments and communicate them to your instructor.* Make sure that you plan ahead, so you will not be late in accomplishing this work and meeting all deadlines for the course.

Other Assignments

page 359 📖 *6*

The final will be a take home exam, and will include questions taken from the first three quizzes, new questions on material drawn from this lesson, and essay questions which will ask for your short answer responses to key integrating questions. Also, you should plan on reciting or writing out the verses memorized for the course on the exam. When you have completed your exam, please notify your mentor and make certain that they get your copy.

Final Exam Notice

4

Please note: Your module grade cannot be determined if you do not take the final exam and turn in all outstanding assignments to your mentor (ministry project, exegetical project, and final exam).

. . . .

The Last Word about this Module

The need of the hour is for a particular kind of effective Christian leader to emerge in the Church. Throughout this module we have explored the NT vision of leadership, based on the model of Christ and the apostles, that can produce maturity in the Church, and advancement of the Kingdom in the world. Your involvement in this course speaks of your potential as a servant leader, whatever the role and ministry God has designed for you. Whether as a layperson or clergy, whether as a deacon, elder, pastor, or bishop, whether in missions or full-time Christian service, God wants you to grow in the grace and in the knowledge of our Lord Jesus Christ (2 Pet. 3.18). Our Lord made himself available to the Father in order to fulfill to the nth degree his command to lay down his life for the world. Now, our Lord is calling men and women to lay down their lives for the sake of his body, the Church.

Our sincere desire is that the Holy Spirit will so inspire and illumine you that you will join that remarkable army of people who have sacrificed all of their lives for Christ. The promise is certain and sure; those who serve our Lord Jesus, the Father himself will honor them. Let Christ's own words bear witness to the truth of this statement:

> John 12.23-26 - And Jesus answered them, "The hour has come for the Son of Man to be glorified. [24] Truly, truly, I say to you, unless a grain of wheat falls into the earth and dies, it remains alone; but if it dies, it bears much fruit. [25] Whoever loves his life loses it, and whoever hates his life in this world will keep it for eternal life. [26] If anyone serves me, he must follow me; and where I am, there will my servant be also. If anyone serves me, the Father will honor him."

May the Lord give you both the courage and integrity to yield your all to Christ, in order that he might be glorified through your service to him, revealed in your selfless sacrifice for his dear bride, the body of Christ. Indeed, *this* kind of service for our risen Lord is the foundation of authentic Christian leadership.

Amen and amen!

4

Appendices

APPENDIX 1

The Nicene Creed

We believe in one God, *(Deut. 6.4-5; Mark 12.29; 1 Cor. 8.6)*
  the Father Almighty, *(Gen. 17.1; Dan. 4.35; Matt. 6.9; Eph. 4.6; Rev. 1.8)*
  Maker of heaven and earth *(Gen 1.1; Isa. 40.28; Rev. 10.6)*
  and of all things visible and invisible. *(Ps. 148; Rom. 11.36; Rev. 4.11)*

We believe in one Lord Jesus Christ, the only Begotten Son of God,
  begotten of the Father before all ages,
  God from God, Light from Light, True God from True God,
  begotten not created,
  of the same essence as the Father, *(John 1.1-2; 3.18; 8.58; 14.9-10; 20.28; Col. 1.15, 17; Heb. 1.3-6)*
  through whom all things were made. *(John 1.3; Col. 1.16)*

Who for us men and for our salvation came down from heaven
  and was incarnate by the Holy Spirit and the virgin Mary
  and became human. *(Matt. 1.20-23; John 1.14; 6.38; Luke 19.10)*
  Who for us too, was crucified under Pontius Pilate,
  suffered, and was buried. *(Matt. 27.1-2; Mark 15.24-39, 43-47; Acts 13.29; Rom. 5.8; Heb. 2.10; 13.12)*
  The third day he rose again
  according to the Scriptures, *(Mark 16.5-7; Luke 24.6-8; Acts 1.3; Rom. 6.9; 10.9; 2 Tim. 2.8)*
  ascended into heaven,
  and is seated at the right hand of the Father. *(Mark 16.19; Eph. 1.19-20)*
  He will come again in glory
  to judge the living and the dead,
  and his Kingdom will have no end.
    (Isa. 9.7; Matt. 24.30; John 5.22; Acts 1.11; 17.31; Rom. 14.9; 2 Cor. 5.10; 2 Tim. 4.1)

We believe in the Holy Spirit, the Lord and life-giver,
    (Gen. 1.1-2; Job 33.4; Ps. 104.30; 139.7-8; Luke 4.18-19; John 3.5-6; Acts 1.1-2; 1 Cor. 2.11; Rev. 3.22)
  who proceeds from the Father and the Son, *(John 14.16-18, 26; 15.26; 20.22)*
  who together with the Father and Son
  is worshiped and glorified, *(Isa. 6.3; Matt. 28.19; 2 Cor. 13.14; Rev. 4.8)*
  who spoke by the prophets. *(Num. 11.29; Mic. 3.8; Acts 2.17-18; 2 Pet. 1.21)*

We believe in one holy, catholic, and apostolic Church.
    (Matt. 16.18; Eph. 5.25-28; 1 Cor. 1.2; 10.17; 1 Tim. 3.15; Rev. 7.9)

We acknowledge one baptism for the forgiveness of sin, *(Acts 22.16; 1 Pet. 3.21; Eph. 4.4-5)*
  And we look for the resurrection of the dead
  And the life of the age to come. *(Isa. 11.6-10; Mic. 4.1-7; Luke 18.29-30; Rev. 21.1-5; 21.22-22.5)*

Amen.

APPENDIX 2

We Believe: Confession of the Nicene Creed (8.7.8.7. meter*)

Rev. Dr. Don L. Davis, 2007. All Rights Reserved.

* This song is adapted from the Nicene Creed, and set to 8.7.8.7. meter, meaning it can be sung to tunes of the same meter, such as: *Joyful, Joyful, We Adore Thee; I Will Sing of My Redeemer; What a Friend We Have in Jesus; Come, Thou Long Expected Jesus*

Father God Almighty rules, the Maker of both earth and heav'n.
All things seen and those unseen, by him were made, by him were giv'n!
We believe in Jesus Christ, the Lord, God's one and only Son,
Begotten, not created, too, he and our Father God are one!

Begotten from the Father, same, in essence, as both God and Light;
Through him by God all things were made, in him all things were giv'n life.
Who for us all, for our salvation, did come down from heav'n to earth,
Incarnate by the Spirit's pow'r, and through the Virgin Mary's birth.

Who for us too, was crucified, by Pontius Pilate's rule and hand,
Suffered, and was buried, yet on the third day, he rose again.
According to the Sacred Scriptures all that happ'ned was meant to be.
Ascended high to God's right hand, in heav'n he sits in glory.

Christ will come again in glory to judge all those alive and dead.
His Kingdom rule shall never end, for he will rule and reign as Head.
We worship God, the Holy Spirit, Lord and the Life-giver known;
With Fath'r and Son is glorified, Who by the prophets ever spoke.

And we believe in one true Church, God's holy people for all time,
Cath'lic in its scope and broadness, built on the Apostles' line!
Acknowledging that one baptism, for forgiv'ness of our sin,
And we look for Resurrection, for the dead shall live again.

Looking for unending days, the life of the bright Age to come,
When Christ's Reign shall come to earth, the will of God shall then be done!
Praise to God, and to Christ Jesus, to the Spirit–triune Lord!
We confess the ancient teachings, clinging to God's holy Word!

APPENDIX 3

The Story of God: Our Sacred Roots

Rev. Dr. Don L. Davis

The Alpha and the Omega	Christus Victor	Come, Holy Spirit	Your Word Is Truth	The Great Confession	His Life in Us	Living in the Way	Reborn to Serve
The LORD God is the source, sustainer, and end of all things in the heavens and earth. All things were formed and exist by his will and for his eternal glory, the triune God, Father, Son, and Holy Spirit. Rom. 11.36.							
	The Triune God's Unfolding Drama — God's Self-Revelation in Creation, Israel, and Christ			The Church's Participation in God's Unfolding Drama — Fidelity to the Apostolic Witness to Christ and His Kingdom			
The Objective Foundation: The Sovereign Love of God — God's Narration of His Saving Work in Christ				The Subjective Practice: Salvation by Grace through Faith — The Redeemed's Joyous Response to God's Saving Work in Christ			
The Author of the Story	*The Champion of the Story*	*The Interpreter of the Story*	*The Testimony of the Story*	*The People of the Story*	*Re-enactment of the Story*	*Embodiment of the Story*	*Continuation of the Story*
The Father as *Director*	Jesus as *Lead Actor*	The Spirit as *Narrator*	Scripture as *Script*	As Saints, *Confessors*	As Worshipers, *Ministers*	As Followers, *Sojourners*	As Servants, *Ambassadors*
Christian *Worldview*	Communal *Identity*	Spiritual *Experience*	Biblical *Authority*	Orthodox *Theology*	Priestly *Worship*	Congregational *Discipleship*	Kingdom *Witness*
Theistic and Trinitarian Vision	Christ-centered Foundation	Spirit-Indwelt and -Filled Community	Canonical and Apostolic Witness	Ancient Creedal Affirmation of Faith	Weekly Gathering in Christian Assembly	Corporate, Ongoing Spiritual Formation	Active Agents of the Reign of God
Sovereign *Willing*	Messianic *Representing*	Divine *Comforting*	Inspired *Testifying*	Truthful *Retelling*	Joyful *Excelling*	Faithful *Indwelling*	Hopeful *Compelling*
Creator True Maker of the Cosmos	Recapitulation Typos and Fulfillment of the Covenant	Life-Giver Regeneration and Adoption	Divine Inspiration God-breathed Word	The Confession of Faith Union with Christ	Song and Celebration Historical Recitation	Pastoral Oversight Shepherding the Flock	Explicit Unity Love for the Saints
Owner Sovereign Disposer of Creation	Revealer Incarnation of the Word	Teacher Illuminator of the Truth	Sacred History Historical Record	Baptism into Christ Communion of Saints	Homilies and Teachings Prophetic Proclamation	Shared Spirituality Common Journey through the Spiritual Disciplines	Radical Hospitality Evidence of God's Kingdom Reign
Ruler Blessed Controller of All Things	Redeemer Reconciler of All Things	Helper Endowment and the Power	Biblical Theology Divine Commentary	The Rule of Faith Apostles' Creed and Nicene Creed	The Lord's Supper Dramatic Re-enactment	Embodiment Anamnesis and Prolepsis through the Church Year	Extravagant Generosity Good Works
Covenant Keeper Faithful Promisor	Restorer Christ, the Victor over the powers of evil	Guide Divine Presence and Shekinah	Spiritual Food Sustenance for the Journey	The Vincentian Canon Ubiquity, antiquity, universality	Eschatological Foreshadowing The Already/Not Yet	Effective Discipling Spiritual Formation in the Believing Assembly	Evangelical Witness Making Disciples of All People Groups

APPENDIX 4

The Theology of Christus Victor

A Christ-Centered Biblical Motif for Integrating and Renewing the Urban Church

Rev. Dr. Don L. Davis

	The Promised Messiah	The Word Made Flesh	The Son of Man	The Suffering Servant	The Lamb of God	The Victorious Conqueror	The Reigning Lord in Heaven	The Bridegroom and Coming King
Biblical Framework	Israel's hope of Yahweh's anointed who would redeem his people	In the person of Jesus of Nazareth, the Lord has come to the world	As the promised king and divine Son of Man, Jesus reveals the Father's glory and salvation to the world	As Inaugurator of the Kingdom of God, Jesus demonstrates God's reign present through his words, wonders, and works	As both High Priest and Paschal Lamb, Jesus offers himself to God on our behalf as a sacrifice for sin	In his resurrection from the dead and ascension to God's right hand, Jesus is proclaimed as Victor over the power of sin and death	Now reigning at God's right hand till his enemies are made his footstool, Jesus pours out his benefits on his body	Soon the risen and ascended Lord will return to gather his Bride, the Church, and consummate his work
Scripture References	Isa. 9.6-7; Jer. 23.5-6; Isa. 11.1-10	John 1.14-18; Matt. 1.20-23; Phil. 2.6-8	Matt. 2.1-11; Num. 24.17; Luke 1.78-79	Mark 1.14-15; Matt. 12.25-30; Luke 17.20-21	2 Cor. 5.18-21; Isa. 52-53; John 1.29	Eph. 1.16-23; Phil. 2.5-11; Col. 1.15-20	1 Cor. 15.25; Eph. 4.15-16; Acts. 2.32-36	Rom. 14.7-9; Rev. 5.9-13; 1 Thess. 4.13-18
Jesus' History	The pre-incarnate, only begotten Son of God in glory	His conception by the Spirit, and birth to Mary	His manifestation to the Magi and to the world	His teaching, exorcisms, miracles, and mighty works among the people	His suffering, crucifixion, death, and burial	His resurrection, with appearances to his witnesses, and his ascension to the Father	The sending of the Holy Spirit and his gifts, and Christ's session in heaven at the Father's right hand	His soon return from heaven to earth as Lord and Christ: the Second Coming
Description	The biblical promise for the seed of Abraham, the prophet like Moses, the son of David	In the Incarnation, God has come to us; Jesus reveals to humankind the Father's glory in fullness	In Jesus, God has shown his salvation to the entire world, including the Gentiles	In Jesus, the promised Kingdom of God has come visibly to earth, demonstrating his binding of Satan and rescinding the Curse	As God's perfect Lamb, Jesus offers himself up to God as a sin offering on behalf of the entire world	In his resurrection and ascension, Jesus destroyed death, disarmed Satan, and rescinded the Curse	Jesus is installed at the Father's right hand as Head of the Church, Firstborn from the dead, and supreme Lord in heaven	As we labor in his harvest field in the world, so we await Christ's return, the fulfillment of his promise
Church Year	Advent	Christmas	Season after Epiphany; Baptism and Transfiguration	Lent	Holy Week; Passion	Eastertide; Easter, Ascension Day, Pentecost	Season after Pentecost; Trinity Sunday	Season after Pentecost; All Saints Day, Reign of Christ the King
	The Coming of Christ	*The Birth of Christ*	*The Manifestation of Christ*	*The Ministry of Christ*	*The Suffering and Death of Christ*	*The Resurrection and Ascension of Christ*	*The Heavenly Session of Christ*	*The Reign of Christ*
Spiritual Formation	As we await his Coming, let us proclaim and affirm the hope of Christ	O Word made flesh, let us every heart prepare him room to dwell	Divine Son of Man, show the nations your salvation and glory	In the person of Christ, the power of the reign of God has come to earth and to the Church	May those who share the Lord's death be resurrected with him	Let us participate by faith in the victory of Christ over the power of sin, Satan, and death	Come, indwell us, Holy Spirit, and empower us to advance Christ's Kingdom in the world	We live and work in expectation of his soon return, seeking to please him in all things

APPENDIX 5

Christus Victor
An Integrated Vision for the Christian Life
Rev. Dr. Don L. Davis

For the Church
- The Church is the primary extension of Jesus in the world
- Ransomed treasure of the victorious, risen Christ
- *Laos:* The people of God
- God's new creation: presence of the future
- Locus and agent of the Already/Not Yet Kingdom

For Theology and Doctrine
- The authoritative Word of Christ's victory: the Apostolic Tradition: the Holy Scriptures
- Theology as commentary on the grand narrative of God
- *Christus Victor* as core theological framework for meaning in the world
- The Nicene Creed: the Story of God's triumphant grace

For Spirituality
- The Holy Spirit's presence and power in the midst of God's people
- Sharing in the disciplines of the Spirit
- Gatherings, lectionary, liturgy, and our observances in the Church Year
- Living the life of the risen Christ in the rhythm of our ordinary lives

For Gifts
- God's gracious endowments and benefits from *Christus Victor*
- Pastoral offices to the Church
- The Holy Spirit's sovereign dispensing of the gifts
- Stewardship: divine, diverse gifts for the common good

Christus Victor
*Destroyer of Evil and Death
Restorer of Creation
Victor o'er Hades and Sin
Crusher of Satan*

For Worship
- People of the Resurrection: unending celebration of the people of God
- Remembering, participating in the Christ event in our worship
- Listen and respond to the Word
- Transformed at the Table, the Lord's Supper
- The presence of the Father through the Son in the Spirit

For Evangelism and Mission
- Evangelism as unashamed declaration and demonstration of *Christus Victor* to the world
- The Gospel as Good News of kingdom pledge
- We proclaim God's Kingdom come in the person of Jesus of Nazareth
- The Great Commission: go to all people groups making disciples of Christ and his Kingdom
- Proclaiming Christ as Lord and Messiah

For Justice and Compassion
- The gracious and generous expressions of Jesus through the Church
- The Church displays the very life of the Kingdom
- The Church demonstrates the very life of the Kingdom of heaven right here and now
- Having freely received, we freely give (no sense of merit or pride)
- Justice as tangible evidence of the Kingdom come

APPENDIX 6

Old Testament Witness to Christ and His Kingdom

Rev. Dr. Don L. Davis

Christ Is Seen in the OT's:	Covenant Promise and Fulfillment	Moral Law	Christophanies	Typology	Tabernacle, Festival, and Levitical Priesthood	Messianic Prophecy	Salvation Promises
Passage	Gen. 12.1-3	Matt. 5.17-18	John 1.18	1 Cor. 15.45	Heb. 8.1-6	Mic. 5.2	Isa. 9.6-7
Example	The Promised Seed of the Abrahamic covenant	The Law given on Mount Sinai	Commander of the Lord's army	Jonah and the great fish	Melchizedek, as both High Priest and King	The Lord's Suffering Servant	Righteous Branch of David
Christ As	Seed of the woman	The Prophet of God	God's present Revelation	Antitype of God's drama	Our eternal High Priest	The coming Son of Man	Israel's Redeemer and King
Where Illustrated	Galatians	Matthew	John	Matthew	Hebrews	Luke and Acts	John and Revelation
Exegetical Goal	To see Christ as heart of God's sacred drama	To see Christ as fulfillment of the Law	To see Christ as God's revealer	To see Christ as antitype of divine typos	To see Christ in the Temple *cultus*	To see Christ as true Messiah	To see Christ as coming King
How Seen in the NT	As fulfillment of God's sacred oath	As *telos* of the Law	As full, final, and superior revelation	As substance behind the historical shadows	As reality behind the rules and roles	As the Kingdom made present	As the One who will rule on David's throne
Our Response in Worship	God's veracity and faithfulness	God's perfect righteousness	God's presence among us	God's inspired Scripture	God's ontology: his realm as primary and determinative	God's anointed servant and mediator	God's resolve to restore his kingdom authority
How God Is Vindicated	God does not lie: he's true to his word	Jesus fulfills all righteousness	God's fulness is revealed to us in Jesus of Nazareth	The Spirit spoke by the prophets	The Lord has provided a mediator for humankind	Every jot and tittle written of him will occur	Evil will be put down, creation restored, under his reign

APPENDIX 7

Summary Outline of the Scriptures

Rev. Dr. Don L. Davis

1. GENESIS - Beginnings
   a. Adam
   b. Noah
   c. Abraham
   d. Isaac
   e. Jacob
   f. Joseph

2. EXODUS - Redemption, (out of)
   a. Slavery
   b. Deliverance
   c. Law
   d. Tabernacle

3. LEVITICUS - Worship and Fellowship
   a. Offerings, sacrifices
   b. Priests
   c. Feasts, festivals

4. NUMBERS - Service and Walk
   a. Organized
   b. Wanderings

5. DEUTERONOMY - Obedience
   a. Moses reviews history and law
   b. Civil and social laws
   c. Palestinian Covenant
   d. Moses' blessing and death

6. JOSHUA - Redemption (into)
   a. Conquer the land
   b. Divide up the land
   c. Joshua's farewell

7. JUDGES - God's Deliverance
   a. Disobedience and judgment
   b. Israel's twelve judges
   c. Lawless conditions

8. RUTH - Love
   a. Ruth chooses
   b. Ruth works
   c. Ruth waits
   d. Ruth rewarded

9. 1 SAMUEL - Kings, Priestly Perspective
   a. Eli
   b. Samuel
   c. Saul
   d. David

10. 2 SAMUEL - David
    a. King of Judah
       (9 years - Hebron)
    b. King of all Israel
       (33 years - Jerusalem)

11. 1 KINGS - Solomon's Glory, Kingdom's Decline
    a. Solomon's glory
    b. Kingdom's decline
    c. Elijah the prophet

12. 2 KINGS- Divided Kingdom
    a. Elisha
    b. Israel (N. Kingdom falls)
    c. Judah (S. Kingdom falls)

13. 1 CHRONICLES - David's Temple Arrangements
    a. Genealogies
    b. End of Saul's reign
    c. Reign of David
    d. Temple preparations

14. 2 CHRONICLES - Temple and Worship Abandoned
    a. Solomon
    b. Kings of Judah

15. EZRA - The Minority (Remnant)
    a. First return from exile - Zerubbabel
    b. Second return from exile - Ezra (priest)

16. NEHEMIAH - Rebuilding by Faith
    a. Rebuild walls
    b. Revival
    c. Religious reform

17. ESTHER - Female Savior
    a. Esther
    b. Haman
    c. Mordecai
    d. Deliverance: Feast of Purim

18. JOB - Why the Righteous Suffer
    a. Godly Job
    b. Satan's attack
    c. Four philosophical friends
    d. God lives

19. PSALMS - Prayer and Praise
    a. Prayers of David
    b. Godly suffer; deliverance
    c. God deals with Israel
    d. Suffering of God's people - end with the Lord's reign
    e. The Word of God (Messiah's suffering and glorious return)

20. PROVERBS - Wisdom
    a. Wisdom versus folly
    b. Solomon
    c. Solomon - Hezekiah
    d. Agur
    e. Lemuel

21. ECCLESIASTES - Vanity
    a. Experimentation
    b. Observation
    c. Consideration

22. SONG OF SOLOMON - Love Story

23. ISAIAH - The Justice (Judgment) and Grace (Comfort) of God
    a. Prophecies of punishment
    b. History
    c. Prophecies of blessing

24. JEREMIAH - Judah's Sin Leads to Babylonian Captivity
    a. Jeremiah's call; empowered
    b. Judah condemned; predicted Babylonian captivity
    c. Restoration promised
    d. Prophesied judgment inflicted
    e. Prophesies against Gentiles
    f. Summary of Judah's captivity

25. LAMENTATIONS - Lament over Jerusalem
    a. Affliction of Jerusalem
    b. Destroyed because of sin
    c. The prophet's suffering
    d. Present desolation versus past splendor
    e. Appeal to God for mercy

26. EZEKIEL - Israel's Captivity and Restoration
    a. Judgment on Judah and Jerusalem
    b. Judgment on Gentile nations
    c. Israel restored; Jerusalem's future glory

27. DANIEL - The Time of the Gentiles
    a. History; Nebuchadnezzar, Belshazzar, Daniel
    b. Prophecy

28. HOSEA - Unfaithfulness
    a. Unfaithfulness
    b. Punishment
    c. Restoration

29. JOEL - The Day of the Lord
    a. Locust plague
    b. Events of the future day of the Lord
    c. Order of the future day of the Lord

30. AMOS - God Judges Sin
    a. Neighbors judged
    b. Israel judged
    c. Visions of future judgment
    d. Israel's past judgment blessings

31. OBADIAH - Edom's Destruction
    a. Destruction prophesied
    b. Reasons for destruction
    c. Israel's future blessing

32. JONAH - Gentile Salvation
    a. Jonah disobeys
    b. Other suffer
    c. Jonah punished
    d. Jonah obeys; thousands saved
    e. Jonah displeased, no love for souls

33. MICAH - Israel's Sins, Judgment, and Restoration
    a. Sin and judgment
    b. Grace and future restoration
    c. Appeal and petition

34. NAHUM - Nineveh Condemned
    a. God hates sin
    b. Nineveh's doom prophesied
    c. Reasons for doom

35. HABAKKUK - The Just Shall Live by Faith
    a. Complaint of Judah's unjudged sin
    b. Chaldeans will punish
    c. Complaint of Chaldeans' wickedness
    d. Punishment promised
    e. Prayer for revival; faith in God

36. ZEPHANIAH - Babylonian Invasion Prefigures the Day of the Lord
    a. Judgment on Judah foreshadows the Great Day of the Lord
    b. Judgment on Jerusalem and neighbors foreshadows final judgment of all nations
    c. Israel restored after judgments

37. HAGGAI - Rebuild the Temple
    a. Negligence
    b. Courage
    c. Separation
    d. Judgment

38. ZECHARIAH - Two Comings of Christ
    a. Zechariah's vision
    b. Bethel's question; Jehovah's answer
    c. Nation's downfall and salvation

39. MALACHI - Neglect
    a. The priest's sins
    b. The people's sins
    c. The faithful few

Summary Outline of the Scriptures (continued)

1. MATTHEW - Jesus the King
   a. The Person of the King
   b. The Preparation of the King
   c. The Propaganda of the King
   d. The Program of the King
   e. The Passion of the King
   f. The Power of the King

2. MARK - Jesus the Servant
   a. John introduces the Servant
   b. God the Father identifies the Servant
   c. The temptation initiates the Servant
   d. Work and word of the Servant
   e. Death, burial, resurrection

3. LUKE - Jesus Christ the Perfect Man
   a. Birth and family of the Perfect Man
   b. Testing of the Perfect Man; hometown
   c. Ministry of the Perfect Man
   d. Betrayal, trial, and death of the Perfect Man
   e. Resurrection of the Perfect Man

4. JOHN - Jesus Christ is God
   a. Prologue - the Incarnation
   b. Introduction
   c. Witness of Jesus to his Apostles
   d. Passion - witness to the world
   e. Epilogue

5. ACTS - The Holy Spirit Working in the Church
   a. The Lord Jesus at work by the Holy Spirit through the Apostles at Jerusalem
   b. In Judea and Samaria
   c. To the uttermost parts of the Earth

6. ROMANS - The Righteousness of God
   a. Salutation
   b. Sin and salvation
   c. Sanctification
   d. Struggle
   e. Spirit-filled living
   f. Security of salvation
   g. Segregation
   h. Sacrifice and service
   i. Separation and salutation

7. 1 CORINTHIANS - The Lordship of Christ
   a. Salutation and thanksgiving
   b. Conditions in the Corinthian body
   c. Concerning the Gospel
   d. Concerning collections

8. 2 CORINTHIANS - The Ministry in the Church
   a. The comfort of God
   b. Collection for the poor
   c. Calling of the Apostle Paul

9. GALATIANS - Justification by Faith
   a. Introduction
   b. Personal - Authority of the Apostle and glory of the Gospel
   c. Doctrinal - Justification by faith
   d. Practical - Sanctification by the Holy Spirit
   e. Autographed conclusion and exhortation

10. EPHESIANS - The Church of Jesus Christ
    a. Doctrinal - the heavenly calling of the Church
       A Body
       A Temple
       A Mystery
    b. Practical - The earthly conduct of the Church
       A New Man
       A Bride
       An Army

11. PHILIPPIANS - Joy in the Christian Life
    a. Philosophy for Christian living
    b. Pattern for Christian living
    c. Prize for Christian living
    d. Power for Christian living

12. COLOSSIANS - Christ the Fullness of God
    a. Doctrinal - In Christ believers are made full
    b. Practical - Christ's life poured out in believers, and through them

13. 1 THESSALONIANS - The Second Coming of Christ:
    a. Is an inspiring hope
    b. Is a working hope
    c. Is a purifying hope
    d. Is a comforting hope
    e. Is a rousing, stimulating hope

14. 2 THESSALONIANS - The Second Coming of Christ
    a. Persecution of believers now; judgment of unbelievers hereafter (at coming of Christ)
    b. Program of the world in connection with the coming of Christ
    c. Practical issues associated with the coming of Christ

15. 1 TIMOTHY - Government and Order in the Local Church
    a. The faith of the Church
    b. Public prayer and women's place in the Church
    c. Officers in the Church
    d. Apostasy in the Church
    e. Duties of the officer of the Church

16. 2 TIMOTHY - Loyalty in the Days of Apostasy
    a. Afflictions of the Gospel
    b. Active in service
    c. Apostasy coming; authority of the Scriptures
    d. Allegiance to the Lord

17. TITUS - The Ideal New Testament Church
    a. The Church is an organization
    b. The Church is to teach and preach the Word of God
    c. The Church is to perform good works

18. PHILEMON - Reveal Christ's Love and Teach Brotherly Love
    a. Genial greeting to Philemon and family
    b. Good reputation of Philemon
    c. Gracious plea for Onesimus
    d. Guiltless illustration of Imputation
    e. General and personal requests

19. HEBREWS - The Superiority of Christ
    a. Doctrinal - Christ is better than the Old Testament economy
    b. Practical - Christ brings better benefits and duties

20. JAMES - Ethics of Christianity
    a. Faith tested
    b. Difficulty of controlling the tongue
    c. Warning against worldliness
    d. Admonitions in view of the Lord's coming

21. 1 PETER - Christian Hope in the Time of Persecution and Trial
    a. Suffering and security of believers
    b. Suffering and the Scriptures
    c. Suffering and the sufferings of Christ
    d. Suffering and the Second Coming of Christ

22. 2 PETER - Warning Against False Teachers
    a. Addition of Christian graces gives assurance
    b. Authority of the Scriptures
    c. Apostasy brought in by false testimony
    d. Attitude toward Return of Christ: test for apostasy
    e. Agenda of God in the world
    f. Admonition to believers

23. 1 JOHN - The Family of God
    a. God is Light
    b. God is Love
    c. God is Life

24. 2 JOHN - Warning against Receiving Deceivers
    a. Walk in truth
    b. Love one another
    c. Receive not deceivers
    d. Find joy in fellowship

25. 3 JOHN - Admonition to Receive True Believers
    a. Gaius, brother in the Church
    b. Diotrephes
    c. Demetrius

26. JUDE - Contending for the Faith
    a. Occasion of the epistle
    b. Occurrences of apostasy
    c. Occupation of believers in the days of apostasy

27. REVELATION - The Unveiling of Christ Glorified
    a. The person of Christ in glory
    b. The possession of Jesus Christ - the Church in the World
    c. The program of Jesus Christ - the scene in Heaven
    d. The seven seals
    e. The seven trumpets
    f. Important persons in the last days
    g. The seven vials
    h. The fall of Babylon
    i. The eternal state

APPENDIX 8

From Before to Beyond Time:

The Plan of God and Human History

*Adapted from: Suzanne de Dietrich. **God's Unfolding Purpose**. Philadelphia: Westminster Press, 1976.*

I. Before Time (Eternity Past) 1 Cor. 2.7

   A. The Eternal Triune God

   B. God's Eternal Purpose

   C. The Mystery of Iniquity

   D. The Principalities and Powers

II. Beginning of Time (Creation and Fall) Gen. 1.1

   A. Creative Word

   B. Humanity

   C. Fall

   D. Reign of Death and First Signs of Grace

III. Unfolding of Time (God's Plan Revealed Through Israel) Gal. 3.8

   A. Promise (Patriarchs)

   B. Exodus and Covenant at Sinai

   C. Promised Land

   D. The City, the Temple, and the Throne (Prophet, Priest, and King)

   E. Exile

   F. Remnant

IV. Fullness of Time (Incarnation of the Messiah) Gal. 4.4-5

   A. The King Comes to His Kingdom

   B. The Present Reality of His Reign

   C. The Secret of the Kingdom: the Already and the Not Yet

   D. The Crucified King

   E. The Risen Lord

V. The Last Times (The Descent of the Holy Spirit) Acts 2.16-18

   A. Between the Times: the Church as Foretaste of the Kingdom

   B. The Church as Agent of the Kingdom

   C. The Conflict Between the Kingdoms of Darkness and Light

VI. The Fulfillment of Time (The Second Coming) Matt. 13.40-43

   A. The Return of Christ

   B. Judgment

   C. The Consummation of His Kingdom

VII. Beyond Time (Eternity Future) 1 Cor. 15.24-28

   A. Kingdom Handed Over to God the Father

   B. God as All in All

From Before to Beyond Time
Scriptures for Major Outline Points

I. Before Time (Eternity Past)

1 Cor. 2.7 (ESV) - But we impart a secret and hidden wisdom of God, *which God decreed before the ages* for our glory (cf. Titus 1.2).

II. Beginning of Time (Creation and Fall)

Gen. 1.1 (ESV) - *In the beginning*, God created the heavens and the earth.

III. Unfolding of Time (God's Plan Revealed Through Israel)

Gal. 3.8 (ESV) - And the Scripture, foreseeing that God would justify the Gentiles by faith, *preached the Gospel beforehand to Abraham*, saying, "In you shall all the nations be blessed" (cf. Rom. 9.4-5).

IV. Fullness of Time (The Incarnation of the Messiah)

Gal. 4.4-5 (ESV) - *But when the fullness of time had come*, God sent forth his Son, born of woman, born under the law, to redeem those who were under the law, so that we might receive adoption as sons.

V. The Last Times (The Descent of the Holy Spirit)

Acts 2.16-18 (ESV) - But this is what was uttered through the prophet Joel: "'*And in the last days it shall be*,' God declares, 'that I will pour out my Spirit on all flesh, and your sons and your daughters shall prophesy, and your young men shall see visions, and your old men shall dream dreams; even on my male servants and female servants in those days I will pour out my Spirit, and they shall prophesy.'"

VI. The Fulfillment of Time (The Second Coming)

Matt. 13.40-43 (ESV) - Just as the weeds are gathered and burned with fire, *so will it be at the close of the age*. The Son of Man will send his angels, and they will gather out of his kingdom all causes of sin and all lawbreakers, and throw them into the fiery furnace. In that place there will be weeping and gnashing of teeth. Then the righteous will shine like the sun in the Kingdom of their Father. He who has ears, let him hear.

VII. Beyond Time (Eternity Future)

1 Cor. 15.24-28 (ESV) - Then comes the end, when he delivers the Kingdom to God the Father after destroying every rule and every authority and power. For he must reign until he has put all his enemies under his feet. The last enemy to be destroyed is death. For "God has put all things in subjection under his feet." But when it says, "all things are put in subjection," it is plain that he is excepted who put all things in subjection under him. When all things are subjected to him, then the Son himself will also be subjected to him who put all things in subjection under him, that God may be all in all.

APPENDIX 9

"There Is a River"

Identifying the Streams of a Revitalized Authentic Christian Community in the City[1]

Rev. Dr. Don L. Davis ● Psalm 46.4 (ESV) - There is a river whose streams make glad the city of God, the holy habitation of the Most High.

Tributaries of Authentic Historic Biblical Faith			
Recognized Biblical Identity	*Revived Urban Spirituality*	*Reaffirmed Historical Connectivity*	*Refocused Kingdom Authority*
The Church Is **One**	The Church Is **Holy**	The Church Is **Catholic**	The Church Is **Apostolic**
A Call to Biblical Fidelity *Recognizing the Scriptures as the anchor and foundation of the Christian faith and practice*	**A Call to the Freedom, Power, and Fullness of the Holy Spirit** *Walking in the holiness, power, gifting, and liberty of the Holy Spirit in the body of Christ*	**A Call to Historic Roots and Continuity** *Confessing the common historical identity and continuity of authentic Christian faith*	**A Call to the Apostolic Faith** *Affirming the apostolic tradition as the authoritative ground of the Christian hope*
A Call to Messianic Kingdom Identity *Rediscovering the story of the promised Messiah and his Kingdom in Jesus of Nazareth*	**A Call to Live as Sojourners and Aliens as the People of God** *Defining authentic Christian discipleship as faithful membership among God's people*	**A Call to Affirm and Express the Global Communion of Saints** *Expressing cooperation and collaboration with all other believers, both local and global*	**A Call to Representative Authority** *Submitting joyfully to God's gifted servants in the Church as undershepherds of true faith*
A Call to Creedal Affinity *Embracing the Nicene Creed as the shared rule of faith of historic orthodoxy*	**A Call to Liturgical, Sacramental, and Catechetical Vitality** *Experiencing God's presence in the context of the Word, sacrament, and instruction*	**A Call to Radical Hospitality and Good Works** *Expressing kingdom love to all, and especially to those of the household of faith*	**A Call to Prophetic and Holistic Witness** *Proclaiming Christ and his Kingdom in word and deed to our neighbors and all peoples*

[1] *This schema is an adaptation and is based on the insights of the **Chicago Call** statement of May 1977, where various leading evangelical scholars and practitioners met to discuss the relationship of modern evangelicalism to the historic Christian faith.*

APPENDIX 10

A Schematic for a Theology of the Kingdom and the Church

The Urban Ministry Institute

The Reign of the One, True, Sovereign, and Triune God, the LORD God, Yahweh, God the Father, Son, and Holy Spirit

The Father	The Son	The Spirit
Love - 1 John 4.8	Faith - Heb. 12.2	Hope - Rom. 15.13
Maker of heaven and earth and of all things visible and invisible	Prophet, Priest, and King	Lord of the Church
Creation — All that exists through the creative action of God.	**Kingdom** — The Reign of God expressed in the rule of his Son Jesus the Messiah.	**Church** — The one, holy, apostolic community which functions as a witness to (Acts 28.31) and a foretaste of (Col. 1.12; James 1.18; 1 Pet. 2.9; Rev. 1.6) the Kingdom of God.
The eternal God, sovereign in power, infinite in wisdom, perfect in holiness, and steadfast in love, is the source and goal of all things.	**Rom. 8.18-21 →** **Freedom** (Slavery) — Jesus answered them, "Truly, truly, I say to you, everyone who commits sin is a slave to sin. The slave does not remain in the house forever; the son remains forever. So if the Son sets you free, you will be free indeed." - John 8.34-36 (ESV)	*The Church is an Apostolic Community Where the Word is Rightly Preached, Therefore it is a Community of:* **Calling** - For freedom Christ has set us free; stand firm therefore, and do not submit again to a yoke of slavery. - Gal. 5.1 (ESV) (cf. Rom. 8.28-30; 1 Cor. 1.26-31; Eph. 1.18; 2 Thess. 2.13-14; Jude 1.1) **Faith** - "... for unless you believe that I am he you will die in your sins" ... So Jesus said to the Jews who had believed in him, "If you abide in my word, you are truly my disciples, and you will know the truth, and the truth will set you free." - John 8.24b, 31-32 (ESV) (cf. Ps. 119.45; Rom. 1.17; 5.1-2; Eph. 2.8-9; 2 Tim. 1.13-14; Heb. 2.14-15; James 1.25) **Witness** - The Spirit of the Lord is upon me, because he has anointed me to proclaim good news to the poor. He has sent me to proclaim liberty to the captives and recovering of sight to the blind, to set at liberty those who are oppressed, to proclaim the year of the Lord's favor. - Luke 4.18-19 (ESV) (cf. Lev. 25.10; Prov. 31.8; Matt. 4.17; 28.18-20; Mark 13.10; Acts 1.8; 8.4, 12; 13.1-3; 25.20; 28.30-31)
O, the depth of the riches and wisdom and knowledge of God! How unsearchable are his judgments, and how inscrutable his ways! For who has known the mind of the Lord, or who has been his counselor? Or who has ever given a gift to him, that he might be repaid? For from him and through him and to him are all things. To him be glory forever! Amen! - Rom. 11.33-36 (ESV) (cf. 1 Cor. 15.23-28; Rev.)	**Rev. 21.1-5 →** **Wholeness** (Sickness) — But he was wounded for our transgressions; he was crushed for our iniquities; upon him was the chastisement that brought us peace, and with his stripes we are healed. - Isa. 53.5 (ESV)	*The Church is One Community Where the Sacraments are Rightly Administered, Therefore it is a Community of:* **Worship** - You shall serve the Lord your God, and he will bless your bread and your water, and I will take sickness away from among you. - Exod. 23.25 (ESV) (cf. Ps. 147.1-3; Heb. 12.28; Col. 3.16; Rev. 15.3-4; 19.5) **Covenant** - And the Holy Spirit also bears witness to us; for after the saying, "This is the covenant that I will make with them after those days, declares the Lord: I will put my laws on their hearts, and write them on their minds," then he adds, "I will remember their sins and their lawless deeds no more." - Heb. 10.15-17 (ESV) (cf. Isa. 54.10-17; Ezek. 34.25-31; 37.26-27; Mal. 2.4-5; Luke 22.20; 2 Cor. 3.6; Col. 3.15; Heb. 8.7-13; 12.22-24; 13.20-21) **Presence** - In him you also are being built together into a dwelling place for God by his Spirit. - Eph. 2.22 (ESV) (cf. Exod. 40.34-38; Ezek. 48.35; Matt. 18.18-20)
	Isa. 11.6-9 → **Justice** (Selfishness) — Behold, my servant whom I have chosen, my beloved with whom my soul is well pleased. I will put my Spirit upon him, and he will proclaim justice to the Gentiles. He will not quarrel or cry aloud, nor will anyone hear his voice in the streets; a bruised reed he will not break, and a smoldering wick he will not quench, until he brings justice to victory. - Matt. 12.18-20 (ESV)	*The Church is a Holy Community Where Discipline is Rightly Ordered, Therefore it is a Community of:* **Reconciliation** - For he himself is our peace, who has made us both one and has broken down in his flesh the dividing wall of hostility by abolishing the law of commandments and ordinances, that he might create in himself one new man in place of the two, so making peace, and might reconcile us both to God in one body through the cross, thereby killing the hostility. And he came and preached peace to you who were far off and peace to those who were near. For through him we both have access in one Spirit to the Father. - Eph. 2.14-18 (ESV) (cf. Exod. 23.4-9; Lev. 19.34; Deut. 10.18-19; Ezek. 22.29; Mic. 6.8; 2 Cor. 5.16-21) **Suffering** - Since therefore Christ suffered in the flesh, arm yourselves with the same way of thinking, for whoever has suffered in the flesh has ceased from sin, so as to live for the rest of the time in the flesh no longer for human passions but for the will of God. - 1 Pet. 4.1-2 (ESV) (cf. Luke 6.22; 10.3; Rom. 8.17; 2 Tim. 2.3; 3.12; 1 Pet. 2.20-24; Heb. 5.8; 13.11-14) **Service** - But Jesus called them to him and said, "You know that the rulers of the Gentiles lord it over them, and their great ones exercise authority over them. It shall not be so among you. But whoever would be great among you must be your servant, and whoever would be first among you must be your slave even as the Son of Man came not to be served but to serve, and to give his life as a ransom for many." - Matt. 20.25-28 (ESV) (cf. 1 John 4.16-18; Gal. 2.10)

Living in the Already and the Not Yet Kingdom
Rev. Dr. Don L. Davis

The Spirit: The pledge of the inheritance (*arrabon*)

The Church: The foretaste (*aparche*) of the Kingdom

"In Christ": The rich life (*en Christos*) we share as citizens of the Kingdom

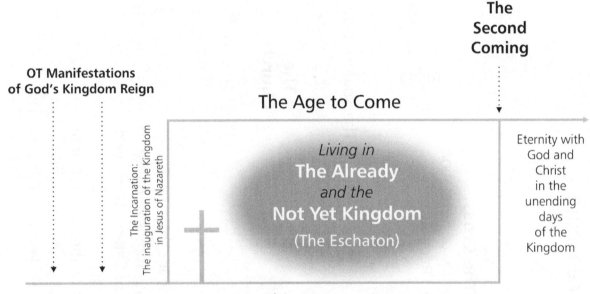

Internal enemy: The flesh (*sarx*) and the sin nature

External enemy: The world (*kosmos*) the systems of greed, lust, and pride

Infernal enemy: The devil (*kakos*) the animating spirit of falsehood and fear

Jewish View of Time

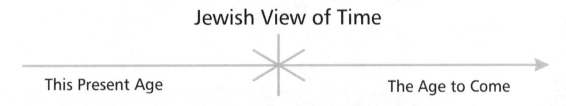

The Coming of Messiah

The restoration of Israel

The end of Gentile oppression

The return of the earth to Edenic glory

Universal knowledge of the Lord

APPENDIX 12

Jesus of Nazareth: The Presence of the Future

Rev. Dr. Don L. Davis

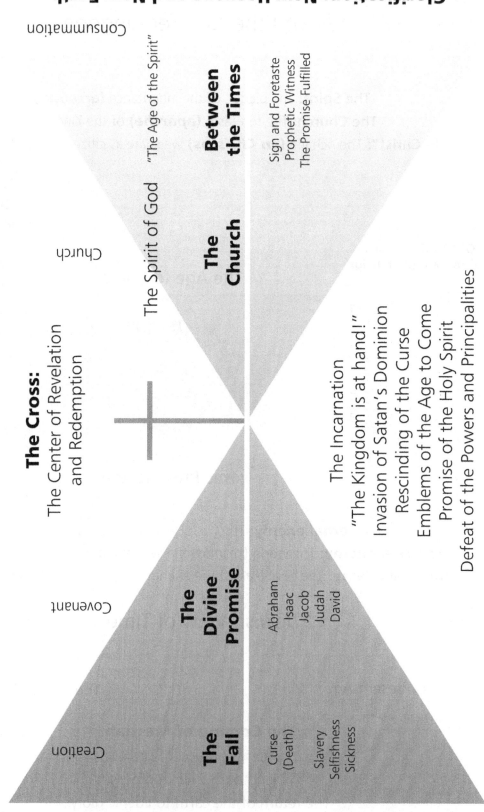

Glorification: New Heavens and New Earth

Consummation

"The Age of the Spirit"

Between the Times

Sign and Foretaste
Prophetic Witness
The Promise Fulfilled

The Spirit of God

The Church

Church

The Cross:
The Center of Revelation
and Redemption

The Incarnation
"The Kingdom is at hand!"
Invasion of Satan's Dominion
Rescinding of the Curse
Emblems of the Age to Come
Promise of the Holy Spirit
Defeat of the Powers and Principalities

The Divine Promise

Covenant

Abraham
Isaac
Jacob
Judah
David

The Fall

Creation

Curse
(Death)

Slavery
Selfishness
Sickness

Creation: The Reign of Almighty God

APPENDIX 13

Traditions
(Paradosis)
Dr. Don L. Davis and Rev. Terry G. Cornett

Strong's Definition

Paradosis. Transmission, i.e. (concretely) a precept; specifically, the Jewish traditionary law

Vine's Explanation

denotes "a tradition," and hence, by metonymy, (a) "the teachings of the rabbis," . . . (b) "apostolic teaching," . . . of instructions concerning the gatherings of believers, of Christian doctrine in general . . . of instructions concerning everyday conduct.

1. The concept of tradition in Scripture is essentially positive.

Jer. 6.16 (ESV) - Thus says the Lord: "Stand by the roads, and look, and ask for the ancient paths, where the good way is; and walk in it, and find rest for your souls. But they said, 'We will not walk in it'" (cf. Exod. 3.15; Judg. 2.17; 1 Kings 8.57-58; Ps. 78.1-6).

2 Chron. 35.25 (ESV) - Jeremiah also uttered a lament for Josiah; and all the singing men and singing women have spoken of Josiah in their laments to this day. They made these a rule in Israel; behold, they are written in the Laments (cf. Gen. 32.32; Judg. 11.38-40).

Jer. 35.14-19 (ESV) - The command that Jonadab the son of Rechab gave to his sons, to drink no wine, has been kept, and they drink none to this day, for they have obeyed their father's command. I have spoken to you persistently, but you have not listened to me. I have sent to you all my servants the prophets, sending them persistently, saying, 'Turn now every one of you from his evil way, and amend your deeds, and do not go after other gods to serve them, and then you shall dwell in the land that I gave to you and your fathers.' But you did not incline your ear or listen to me. The sons of Jonadab the son of Rechab have kept the command that their father gave them, but this people has not obeyed me. Therefore, thus says the

Traditions (continued)

Lord, the God of hosts, the God of Israel: Behold, I am bringing upon Judah and all the inhabitants of Jerusalem all the disaster that I have pronounced against them, because I have spoken to them and they have not listened, I have called to them and they have not answered." But to the house of the Rechabites Jeremiah said, "Thus says the Lord of hosts, the God of Israel: Because you have obeyed the command of Jonadab your father and kept all his precepts and done all that he commanded you, therefore thus says the Lord of hosts, the God of Israel: Jonadab the son of Rechab shall never lack a man to stand before me."

2. **Godly tradition is a wonderful thing, but not all tradition is godly.**

Any individual tradition must be judged by its faithfulness to the Word of God and its usefulness in helping people maintain obedience to Christ's example and teaching.[1] In the Gospels, Jesus frequently rebukes the Pharisees for establishing traditions that nullify rather than uphold God's commands.

Mark 7.8 (ESV) - You leave the commandment of God and hold to the tradition of men" (cf. Matt. 15.2-6; Mark 7.13).

Col. 2.8 (ESV) - See to it that no one takes you captive by philosophy and empty deceit, according to human tradition, according to the elemental spirits of the world, and not according to Christ.

3. **Without the fullness of the Holy Spirit, and the constant edification provided to us by the Word of God, tradition will inevitably lead to dead formalism.**

Those who are spiritual are filled with the Holy Spirit, whose power and leading alone provides individuals and congregations a sense of freedom and vitality in all they practice and believe. However, when the practices and teachings of any given tradition are no longer infused by the power of the Holy Spirit and the Word of God, tradition loses its effectiveness, and may actually become counterproductive to our discipleship in Jesus Christ.

Eph. 5.18 (ESV) - And do not get drunk with wine, for that is debauchery, but be filled with the Spirit.

---

[1] *"All Protestants insist that these traditions must ever be tested against Scripture and can never possess an independent apostolic authority over or alongside of Scripture." (J. Van Engen, "Tradition," **Evangelical Dictionary of Theology**, Walter Elwell, Gen. ed.) We would add that Scripture is itself the "authoritative tradition" by which all other traditions are judged. See "Appendix A, The Founders of Tradition: Three Levels of Christian Authority," p. 4.*

Gal. 5.22-25 (ESV) - But the fruit of the Spirit is love, joy, peace, patience, kindness, goodness, faithfulness, gentleness, self-control; against such things there is no law. And those who belong to Christ Jesus have crucified the flesh with its passions and desires. If we live by the Spirit, let us also walk by the Spirit.

2 Cor. 3.5-6 (ESV) - Not that we are sufficient in ourselves to claim anything as coming from us, but our sufficiency is from God, who has made us competent to be ministers of a new covenant, not of the letter but of the Spirit. For the letter kills, but the Spirit gives life.

4. **Fidelity to the Apostolic Tradition (teaching and modeling) is the essence of Christian maturity.**

2 Tim. 2.2 (ESV) - and what you have heard from me in the presence of many witnesses entrust to faithful men who will be able to teach others also.

1 Cor. 11.1-2 (ESV) - Be imitators of me, as I am of Christ. Now I commend you because you remember me in everything and maintain the traditions even as I delivered them to you (cf.1 Cor. 4.16-17, 2 Tim. 1.13-14, 2 Thess. 3.7-9, Phil. 4.9).

1 Cor. 15.3-8 (ESV) - For I delivered to you as of first importance what I also received: that Christ died for our sins in accordance with the Scriptures, that he was buried, that he was raised on the third day in accordance with the Scriptures, and that he appeared to Cephas, then to the twelve. Then he appeared to more than five hundred brothers at one time, most of whom are still alive, though some have fallen asleep. Then he appeared to James, then to all the apostles. Last of all, as to one untimely born, he appeared also to me.

5. **The Apostle Paul often includes an appeal to the tradition for support in doctrinal practices.**

1 Cor. 11.16 (ESV) - If anyone is inclined to be contentious, we have no such practice, nor do the churches of God (cf. 1 Cor. 1.2, 7.17, 15.3).

Traditions (continued)

1 Cor. 14.33-34 (ESV) - For God is not a God of confusion but of peace. As in all the churches of the saints, the women should keep silent in the churches. For they are not permitted to speak, but should be in submission, as the Law also says.

6. **When a congregation uses received tradition to remain faithful to the "Word of God," they are commended by the apostles.**

   1 Cor. 11.2 (ESV) - Now I commend you because you remember me in everything and maintain the traditions even as I delivered them to you.

   2 Thess. 2.15 (ESV) - So then, brothers, stand firm and hold to the traditions that you were taught by us, either by our spoken word or by our letter.

   2 Thess. 3.6 (ESV) - Now we command you, brothers, in the name of our Lord Jesus Christ, that you keep away from any brother who is walking in idleness and not in accord with the tradition that you received from us.

Appendix A

The Founders of Tradition: Three Levels of Christian Authority

Exod. 3.15 (ESV) - God also said to Moses, "Say this to the people of Israel, 'The Lord, the God of your fathers, the God of Abraham, the God of Isaac, and the God of Jacob, has sent me to you.' This is my name forever, and thus I am to be remembered throughout all generations."

1. **The Authoritative Tradition: the Apostles and the Prophets (The Holy Scriptures)**

   Eph. 2.19-21 (ESV) - So then you are no longer strangers and aliens, but you are fellow citizens with the saints and members of the household of God, built on the foundation of the apostles and prophets, Christ Jesus himself being the cornerstone, in whom the whole structure, being joined together, grows into a holy temple in the Lord.

   ~ The Apostle Paul

Those who gave eyewitness testimony to the revelation and saving acts of Yahweh, first in Israel, and ultimately in Jesus Christ the Messiah. This testimony is binding for all people, at all times, and in all places. It is the authoritative tradition by which all subsequent tradition is judged.

2. The Great Tradition: the Ecumenical Councils and their Creeds[2]

2 See Appendix B, "Defining the Great Tradition."

What has been believed everywhere, always, and by all.

~ Vincent of Lerins

The Great Tradition is the core dogma (doctrine) of the Church. It represents the teaching of the Church as it has understood the Authoritative Tradition (the Holy Scriptures), and summarizes those essential truths that Christians of all ages have confessed and believed. To these doctrinal statements the whole Church, (Catholic, Orthodox, and Protestant)[3] gives its assent. The worship and theology of the Church reflects this core dogma, which finds its summation and fulfillment in the person and work of Jesus Christ. From earliest times, Christians have expressed their devotion to God in its Church calendar, a yearly pattern of worship which summarizes and reenacts the events of Christ's life.

*3 Even the more radical wing of the Protestant reformation (Anabaptists) who were the most reluctant to embrace the creeds as dogmatic instruments of faith, did not disagree with the essential content found in them. "They assumed the Apostolic Creed–they called it 'The Faith,' **Der Glaube**, as did most people." See John Howard Yoder, **Preface to Theology: Christology and Theological Method.** Grand Rapids: Brazos Press, 2002. pp. 222-223.*

3. Specific Church Traditions: the Founders of Denominations and Orders

The Presbyterian Church (U.S.A.) has approximately 2.5 million members, 11,200 congregations and 21,000 ordained ministers. Presbyterians trace their history to the 16th century and the Protestant Reformation. Our heritage, and much of what we believe, began with the French lawyer John Calvin (1509-1564), whose writings crystallized much of the Reformed thinking that came before him.

~ The Presbyterian Church, U.S.A.

Christians have expressed their faith in Jesus Christ in various ways through specific movements and traditions which embrace and express the Authoritative Tradition and the Great Tradition in unique ways. For instance,

Traditions (continued)

Catholic movements have arisen around people like Benedict, Francis, or Dominic, and among Protestants people like Martin Luther, John Calvin, Ulrich Zwingli, and John Wesley. Women have founded vital movements of Christian faith (e.g., Aimee Semple McPherson of the Foursquare Church), as well as minorities (e.g., Richard Allen of the African Methodist Episcopal Church or Charles H. Mason of the Church of God in Christ, who also helped to spawn the Assemblies of God), all which attempted to express the Authoritative Tradition and the Great Tradition in a specific way consistent with their time and expression.

The emergence of vital, dynamic movements of the faith at different times and among different peoples reveal the fresh working of the Holy Spirit throughout history. Thus, inside Catholicism, new communities have arisen such as the Benedictines, Franciscans, and Dominicans; and outside Catholicism, new denominations have emerged (Lutherans, Presbyterians, Methodists, Church of God in Christ, etc.). Each of these specific traditions have "founders," key leaders whose energy and vision helped to establish a unique expression of Christian faith and practice. Of course, to be legitimate, these movements must adhere to and faithfully express both the Authoritative Tradition and the Great Tradition. Members of these specific traditions embrace their own unique practices and patterns of spirituality, but these unique features are not necessarily binding on the Church at large. They represent the unique expressions of that community's understanding of and faithfulness to the Authoritative and Great Traditions.

Specific traditions seek to express and live out this faithfulness to the Authoritative and Great Traditions through their worship, teaching, and service. They seek to make the Gospel clear within new cultures or sub-cultures, speaking and modeling the hope of Christ into new situations shaped by their own set of questions posed in light of their own unique circumstances. These movements, therefore, seek to contextualize the Authoritative tradition in a way that faithfully and effectively leads new groups of people to faith in Jesus Christ, and incorporates those who believe into the community of faith that obeys his teachings and gives witness of him to others.

Appendix B

Defining the "Great Tradition"

The Great Tradition (sometimes called the "classical Christian tradition") is defined by Robert E. Webber as follows:

[It is] the broad outline of Christian belief and practice developed from the Scriptures between the time of Christ and the middle of the fifth century

~ Webber. **The Majestic Tapestry**.
Nashville: Thomas Nelson Publishers, 1986. p. 10.

This tradition is widely affirmed by Protestant theologians both ancient and modern.

Thus those ancient Councils of Nicea, Constantinople, the first of Ephesus, Chalcedon, and the like, which were held for refuting errors, we willingly embrace, and reverence as sacred, in so far as relates to doctrines of faith, for they contain nothing but the pure and genuine interpretation of Scripture, which the holy Fathers with spiritual prudence adopted to crush the enemies of religion who had then arisen.

~ John Calvin. **Institutes**. IV, ix. 8.

. . . most of what is enduringly valuable in contemporary biblical exegesis was discovered by the fifth century.

~ Thomas C. Oden. **The Word of Life**.
San Francisco: HarperSanFrancisco, 1989. p. xi

The first four Councils are by far the most important, as they settled the orthodox faith on the Trinity and the Incarnation.

~ Philip Schaff. **The Creeds of Christendom**. Vol. 1.
Grand Rapids: Baker Book House, 1996. p. 44.

Our reference to the Ecumenical Councils and Creeds is, therefore, focused on those Councils which retain a widespread agreement in the Church among Catholics, Orthodox, and Protestants. While Catholic and Orthodox share common agreement on the first seven councils, Protestants tend to affirm and use primarily the first four. Therefore, those councils which continue to be shared by the whole Church are completed with the Council of Chalcedon in 451.

Traditions (continued)

It is worth noting that each of these four Ecumenical Councils took place in a pre-European cultural context and that none of them were held in Europe. They were councils of the whole Church and they reflected a time in which Christianity was primarily an eastern religion in it's geographic core. By modern reckoning, their participants were African, Asian, and European. The councils reflected a church that ". . . has roots in cultures far distant from Europe and preceded the development of modern European identity, and [of which] some of its greatest minds have been African" (Oden, *The Living God*, San Francisco: HarperSanFrancisco, 1987, p. 9).

Perhaps the most important achievement of the Councils was the creation of what is now commonly called the Nicene Creed. It serves as a summary statement of the Christian faith that can be agreed on by Catholic, Orthodox, and Protestant Christians.

The first four Ecumenical Councils are summarized in the following chart:

Name/Date/Location	Purpose
First Ecumenical Council 325 A.D. Nicea, Asia Minor	Defending against: *Arianism* Question answered: *Was Jesus God?* Action: *Developed the initial form of the Nicene Creed to serve as a summary of the Christian faith*
Second Ecumenical Council 381 A.D. Constantinople, Asia Minor	Defending against: *Macedonianism* Question answered: *Is the Holy Spirit a personal and equal part of the Godhead?* Action: *Completed the Nicene Creed by expanding the article dealing with the Holy Spirit*
Third Ecumenical Council 431 A.D. Ephesus, Asia Minor	Defending against: *Nestorianism* Question answered: *Is Jesus Christ both God and man in one person?* Action: *Defined Christ as the Incarnate Word of God and affirmed his mother Mary as* **theotokos** *(God-bearer)*
Fourth Ecumenical Council 451 A.D. Chalcedon, Asia Minor	Defending against: *Monophysitism* Question answered: *How can Jesus be both God and man?* Action: *Explained the relationship between Jesus' two natures (human and Divine)*

33 Blessings in Christ

Rev. Dr. Don L. Davis

Did you know that 33 things happened to you at the moment you became a believer in Jesus Christ? Lewis Sperry Chafer, the first president of Dallas Theological Seminary, listed these benefits of salvation in his *Systematic Theology, Volume III* (pp. 234-266). These points, along with brief explanations, give the born-again Christian a better understanding of the work of grace accomplished in his life as well as a greater appreciation of his new life.

1. In the eternal plan of God, the believer is:

    a. *Foreknown* - Acts 2.23; 1 Pet. 1.2, 20. God knew from all eternity every step in the entire program of the universe.

    b. *Predestined* - Rom. 8.29-30. A believer's destiny has been appointed through foreknowledge to the unending realization of all God's riches of grace.

    c. *Elected* - Rom. 8.38; Col. 3.12. He/she is chosen of God in the present age and will manifest the grace of God in future ages.

    d. *Chosen* - Eph. 1.4. God has separated unto himself his elect who are both foreknown and predestined.

    e. *Called* - 1 Thess. 5.23-24. God invites man to enjoy the benefits of his redemptive purposes. This term may include those whom God has selected for salvation, but who are still in their unregenerate state.

2. A believer has been *redeemed* - Rom. 3.24. The price required to set him/her free from sin has been paid.

3. A believer has been *reconciled* - 2 Cor. 5.18-21; Rom. 5.10. He/she is both restored to fellowship by God and restored to fellowship with God.

4. A believer is related to God through *propitiation* - Rom. 3.24-26. He/she has been set free from judgment by God's satisfaction with his Son's death for sinners.

5. A believer has been *forgiven* all trespasses - Eph. 1.7. All his/her sins are taken care of - past, present, and future.

6. A believer is vitally *conjoined to Christ* for the judgment of the old man "unto a new walk" - Rom. 6.1-10. He/she is brought into a union with Christ.

33 Blessings in Christ (continued)

7. A believer is *"free from the law"* - Rom. 7.2-6. He/she is both dead to its condemnation, and delivered from its jurisdiction.

8. A believer has been made a *child of God* - Gal. 3.26. He/she is born anew by the regenerating power of the Holy Spirit into a relationship in which God the First Person becomes a legitimate Father and the saved one becomes a legitimate child with every right and title - an heir of God and a joint heir with Jesus Christ.

9. A believer has been *adopted as an adult child* into the Father's household - Rom. 8.15, 23.

10. A believer has been *made acceptable to God* by Jesus Christ - Eph. 1.6. He/she is made *righteous* (Rom. 3.22), *sanctified* (set apart) positionally (1 Cor. 1.30, 6.11); *perfected forever in his/her standing and position* (Heb. 10.14), and *made acceptable* in the Beloved (Col. 1.12).

11. A believer has been *justified* - Rom. 5.1. He/she has been declared righteous by God's decree.

12. A believer is *"made right"* - Eph. 2.13. A close relation is set up and exists between God and the believer.

13. A believer has been *delivered from the power of darkness* - Col. 1.13; 2.13. A Christian has been delivered from Satan and his evil spirits. Yet the disciple must continue to wage a warfare against these powers.

14. A believer has been *translated into the Kingdom of God* - Col. 1.13. The Christian has been transferred from Satan's kingdom to Christ's Kingdom.

15. A believer is *planted* on the Rock, Jesus Christ - 1 Cor. 3.9-15. Christ is the foundation on which the believer stands and on which he/she builds his/her Christian life.

16. A believer is *a gift from God to Jesus Christ* - John 17.6, 11, 12, 20. He/she is the Father's love gift to Jesus Christ.

17. A believer is *circumcised in Christ* - Col. 2.11. He/she has been delivered from the power of the old sin nature.

18. A believer has been made a *partaker of the Holy and Royal Priesthood* - 1 Pet. 2.5, 9. He/she is a priest because of his/her relation to Christ, the High Priest, and will reign on earth with Christ.

19. A believer is part of a ***chosen generation, a holy nation and a peculiar people*** - 1 Pet. 2.9. This is the company of believers in this age.

20. A believer is a ***heavenly citizen*** - Phil. 3.20. Therefore he/she is called a stranger as far as his/her life on earth is concerned (1 Pet. 2.13), and will enjoy his/her true home in heaven forever.

21. A believer is in ***the family and household of God*** - Eph. 2.1, 9. He/she is part of God's "family" which is composed only of true believers.

22. A believer is in ***the fellowship of the saints***. John 17.11, 21-23. He/she can be a part of the fellowship of believers with one another.

23. A believer is in ***a heavenly association*** - Col. 1.27; 3.1; 2 Cor. 6.1; Col. 1.24; John 14.12-14; Eph. 5.25-27; Titus 2.13. He/she is ***a partner with Christ*** now in life, position, service, suffering, prayer, betrothal as a bride to Christ, and expectation of the coming again of Christ.

24. A believer has ***access to God*** - Eph. 2.18. He/she has access to God's grace which enables him/her to grow spiritually, and he/she has unhindered approach to the Father (Heb. 4.16).

25. A believer is within ***the "much more" care of God*** - Rom. 5.8-10. He/she is an object of God's love (John 3.16), God's grace (Eph. 2.7-9), God's power (Eph. 1.19), God's faithfulness (Phil. 1.6), God's peace (Rom. 5.1), God's consolation (2 Thess. 2.16-17), and God's intercession (Rom. 8.26).

26. A believer is ***God's inheritance*** - Eph. 1.18. He/she is given to Christ as a gift from the Father.

27. A believer ***has the inheritance of God himself*** and all that God bestows - 1 Pet. 1.4.

28. A believer has ***light in the Lord*** - 2 Cor. 4.6. He/she not only has this light, but is commanded to walk in the light.

29. A believer is ***vitally united to the Father, the Son and the Holy Spirit*** - 1 Thess. 1.1; Eph. 4.6; Rom. 8.1; John 14.20; Rom. 8.9; 1 Cor. 2.12.

30. A believer is blessed with ***the earnest or firstfruits of the Spirit*** - Eph. 1.14; 8.23. He/she is born of the Spirit (John 3.6), and baptized by the Spirit (1 Cor. 12.13), which is a work of the Holy Spirit by which the believer is joined to Christ's body and comes to be "in Christ," and therefore is a partaker of all that Christ is.

33 Blessings in Christ (continued)

The disciple is also indwelt by the Spirit (Rom. 8.9), sealed by the Spirit (2 Cor. 1.22), making him/her eternally secure, and filled with the Spirit (Eph. 5.18) whose ministry releases his Power and effectiveness in the heart in which he dwells.

31. A believer is *glorified* - Rom. 8.18. He/she will be a partaker of the infinite story of the Godhead.

32. A believer is *complete in God* - Col. 2.9, 10. He/she partakes of all that Christ is.

33. A believer *possesses every spiritual blessing* - Eph. 1.3. All the riches tabulated in the other 32 points made before are to be included in this sweeping term, "all spiritual blessings."

Come Thou Fount of every blessing
Tune my heart to sing Thy grace;
Streams of mercy, never ceasing,
Call for songs of loudest praise
Teach me some melodious sonnet,
Sung by flaming tongues above.
Praise the mount! I'm fixed upon it,
Mount of God's unchanging love.

Here I raise my Ebenezer;
Hither by Thy help I'm come;
And I hope, by Thy good pleasure,
Safely to arrive at home.
Jesus sought me when a stranger,
Wandering from the fold of God;
He, to rescue me from danger,
Interposed His precious blood.

O to grace how great a debtor
Daily I'm constrained to be!
Let that grace now like a fetter,
Bind my wandering heart to Thee.
Prone to wander, Lord, I feel it,
Prone to leave the God I love;
Here's my heart, O take and seal it,
Seal it for Thy courts above.

Come, Thou Fount
of Every Blessing,
Robert Robinson, 1757

APPENDIX 15

Paul's Partnership Theology

Our Union with Christ and Partnership in Kingdom Ministry

*Adapted from Brian J. Dodd. **Empowered Church Leadership**. Downers Grove: InterVarsity Press, 2003.*

The Apostolic fondness for Greek terms compounded with the prefix syn (with or co-)

English Translation of the Greek Term	Scripture References
Co-worker (*Synergos*)	Rom 16.3, 7, 9, 21; 2 Cor. 8.23; Phil. 2.25; 4.3; Col. 4.7, 10, 11, 14; Philem. 1, 24
Co-prisoner (*Synaichmalotos*)	Col. 4.10; Philem. 23
Co-slave (*Syndoulous*)	Col. 1.7; 4.7
Co-soldier (*Systratiotes*)	Phil. 2.25; Philem. 2
Co-laborer (*Synathleo*)	Phil. 4.2-3

APPENDIX 16

Six Kinds of New Testament Ministry for Community

Rev. Dr. Don L. Davis

Type	Greek	Text	Task
Proclamation	*evanggelion*	Rom. 1.15-17	Preaching the Good News
Teaching	*didasko*	Matt. 28.19	To make disciples of Jesus
Worship	*latreuo*	John 4.20-24	Ushering into God's presence
Fellowship	*agape*	Rom. 13.8-10	The communion of saints
Witness	*martyria*	Acts 1.8	Compelling testimony to the lost
Service	*diakonia*	Matt. 10.43-45	Caring for the needs of others

APPENDIX 17

Spiritual Gifts Specifically Mentioned in the New Testament

Rev. Terry G. Cornett

Administration	1 Cor. 12.28	The ability to bring order to Church life.
Apostleship	1 Cor. 12.28; Eph. 4.11	The ability to establish new churches among the unreached, nurture them to maturity, and exercise the authority and wisdom necessary to see them permanently established and able to reproduce; and/or A gift unique to the founding of the Church age which included the reception of special revelation and uniquely binding leadership authority
Discernment	1 Cor. 12.10	The ability to serve the Church through a Spirit-given ability to distinguish between God's truth (his presence, working, and doctrine) and fleshly error or satanic counterfeits
Evangelism	Eph. 4.11	The passion and the ability to effectively proclaim the Gospel so that people understand it
Exhortation	Rom. 12.8	The ability to give encouragement or rebuke that helps others obey Christ
Faith	1 Cor. 12.9	The ability to build up the Church through a unique ability to see the unrealized purposes of God and unwaveringly trust God to accomplish them
Giving	Rom. 12.8	The ability to build up a church through taking delight in the consistent, generous sharing of spiritual and physical resources
Healing	1 Cor. 12.9; 12.28	The ability to exercise faith that results in restoring people to physical, emotional, and spiritual health
Interpretation	1 Cor. 12.10	The ability to explain the meaning of an ecstatic utterance so that the Church is edified
Knowledge	1 Cor. 12.8	The ability to understand scriptural truth, through the illumination of the Holy Spirit, and speak it out to edify the body; and/or The supernatural revelation of the existence, or nature, of a person or thing which would not be known through natural means

Spiritual Gifts Specifically Mentioned in the New Testament (continued)

Leadership	Rom. 12.8	Spiritually-inspired courage, wisdom, zeal, and hard work which motivate and guide others so that they can effectively participate in building the Church
Mercy	Rom. 12.8	Sympathy of heart which enables a person to empathize with and cheerfully serve those who are sick, hurting, or discouraged
Ministering (or Service, or Helping, or Hospitality)	Rom. 12.7; 1 Pet. 4.9	The ability to joyfully perform any task which benefits others and meets their practical and material needs (especially on behalf of the poor or afflicted)
Miracles	1 Cor. 12.10; 12.28	The ability to confront evil and do good in ways that make visible the awesome power and presence of God
Pastoring	Eph. 4.11	The desire and ability to guide, protect, and equip the members of a congregation for ministry
Prophecy	1 Cor. 12.28; Rom. 12.6	The ability to receive and proclaim openly a revealed message from God which prepares the Church for obedience to him and to the Scriptures
Teaching	1 Cor. 12.28; Rom. 12.7; Eph. 4.11	The ability to explain the meaning of the Word of God and its application through careful instruction
Tongues	1 Cor. 12.10; 12.28	Ecstatic utterance by which a person speaks to God (or others) under the direction of the Holy Spirit
Wisdom	1 Cor. 12.8	Spirit-revealed insight that allows a person to speak godly instruction for solving problems; and/or Spirit-revealed insight that allows a person to explain the central mysteries of the Christian faith

APPENDIX 18

Paul's Team Members

Don L. Davis

Achaicus, A Corinthian who visited Paul at Philippi, 1 Cor. 16.17.

Archippus, Colossian disciple whom Paul exhorted to fulfill his ministry, Col. 4.17; Philem. 2.

Aquila, Jewish disciple Paul found at Corinth, Acts 18.2, 18, 26; Rom. 16.3; 1 Cor. 16.19; 2 Tim. 4.19.

Aristarchus, With Paul on 3rd journey, Acts 19.29; 20.4; 27.2; Col. 4.10; Philem. 24.

Artemas, Companion of Paul at Nicopolis, Titus 3.12.

Barnabas, A Levite, cousin of John Mark, and companion with Paul in several of his journeys, cf. Acts 4.36, 9.27; 11.22, 25, 30; 12.25; chs. 13, 14, and 15; 1 Cor. 9.6; Gal. 2.1, 9, 13; Col. 4.13.

Carpus, Disciple of Troas, 2 Tim. 4.13.

Claudia, Female disciple of Rome, 2 Tim. 4.21.

Clement, Fellow-laborer at Phillipi, Phil. 4.3.

Crescens, A disciple at Rome, 2 Tim. 4.10.

Demas, A laborer of Paul at Rome, Col. 4.14; Philem. 24; 2 Tim. 4.10.

Epaphras, Fellow laborer and prisoner, Col. 1.7, 4.12; Philem. 23.

Epaphroditus, Messenger between Paul and the churches, Phil. 2.25, 4.18.

Eubulus, Disciple of Rome, 2 Tim. 4.21.

Euodia, Christian woman of Philippi, Phil. 4.2

Fortunatus, Part of the Corinthian team, 1 Cor. 16.17.

Gaius, 1) A Macedonian companion, Acts 19.29; 2) A disciple/companion in Derbe, Acts 20.4.

Jesus (Justus), A Jewish disciple at Colossae, Col. 4.11.

John Mark, Companion of Paul and cousin of Barnabas, Acts 12.12, 15; 15.37, 39; Col. 4.10; 2 Tim. 4.11; Philem. 24.

Linus, A Roman Companion of Paul, 2 Tim. 4.21.

Luke, Physician and fellow-traveler with Paul, Col. 4.14; 2 Tim. 4.11; Philem. 24.

Paul's Team Members (continued)

Onesimus, Native of Colossae and slave of Philemon who served Paul, Col. 4.9; Philem. 10.

Hermogenes, A team member who abandoned Paul in prison, 2 Tim. 1.15.

Phygellus, One with Hermogenes turned from Paul in Asia, 2 Tim. 1.15.

Priscilla (Prisca), Wife of Aquila of Pontus and fellow-worker in the Gospel, Acts 18.2, 18, 26; Rom. 16.3; 1 Cor. 16.19.

Pudens, A Roman companion of Paul, 2 Tim. 4.21.

Secundus, Companion of Paul on his way from Greece to Syria, Acts 20.4.

Silas, Disciple, fellow laborer, and prisoner with Paul, Acts 15.22, 27, 32, 34, 40; 16.19, 25, 29; 17.4, 10, etc.

Sopater, Accompanied Paul to Syria, Acts 20.4.

Sosipater, Kinsman of Paul, Rom. 16.21.

Silvanus, Probably same as Silas, 2 Cor. 1.19; 1 Thess. 1.1; 2 Thess. 1.1.

Sosthenes, Chief Ruler of the Synagogue of Corinth, laborer with Paul there, Acts 18.17.

Stephanus, One of the first believers of Achaia and visitor to Paul, 1 Cor. 1.16; 16.15; 16.17.

Syntyche, One of Paul's female "fellow workers" in Philippi, Phil. 4.2.

Tertius, Slave and person who wrote the Epistle to the Romans, Rom. 16.22.

Timothy, A young man of Lystra with a Jewish mother and Greek father who labored on with Paul in his ministry, Acts 16.1;17.14, 15; 18.5; 19.22; 20.4; Rom. 16.21; 1 Cor. 4.17; 16.10; 2 Cor. 1.1, 19; Phil. 1.1; 2.19; Col. 1.1; 1 Thess. 1.1; 3.2, 6; 2 Thess. 1.1; 1 Tim. 1.2, 18; 6.20; 2 Tim. 1.2; Philem. 1; Heb. 13.23.

Titus, Greek disciple and co-laborer of Paul, 2 Cor. 2.13; 7.6, 13, 14; 8.6, 16, 23; 12.18; Gal. 2.1, 3; 2 Tim. 4.10; Titus 1.4.

Trophimus, A Ephesian disciple who accompanied Paul to Jerusalem from Greece, Acts 20.4; 21.29; 2 Tim. 4.20.

Tryphena and Tryphosa, Female disciples of Rome, probably twins, who Paul calls laborers in the Lord, Rom. 16.12.

Tychicus, A disciple of Asia Minor who accompanied Paul in various trips, Acts 20.4; Eph. 6.21; Col. 4.7; 2 Tim. 4.12; Titus 3.12.

Urbanus, Roman disciple and aid to Paul, Rom. 16.9.

APPENDIX 19

Nurturing Authentic Christian Leadership

Rev. Dr. Don L. Davis

Cliff On-One-Side	Cliff On-the-Other-Side
Laying on hands too quickly	Always postponing delegation to the indigenous
Ignoring culture in leadership training	Elevating culture above truth
Demoting doctrine and theology	Supposing doctrine and theology as only criteria
Highlighting skills and gifts above availability and character	Substituting availability and character for genuine giftedness
Emphasizing administrative abilities above spiritual dynamism	Ignoring administration's role in spiritual vitality and power
Equating readiness with Christian perfection	Ignoring the importance of biblical standards
Limiting candidacy for leadership based on gender and ethnicity	Setting quotas of leadership based on gender and ethnicity
Seeing everyone as a leader	Seeing virtually no one as worthy to lead

The Role of Women in Ministry
Dr. Don L. Davis

While it is plain that God has established a clearly designed order of responsibility within the home, it is equally clear that women are called and gifted by God, led by his own Spirit to bear fruit worthy of their calling in Christ. Throughout the NT, commands are directed specifically to women to submit, with the particular Greek verb *hupotasso*, occurring frequently which means "to place under" or "to submit" (cf. 1 Tim. 2.11). The word also translated into our English word "subjection" is from the same root. In such contexts these Greek renderings ought not to be understood in any way except as positive admonitions towards God's designed framework for the home, where women are charged to learn quietly and submissively, trusting and working within the Lord's own plan.

This ordering of the woman's submission in the home, however, must not be misinterpreted to mean that women are disallowed from ministering their gifts under the Spirit's direction. Indeed, it is the Holy Spirit through Christ's gracious endowment who assigns the gifts as he wills, for the edification of the Church (1 Cor. 12.1-27; Eph. 4.1-16). The gifts are not given to believers on the criteria of gender; in other words, there is no indication from the Scriptures that some gifts are for men only, and the others reserved for women. On the contrary, Paul affirms that Christ provided gifts as a direct result of his own personal victory over the devil and his minions (cf. Eph. 4.6ff.). This was his own personal choice, given by his Spirit to whomever he wills (cf. 1 Cor. 12.1-11). In affirming the ministry of women we affirm the right of the Spirit to be creative in all saints for the well-being of all and the expansion of his Kingdom, as he sees fit, and not necessarily as we determine (Rom. 12.4-8; 1 Pet. 4.10-11).

Furthermore, a careful study of the Scriptures as a whole indicates that God's ordering of the home in no way undermines his intention for men and women to serve Christ as disciples and laborers together, under Christ's leading. The clear NT teaching of Christ as head of the man, and the man of the woman (see 1 Cor. 11.4) shows God's esteem for godly spiritual representation within the home. The apparent forbidding of women to hold teaching/ruling positions appears to be an admonition to protect God's assigned lines of responsibility and authority within the home. For instance, the particular Greek term in the highly debated passage in 1 Timothy 2.12, *andros*, which has often times been translated "man," may also be

The Role of Women in Ministry (continued)

translated "husband." With such a translation, then, the teaching would be that a wife ought not to rule over her husband.

This doctrine of a woman who, in choosing to marry, makes herself voluntarily submissive to "line up under" her husband is entirely consistent with the gist of the NT teaching on the role of authority in the Christian home. The Greek word *hupotasso*, which means to "line up under" refers to a wife's voluntary submission to her own husband (cf. Eph. 5.22, 23; Col. 3.18; Titus 2.5; 1 Pet. 3.1). This has nothing to do with any supposed superior status or capacity of the husband; rather, this refers to God's design of godly headship, authority which is given for comfort, protection, and care, not for destruction or domination (cf. Gen. 2.15-17; 3.16; 1 Cor. 11.3). Indeed, that this headship is interpreted in light of Christ's headship over the Church signifies the kind of godly headship that must be given, that sense of tireless care, service, and protection required from godly leadership.

Of course, such an admonition for a wife to submit to a husband would not in any way rule out that women be involved in a teaching ministry (e.g., Titus 2.4), but, rather, that in the particular case of married women, that their own ministries would come under the protection and direction of their respective husbands (Acts 18.26). This would assert that a married woman's ministry in the Church would be given serving, protective oversight by her husband, not due to any notion of inferior capacity or defective spirituality, but for the sake of, as one commentator has put it, "avoiding confusion and maintaining orderliness" (cf. 1 Cor. 14.40).

In both Corinth and Ephesus (which represent the contested Corinthian and Timothy epistolary comments), it appears that Paul's restriction upon women's participation was prompted by occasional happenings, issues which grew particularly out of these contexts, and therefore are meant to be understood in those lights. For instance, the hotly-contested test of a women's "silence" in the church (see both 1 Cor. 14 and 1 Tim. 2) does not appear in any way to undermine the prominent role women played in the expansion of the Kingdom and development of the Church in the first century. Women were involved in the ministries of prophecy and prayer (1 Cor. 11.5), personal instruction (Acts 18.26), teaching (Titus 2.4,5), giving testimony (John 4.28, 29), offering hospitality (Acts 12.12), and serving as co-laborers with the Apostles in the cause of the Gospel (Phil. 4.2-3). Paul did not relegate women to an inferior role or hidden status but served side-by-side with women for the sake of Christ "I urge Euodia and I urge Syntyche to live in harmony in the Lord. Indeed, true companion, I ask you also to help these women

The Role of Women in Ministry (continued)

who have shared my struggle in *the cause of* the Gospel, together with Clement also and the rest of my fellow workers, whose names are in the book of life" (Phil. 4.2-3).

Furthermore, we must be careful in subordinating the personage of women *per se* (that is, their nature as women) versus their subordinated role in the marriage relationship. Notwithstanding the clear description of the role of women as heirs together of the grace of life in the marriage relationship (1 Pet. 3.7), it is equally plain that the Kingdom of God has created a dramatic shift in how women are to be viewed, understood, and embraced in the kingdom community. It is plain that in Christ there is now no difference between rich and poor, Jew and Gentile, barbarian, Scythian, bondman and freemen, as well as man and woman (cf. Gal. 3.28; Col. 3.11). Women were allowed to be disciples of a Rabbi (which was foreign and disallowed at the time of Jesus), and played prominent roles in the NT church, including being fellow laborers side by side with the Apostles in ministry (e.g., see Euodia and Syntyche in Phil. 4.1ff.), as well as hosting a church in their houses (cf. Phoebe in Rom. 16.1-2, and Apphia in Philem. 1).

In regards to the issue of pastoral authority, I am convinced that Paul's understanding of the role of equippers (of which the pastor-teacher is one such role, cf. Eph. 4.9-15) is not gender specific. In other words, the decisive and seminal text for me on the operation of gifts and the status and function of offices are those NT texts which deal with the gifts (1 Cor. 12.1-27; Rom. 12.4-8; 1 Pet. 4.10-11, and Eph. 4.9-15). There is no indication in any of these formative texts that gifts are gender-specific. In other words, for the argument to hold decisively that women were never to be in roles that were pastoral or equipping in nature, the simplest and most effective argument would be to show that the Spirit simply would never even consider giving a woman a gift which was not suited to the range of callings which she felt a calling towards. Women would be forbidden from leadership because the Holy Spirit would never grant to a woman a calling and its requisite gifts because she was a woman. Some gifts would be reserved for men, and women would never receive those gifts.

A careful reading of these and other related texts show no such prohibition. It appears that it is up to the Holy Spirit to give any person, man or woman, any gift that suits him for any ministry he wishes them to do, as he wills (1 Cor. 12.11 "But one and the same Spirit works all these things, distributing to each one individually as he wills"). Building upon this point, Terry Cornett has even written a fine theological essay showing how the NT Greek for the word "apostle" is unequivocally applied to women, most clearly shown in the rendering of the female noun, "Junia" applied to "apostle" in Romans 16.7, as well as allusions to co-laboring, for instance, with the twins, Tryphena and Tryphosa, who "labored" with Paul in the Lord (16.12).

Believing that every God-called, Christ-endowed, and Spirit-gifted and led Christian ought to fulfill their role in the body, we affirm the role of women to lead and instruct under godly authority that submits to the Holy Spirit, the Word of God, and is informed by the tradition of the Church and spiritual reasoning. We ought to expect God to give women supernatural endowments of grace to carry out his bidding on behalf of his Church, and his reign in the Kingdom of God. Since men and women both reflect the *Imago Dei* (i.e., image of God), and both stand as heirs together of God's grace (cf. Gen. 1.27; 5.2; Matt. 19.4; Gal. 3.28; 1 Pet. 3.7), they are given the high privilege of representing Christ together as his ambassadors (2 Cor. 5.20), and through their partnership to bring to completion our obedience to Christ's Great Commission of making disciples of all nations (Matt. 28.18-20).

APPENDIX 21

Discerning the Call: The Profile of a Godly Christian Leader

Rev. Dr. Don L. Davis

	Commission	Character	Community	Competence
Definition	Recognizes the call of God and replies with prompt obedience to his lordship and leading	Reflects the character of Christ in their personal convictions, conduct, and lifestyle	Regards multiplying disciples in the body of Christ as the primary role of ministry	Responds in the power of the Spirit with excellence in carrying out their appointed tasks and ministry
Key Scripture	2 Tim. 1.6-14; 1 Tim. 4.14; Acts 1.8; Matt. 28.18-20	John 15.4-5; 2 Tim. 2.2; 1 Cor. 4.2; Gal. 5.16-23	Eph. 4.9-15; 1 Cor. 12.1-27	2 Tim. 2.15; 3.16-17; Rom. 15.14; 1 Cor. 12
Critical Concept	The Authority of God: God's leader acts on God's recognized call and authority, acknowledged by the saints and God's leaders	The Humility of Christ: God's leader demonstrates the mind and lifestyle of Christ in his or her actions and relationships	The Growth of the Church: God's leader uses all of his or her resources to equip and empower the body of Christ for his/her goal and task	The Power of the Spirit: God's leader operates in the gifting and anointing of the Holy Spirit
Central Elements	A clear call from God Authentic testimony before God and others Deep sense of personal conviction based on Scripture Personal burden for a particular task or people Confirmation by leaders and the body	Passion for Christlikeness Radical lifestyle for the Kingdom Serious pursuit of holiness Discipline in the personal life Fulfills role-relationships as bondslave of Jesus Christ Provides an attractive model for others in their conduct, speech, and lifestyle (the fruit of the Spirit)	Genuine love for and desire to serve God's people Disciples faithful individuals Facilitates growth in small groups Pastors and equips believers in the congregation Nurtures associations and networks among Christians and churches Advances new movements among God's people locally	Endowments and gifts from the Spirit Sound discipling from an able mentor Skill in the spiritual disciplines Ability in the Word Able to evangelize, follow up, and disciple new converts Strategic in the use of resources and people to accomplish God's task
Satanic Strategy to Abort	Operates on the basis of personality or position rather than on God's appointed call and ongoing authority	Substitutes ministry activity and/or hard work and industry for godliness and Christlikeness	Exalts tasks and activities above equipping the saints and developing Christian community	Functions on natural gifting and personal ingenuity rather than on the Spirit's leading and gifting
Key Steps	Identify God's call Discover your burden Be confirmed by leaders	Abide in Christ Discipline for godliness Pursue holiness in all	Embrace God's Church Learn leadership's contexts Equip concentrically	Discover the Spirit's gifts Receive excellent training Hone your performance
Results	Deep confidence in God arising from God's call	Powerful Christlike example provided for others to follow	Multiplying disciples in the Church	Dynamic working of the Holy Spirit

APPENDIX 22

Suffering: The Cost of Discipleship and Servant-Leadership

Don L. Davis

To be a disciple is to bear the stigma and reproach of the One who called you into service (2 Tim. 3.12). Practically, this may mean the loss of comfort, convenience, and even life itself (John 12.24-25).

All of Christ's Apostles endured insults, rebukes, lashes, and rejections by the enemies of their Master. Each of them sealed their doctrines with their blood in exile, torture, and martyrdom. Listed below are the fates of the Apostles according to traditional accounts.

- Matthew suffered martyrdom by being slain with a sword at a distant city of Ethiopia.

- Mark expired at Alexandria, after being cruelly dragged through the streets of that city.

- Luke was hanged upon an olive tree in the classic land of Greece.

- John was put in a caldron of boiling oil, but escaped death in a miraculous manner, and was afterward branded at Patmos.

- Peter was crucified at Rome with his head downward.

- James, the Greater, was beheaded at Jerusalem.

- James, the Less, was thrown from a lofty pinnacle of the temple, and then beaten to death with a fuller's club.

- Bartholomew was flayed alive.

- Andrew was bound to a cross, whence he preached to his persecutors until he died.

- Thomas was run through the body with a lance at Coromandel in the East Indies.

- Jude was shot to death with arrows.

- Matthias was first stoned and then beheaded.

- Barnabas of the Gentiles was stoned to death at Salonica.

- Paul, after various tortures and persecutions, was at length beheaded at Rome by the Emperor Nero.

APPENDIX 23

Our Declaration of Dependence: Freedom in Christ

It is important to teach morality within the realm of freedom (i.e., Gal. 5.1, "It is for freedom Christ has set you free"), and always in the context of using your freedom in the framework of bringing God glory and advancing Christ's Kingdom. I emphasize the "6-8-10" principles of 1 Corinthians, and apply them to all moral issues.

1. 1 Cor. 6.9-11, Christianity is about transformation in Christ; no amount of excuses will get a person into the Kingdom.

2. 1 Cor. 6.12a, We are free in Christ, but not everything one does is edifying or helpful.

3. 1 Cor. 6.12b, We are free in Christ, but anything that is addictive and exercising control over you is counter to Christ and his Kingdom.

4. 1 Cor. 8.7-13, We are free in Christ, but we ought never to flaunt our freedom, especially in the face of Christians whose conscience would be marred and who would stumble if they saw us doing something they found offensive.

5. 1 Cor. 10.23, We are free in Christ; all things are lawful for us, but neither is everything helpful, nor does doing everything build oneself up.

6. 1 Cor. 10.24, We are free in Christ, and ought to use our freedom to love our brothers and sisters in Christ, and nurture them for other's well being (cf. Gal. 5.13).

7. 1 Cor. 10.31, We are free in Christ, and are given that freedom in order that we might glorify God in all that we do, whether we eat or drink, or anything else.

8. 1 Cor. 10.32-33, We are free in Christ, and ought to use our freedom in order to do what we can to give no offense to people in the world or the Church, but do what we do in order to influence them to know and love Christ, i.e., that they might be saved.

This focus on freedom, in my mind, places all things that we say to adults or teens in context. Often, the way in which many new Christians are discipled is through a rigorous taxonomy (listing) of different vices and moral ills, and this can at times give them the sense that Christianity is an anti-act religion (a religion of simply not doing things), and/or a faith overly concerned with not sinning. Actually, the moral focus in Christianity is on freedom, a freedom won at a high price, a freedom to love God and advance the Kingdom, a freedom to live a surrendered life before the Lord. The moral responsibility of urban Christians is to live free in Jesus Christ, to live free unto God's glory, and to not use their freedom from the law as a license for sin.

The core of the teaching, then, is to focus on the freedom won for us through Christ's death and resurrection, and our union with him. We are now set free from the law, the principle of sin and death, the condemnation and guilt of our own sin, and the conviction of the law on us. We serve God now out of gratitude and thankfulness, and the moral impulse is living free in Christ. Yet, we do not use our freedom to be wiseguys or knuckle-heads, but to glorify God and love others. This is the context in which we address the thorny issues of homosexuality, abortion, and other social ills. Those who engage in such acts feign freedom, but, lacking a knowledge of God in Christ, they are merely following their own internal predispositions, which are not informed either by God's moral will or his love.

Freedom in Christ is a banner call to live holy and joyously as urban disciples. This freedom will enable them to see how creative they can be as Christians in the midst of so-called "free" living which only leads to bondage, shame, and remorse.

"You Got To Serve Somebody!"

Over half of the metaphors chosen by Jesus describe someone who is under the authority of another. Often the word selected is one member of a familiar role pair, such as child (of a father, *pater*), servant (of a master, *kyrios*), or disciple (of a teacher, *didaskalos*). Other images of those under authority include the shepherd (*poimen*) who tends a flock that belongs to another, the worker (*ergates*) hired by the landowner (*oikodespotes*), the apostle (*apostolos*) commissioned by his superior, and the sheep (*probaton*) obeying the voice of the shepherd. It is interesting to note that even though the disciples are being prepared for spiritual leadership in the Church, Jesus places far more emphasis on their responsibility to God's authority, than on the authority which they themselves will exercise. There is far more instruction about the role of *following* than about the role of *leading* [emphasis added].

~ David Bennett, **The Metaphors of Ministry**, p. 62.

APPENDIX 25

Spiritual Service Checklist

Rev. Dr. Don L. Davis

1. *Salvation*: Has this person believed the Gospel, confessed Jesus as Lord and Savior, been baptized, and formally joined our church as a member?

2. *Personal integrity*: Are they walking with God, growing in their personal life, and demonstrating love and faithfulness in their family, work, and in the community?

3. *Equipped in the Word*: How equipped is this person in the Word of God to share and teach with others?

4. *Support of our church*: Do they support the church through their presence, pray for the leaders and members, and give financially to its support?

5. *Submission to authority*: Does this person joyfully submit to spiritual authority?

6. *Identification of spiritual gifts*: What gifts, talents, abilities, or special resources does this person have for service, and what is their particular burden for ministry now?

7. *Present availability*: Are they open to be assigned to a task or project where we could use their service to build up the body?

8. *Reputation amongst leaders*: How do the other leaders feel about this person's readiness for a new role of leadership?

9. *Resources needed to accomplish*: If appointed to this role, what particular training, monies, resources, and/or input will they need to accomplish the task?

10. *Formal commissioning*: When and how will we make known to others that we have appointed this person to their task or project?

11. *Timing and reporting*: Also, if we dedicate this person to this role/task, when will they be able to start, and how long ought they serve before we evaluate them.

12. *Evaluate and re-commission*: When will we evaluate the performance of the person, and determine what next steps we ought to take in their leadership role at the church?

Lording Over vs. Serving Among
Differing Styles and Models of Leadership
*Adapted from George Mallone, **Furnace of Renewal.***

Secular Authority	Servant Authority
Functions on the basis of power	Functions on basis of love and obedience
Primarily rules by giving orders	Serves as one who is under orders of another
Unwilling to fail: blame-shifts for leverage	Unafraid to receive responsibility for failure
Sees itself as absolutely necessary	Willing to be used and expended for the body
Drives others (cow-punching mentality)	Leads others (shepherding mentality)
Subjects others to threat of loss and pain	Builds others by encouragement and challenge
Consolidates power for maximum impact	Stewards authority for greatest good
Has gold, makes rules	Follows the Golden Rule
Uses position for personal advancement	Exercises authority to please the Master
Expects benefits from service	Expects to expend oneself in service to others
Strength, not character, is decisive	Character, not strength, carries most weight

APPENDIX 27

From Deep Ignorance to Credible Witness

Rev. Dr. Don L. Davis

Witness - Ability to give witness and teach
2 Tim. 2.2
Matt. 28.18-20
1 John 1.1-4
Prov. 20.6
2 Cor. 5.18-21

And the things you have heard me say in the presence of many witnesses entrust to reliable men who will also be qualified to teach others. - 2 Tim. 2.2

8

Lifestyle - Consistent appropriation and habitual practice based on beliefs
Heb. 5.11-6.2
Eph. 4.11-16
2 Pet. 3.18
1 Tim. 4.7-10

And Jesus increased in wisdom and in stature, and in favor with God and man. - Luke 2.52

7

Demonstration - Expressing conviction in corresponding conduct, speech, and behavior
James 2.14-26
2 Cor. 4.13
2 Pet. 1.5-9
1 Thess. 1.3-10

Nevertheless, at your word I will let down the net. - Luke 5.5

6

Conviction - Committing oneself to think, speak, and act in light of information
Heb. 2.3-4
Heb. 11.1, 6
Heb. 3.15-19
Heb. 4.2-6

Do you believe this? - John 11.26

5

Discernment - Understanding the meaning and implications of information
John 16.13
Eph. 1.15-18
Col. 1.9-10
Isa. 6.10; 29.10

Do you understand what you are reading? - Acts 8.30

4

Knowledge - Ability to recall and recite information
2 Tim. 3.16-17
1 Cor. 2.9-16
1 John 2.20-27
John 14.26

For what does the Scripture say? - Rom. 4.3

3

Interest - Responding to ideas or information with both curiosity and openness
Ps. 42.1-2
Acts 9.4-5
John 12.21
1 Sam. 3.4-10

We will hear you again on this matter. - Acts 17.32

2

Awareness - General exposure to ideas and information
Mark 7.6-8
Acts 19.1-7
John 5.39-40
Matt. 7.21-23

At that time, Herod the tetrarch heard about the fame of Jesus. - Matt. 14.1

1

Ignorance - Unfamiliarity with information due to naivete, indifference, or hardness
Eph. 4.17-19
Ps. 2.1-3
Rom. 1.21; 2.19
1 John 2.11

Who is the Lord that I should heed his voice? - Exod. 5.2

0

APPENDIX 28

Ethics of the New Testament: Living in the Upside-Down Kingdom of God
True Myth and Biblical Fairy Tale
Dr. Don L. Davis

The Principle of Reversal

The Principle Expressed	Scripture
The poor shall become rich, and the rich shall become poor	Luke 6.20-26
The law breaker and the undeserving are saved	Matt. 21.31-32
Those who humble themselves shall be exalted	1 Pet. 5.5-6
Those who exalt themselves shall be brought low	Luke 18.14
The blind shall be given sight	John 9.39
Those claiming to see shall be made blind	John 9.40-41
We become free by being Christ's slave	Rom. 12.1-2
God has chosen what is foolish in the world to shame the wise	1 Cor. 1.27
God has chosen what is weak in the world to shame the strong	1 Cor. 1.27
God has chosen the low and despised to bring to nothing things that are	1 Cor. 1.28
We gain the next world by losing this one	1 Tim. 6.7
Love this life and you'll lose it; hate this life, and you'll keep the next	John 12.25
You become the greatest by being the servant of all	Matt. 10.42-45
Store up treasures here, you forfeit heaven's reward	Matt. 6.19
Store up treasures above, you gain Heaven's wealth	Matt. 6.20
Accept your own death to yourself in order to live fully	John 12.24
Release all earthly reputation to gain Heaven's favor	Phil. 3.3-7
The first shall be last, and the last shall become first	Mark 9.35
The grace of Jesus is perfected in your weakness, not your strength	2 Cor. 12.9
God's highest sacrifice is contrition and brokenness	Ps. 51.17
It is better to give to others than to receive from them	Acts 20.35
Give away all you have in order to receive God's best	Luke 6.38

APPENDIX 29

Substitute Centers to a Christ-Centered Vision

Goods and Effects Which Our Culture Substitutes as the Ultimate Concern

Rev. Dr. Don L. Davis

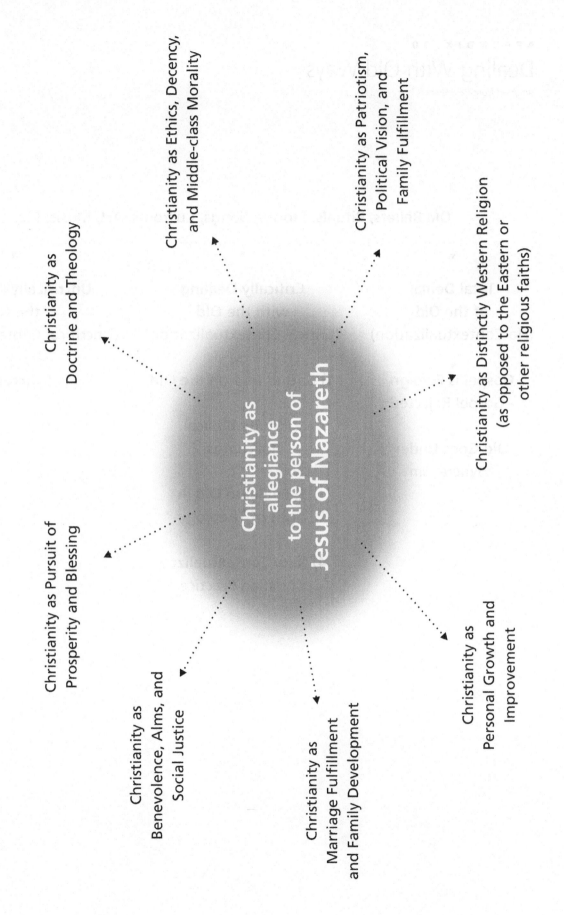

Christianity as
Doctrine and Theology

Christianity as Ethics, Decency,
and Middle-class Morality

Christianity as Patriotism,
Political Vision, and
Family Fulfillment

Christianity as Pursuit of
Prosperity and Blessing

Christianity as
allegiance
to the person of
Jesus of Nazareth

Christianity as Distinctly Western Religion
(as opposed to the Eastern or
other religious faiths)

Christianity as
Benevolence, Alms, and
Social Justice

Christianity as
Marriage Fulfillment
and Family Development

Christianity as
Personal Growth and
Improvement

APPENDIX 30

Dealing With Old Ways
Adapted from Paul Hiebert

Old Beliefs, Rituals, Stories, Songs, Customs, Art, Music, Etc.

Total Denial of the Old (No Contextualization)	**Critically Dealing with the Old** (Critical Contextualization)	**Uncritically Accepting the Old** (Uncritical Contextualization)
Gospel Is Foreign - Gospel Rejected	**1) Gather Info on the Old**	**Syncretism**
Old Goes Under - Syncretism	**2) Study Biblical Teachings**	
	3) Evaluate Old in Light of Theology	
	4) New Contextualized Christian Practice	

APPENDIX 3 1
Three Contexts of Urban Christian Leadership Development

Rev. Dr. Don L. Davis

Ephesians 4.11 (ESV) - And he himself gave some to be apostles, some prophets, some evangelists, and some pastors and teachers,

12. for the equipping of the saints for the work of ministry, for the edifying of the body of Christ

God has appointed leaders in the Church to equip Christians for "the work of the ministry," that they might walk worthy of the Lord in all things, bear abundant fruit in Christ, to win, follow-up, and disciple members within their *oikos* (their family, friends, and associates), and to be zealous in good works to reveal the Kingdom's life

Three Contexts of Leadership Function

I. Forming, Leading, and Reproducing Dynamic Small Group Life and Ministry
- Inreach (discipling, fellowship, care giving, etc.)
- Outreach (evangelism, service, witness)

II. Facilitating and Reproducing Vital Congregational Life and Ministry

III. Nurturing and Cultivating Inter-congregational Support, Cooperation, and Collaboration

Any recognized part of a larger assembly, e.g., Cell group, Women's study, Prayer group, BibleStudy, Sunday School class, Street Ministry team, Prison outreach team, etc.

The church together as one, from house church to mega-church (i.e., Any distinct gathering of believers who identify with one another, give and serve together, under one pastoral head, where their presence and allegiance are shown and known)

According to some biblical linguists, the phrase in the NT for the church in assembly, *en ekklesia*, applies to the local expressions of the people of God when they "come together as a church," cf. 1 Cor. 11.18. The people of God can thus be called the "church/assembly," that is, those who by faith in Jesus Christ and his Holy Spirit now represent his called ones in a particular place and locale.

Clusters of churches which band together in partnership for mutual support, refreshment, service, and mission (e.g., Associations, denominations, conferences, etc.)

God has given to the Church leaders of unique gifting - apostles, prophets, evangelists, pastors and teachers in order that the "Church Assembled" might be edified and equipped to fulfill its mission and ministry as it scatters, as individuals, into the world. **Luke 10.2-3 (ESV)**, And he said to them, "The harvest is plentiful but the laborers are few. Therefore pray earnestly to the Lord of the harvest to send out laborers into his harvest. **[3]** Go your way; behold, I am sending you out as lambs in the midst of wolves").

Small Group / Congregational Form / The Locale Church / "The Church Assembled"

Less than all of us • **"Us"** (My church) • **More** than all of us

Four Contexts of Urban Christian Leadership Development
Rev. Dr. Don L. Davis

1. Personal Friendships, Mentoring, and Discipleship

2. Small Group Nurture and Cell Groups

3. Congregational Life and Governance

4. Inter-congregational Cooperation and Collaboration

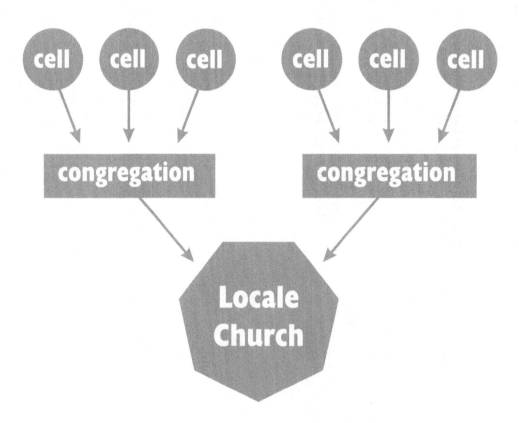

APPENDIX 33

Investment, Empowerment, and Assessment

How Leadership as Representation Provides Freedom to Innovate

Rev. Dr. Don L. Davis

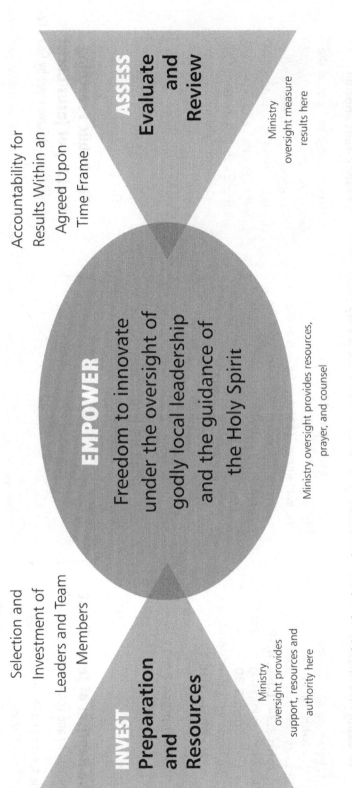

ASSESS

Evaluate and Review

Accountability for Results Within an Agreed Upon Time Frame

Ministry oversight measure results here

EMPOWER

Freedom to innovate under the oversight of godly local leadership and the guidance of the Holy Spirit

Ministry oversight provides resources, prayer, and counsel

Selection and Investment of Leaders and Team Members

INVEST

Preparation and Resources

Ministry oversight provides support, resources and authority here

Evaluation by sending authority
Review of results in light of task
Faithfulness and loyalty assessed
Overall evaluation of plan and strategy
Critical evaluation of leadership performance
Formal determination of operation's "success"
Reassignment in light of evaluation

Formal leadership selection
Acknowledgment of personal call
Determination of task and assignment
Training in spiritual warfare
Authorization to act defined and given
Necessary resources given and logistics planned
Commissioning: deputization formally recognized

APPENDIX 34

Representin'

Jesus as God's Chosen Representative

Rev. Dr. Don L. Davis

To represent another

Is to be selected to stand in the place of another, and thereby fulfill the assigned duties, exercise the rights and serve as deputy for, as well as to speak and act with another's authority on behalf of their interests and reputation.

The Temptation of Jesus Christ
Challenge to and Contention with God's Rep

Mark 1.12-13 (ESV)
The Spirit immediately drove him out into the wilderness. **[13]** *And he was in the wilderness forty days, being tempted by Satan. And he was with the wild animals,* and the angels were ministering to him.

The Public Preaching Ministry of Jesus Christ
Communication and Conveyance by God's Rep

Mark 1.14-15 (ESV) Now after John was arrested, Jesus came into Galilee, proclaiming the gospel of God, **[15]** and saying, "The time is fulfilled, and the kingdom of God is at hand; repent and believe in the gospel."

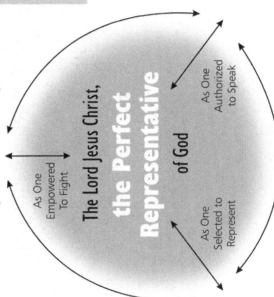

The Lord Jesus Christ, **the Perfect Representative** of God

As One Empowered To Fight

As One Authorized to Speak

As One Selected to Represent

Jesus Fulfills The Duties Of Being an Emissary

1. Receiving an *Assignment,*
   John 10.17-18
2. Resourced with an *Entrustment,*
   John 3.34; Luke. 4.18
3. Launched into *Engagement,*
   John 5.30
4. Answered with an *Assessment,*
   Matthew 3.16-17
5. New assignment after *Assessment,*
   Philippians 2.9-11

The Baptism of Jesus Christ
Commissioning and Confirmation of God's Rep

Mark 1.9-11 (ESV) *In those days Jesus came from Nazareth of Galilee and was baptized by John in the Jordan.* **[10]** And when he came up out of the water, immediately he saw the heavens opening and the Spirit descending on him like a dove. **[11]** And a voice came from heaven, "You are my beloved Son; with you I am well pleased."

APPENDIX 3 5

Delegation and Authority in Christian Leadership

Rev. Dr. Don L. Davis

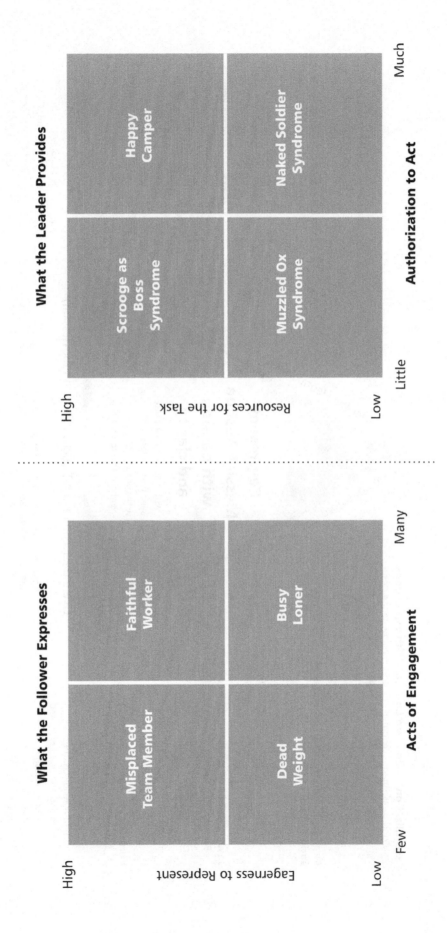

What the Leader Provides

| Scrooge as Boss Syndrome | Happy Camper |
| Muzzled Ox Syndrome | Naked Soldier Syndrome |

Resources for the Task — High / Low

Authorization to Act — Little / Much

What the Follower Expresses

| Misplaced Team Member | Faithful Worker |
| Dead Weight | Busy Loner |

Eagerness to Represent — High / Low

Acts of Engagement — Few / Many

APPENDIX 36

Re-presenting Messiah

Don L. Davis

"Gentilization" of modern Christian faith expressions

Contextualization: freedom in Christ to enculturate the gospel
Common modern portrayal of Messianic hope as Gentile faith
Tendency of tradition/culture to usurp biblical authority
Present day eclipse of biblical framework by "captivities"

Strange fires on the altar: examples of socio-cultural captivities

Nationalism	Personal existentialism
Capitalism	Asceticism/moralism
Scientific rationalism	Ethnocentrism
Denominationalism	Nuclear family life

Jesus' critique of socio-cultural captivity

Bondage to religious tradition, Matt. 15.3-9
Ignorance of Scripture and God's power, Matt. 22.29
Zealous effort without knowledge, Romans 10.1-3

Hermeneutic habits that lead toward a syncretistic faith

Selective choice of texts
Tradition viewed as canon
Cultural readings of texts
Preaching and teaching based on eisegesis and audience
Uncritical approaches to one's own doctrine and practice
Apologetics for socio-cultural identity

"Paradigm paralysis" & biblical faith

Blind to one's own historical conditionedness
Limited vantage point and perspective
Privilege and power: political manipulation
Inability to receive criticism
Persecution of opposite viewpoints and new interpretations of faith

---

Rediscover the Hebraic roots of the biblical Messianic hope (return)

Recognize the socio-cultural captivity of Christian profession (exile)

Re-present Messiah Yeshua with passion and clarity

with fidelity to Scripture in sync with historic orthodoxy without cultural distortion without theological bias

---

Rediscovery of the Jewish origins of biblical faith, John 4.22

YHWH as God of lovingkindness in covenant faithfulness

Messianic fulfillment in OT: prophecy, type, story, ceremony, and symbol

Hebraic roots of the Promise: YHWH as a Warrior God

People of Israel as community of Messianic hope

Psalms and Prophets emphasize divine rulership of Messiah

Tracing the Seed
Seed of the Woman, Gen. 3.15
Seed of Shem, Gen. 9.26-27
Seed of Abraham, Gen. 12.3
Seed of Isaac and Jacob, Gen. 26.2-5; 28.10-15
Seed of Judah, Gen. 49.10
Seed of David, 2 Sam. 7

Suffering Servant of YHWH: humiliation and lowliness of God's Davidic king

Glimmers of Gentile salvation and global transformation

Live the adventure of NT apocalyptic myth (possession)

Apocalyptic as the "mother tongue and native language" of the apostles and early Church as eschatological community

Yeshua Messiah as the Cosmic Warrior: YHWH as God who wins ultimate victory over his enemies

Messiah Yeshua as Anointed One and Binder of the Strong Man: the Messianic Age to come inaugurated in Jesus of Nazareth

"Already/Not Yet" Kingdom orientation:
The Reign of God as both manifest but not consummated

The Evidence and Guarantee of the Age to Come:
The Spirit as down payment, first fruits, and seal of God

APPENDIX 37

"You Can Pay Me Now, Or You Can Pay Me Later"

Don L. Davis

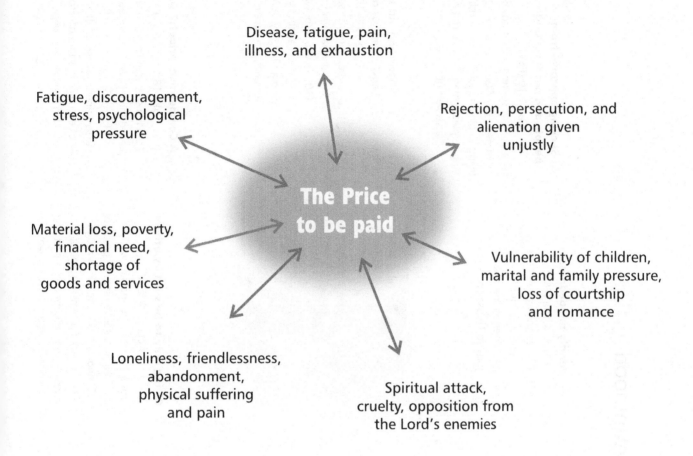

Disease, fatigue, pain, illness, and exhaustion

Fatigue, discouragement, stress, psychological pressure

Rejection, persecution, and alienation given unjustly

The Price to be paid

Material loss, poverty, financial need, shortage of goods and services

Vulnerability of children, marital and family pressure, loss of courtship and romance

Loneliness, friendlessness, abandonment, physical suffering and pain

Spiritual attack, cruelty, opposition from the Lord's enemies

APPENDIX 38

Hindrances to Christlike Servanthood

Don L. Davis

Seeking approval from people and not from God
Gal. 1.10 (ESV)

For am I now seeking the approval of man, or of God? Or am I trying to please man? If I were still trying to please man, I would not be a servant of Christ.

Scripting out the order and extent of our service
Luke 17.9-10 (ESV)

Does he thank the servant because he did what was commanded? [10] So you also, when you have done all that you were commanded, say, "We are unworthy servants; we have only done what was our duty."

A Competitive, prideful spirit
Luke 18.11-12 (ESV)

The Pharisee, standing by himself, prayed thus: "God I thank you that I am not like other men, extortioners, unjust, adulterers, or even like this tax collector. [12] I fast twice a week; I give tithes of all that I get."

Worldly-mindedness
2 Tim. 4.10a (ESV)

For Demas, in love with this present world, has deserted me and gone to Thessalonica.

Hindrances to Christ-like Servanthood

Giving only to be seen by others
Acts 5.12 (ESV)

But a man named Ananias, with his wife Sapphira, sold a piece of property, [2] and with his wife's knowledge he kept back for himself some of the proceeds and brought only a part of it and laid it at the apostles' feet.

Preoccupation with self-interest
Phil. 2.21 (ESV)

They all seek their own interests, not those of Jesus Christ.

Insistence on others not doing their fair share
Luke 10.40 (ESV)

But Martha was distracted with much serving. And she went up to him and said, "Lord, do you not care that my sister has left me to serve alone? Tell her then to help me."

Responding with touchiness and defensiveness
2 Cor. 12.19 (ESV)

Have you been thinking all along that we have been defending ourselves to you? It is in the sight of God that we have been speaking in Christ, and all for your upbuilding, beloved.

APPENDIX 39

The Ministry of Praise and Worship

Rev. Dr. Don L. Davis

The Special Call to the Ministry of Praise and Worship

*The praise which overcomes is not merely occasional or spasmodic praise, praise that fluctuates with moods and circumstances. It is continuous praise, praise that is a vocation, a way of life. "I will bless [praise] the Lord at **all times**; his praise shall **continually** be in my mouth" (Psalms 34.1). Blessed are they that dwell in thy house; they will be still [always] praising thee" (Psalms 84.4). It has been pointed out that in heaven praise is so important that it constitutes the total occupation of a certain order of beings (Revelation 4.8). God gave to King David such a revelation of the importance and power of praise upon earth that, following the heavenly pattern, he set aside and dedicated an army of four thousand Levites whose sole occupation was to praise the Lord! (1 Chronicles 23.5). They did nothing else. One of the last official acts of King David before his death was the organization of a formal program of praise. Each morning and each evening a contingent of these four thousand Levites engaged in this service. "And to stand every morning to thank and praise the Lord, and likewise at evening," (1 Chronicles 23.30, New Scofield). To the shame and defeat of the Church, the significance of the massive praise content of the Word has been largely overlooked. To be most effective, then, praise must be massive, continuous, a fixed habit, a full-time occupation, a diligently pursued vocation, a total way of life. This principle is emphasized in Psalm 57.7: "My hearted is fixed, O God, my heart is fixed; I will sing and give praise." This suggests a premeditated and predetermined habit of praise. "My heart is FIXED." This kind of praise depends on something more than temporary euphoria.*

~ Paul Billheimer, **Destined for the Throne**, pp. 121-22.

I. **Exalted God-centered Purpose, Ps. 150.5; Rev. 4.11; Ps. 29.1-2**

   A. "That's why we praise him, that's why we sing!"

      1. To express our joy in God in the Holy Spirit

      2. To acknowledge the grace of God in the person of Jesus Christ

      3. To experience the presence of God

      4. To see the beauty of God in the midst of his people

The Ministry of Praise and Worship (continued)

B. Worship is not

1. Good music alone

2. Professionally performed liturgies

3. Outstanding gear and equipment

C. Worship represents the expression of the saved heart who approaches the Father through the Son in the power of the Holy Spirit for his praise and glory alone! (John 4.24)

D. Worship leading is imitating a GE light bulb

1. When it is most effective, you never notice it, only the effects of its working

2. When it is not working is the only time you give attention to it!

II. **The Goal: to Acknowledge and Extol the Excellence of God in Every Dimension of Our Lives, Our Praises of God, 1 Pet. 2.8-9**

Principles of Effective Worship Leading

I. **To Be an Effective Worship Leader One Must Understand the Nature, Design, and Importance of Worship**

A. Worship as spiritual inquiry (*darash*), Ezra 4.2, 6.21

B. Worship as reverent obedience (*yare*), Exod.14.31; Deut.31.12-13

C. Worship as loyal service (*abad*), Exod. 5.18; Num. 8.25

D. Worship as personal ministry (*sharat*), Deut. 10.8, 18.5-7

E. Worship as genuine humility (*shaha*), most common Isa. 49.7; Gen.47.31; Exod. 34.8 cf. Isa. 66.2

F. Worship as prostration in prayer (*segid*), Dan.3.5-7, 10-12, 14-18, 28

G. Worship as nearness to God (*nagash*), Ps. 69.18; Isa. 58.2

II. **To Be an Effective Worship Leader One Must above All Else Become an Effective Worshiper**

A. Modeling: the cardinal principle of Christian discipleship

1. Luke 6.40

2. 1 Tim. 4.6-16

3. 1 Cor. 11.1

4. 1 Cor. 15.1-4

5. Phil. 3.12-15

6. Phil. 4.6-9

7. 1 Pet. 5.1-4

B. God desires that we worship him in spirit and in truth (John 4.34)

C. With wholehearted passion: the big three

1. Moses, Exod. 33-34

2. David, Ps. 27.1ff; 34.1-3; 104

3. Paul, Phil.1.18-21

III. **To Be an Effective Worship Leader One Must Understand the Principles and Practice of Worship as They Have Displayed Themselves in the History of the Saints**

A. Liturgical Theology

1. Liturgical theology does not focus primarily on the data of the Bible

The Ministry of Praise and Worship (continued)

2. It concentrates on the history of the Church, that is, what the Church has done in its historical practice to bring glory and honor to God

3. Use of reason and sociology

B. Tendencies toward shallowness: the problem of ignoring historical worship practice of the Church

1. Create the rut of ignoring everything that has gone on before, concentrate on what we like and have done

2. Ignore the power of the Spirit to work in the past

3. Deny the anointing that God has given to his people throughout every era

4. Short-change those you lead by isolating them from their brothers and sisters of long ago

C. Views regarding Liturgical Theology

1. *Anabaptist view*: reproduce NT practice unchanged

2. *Lutheran, Anglican, Reformed view*: biblical principles and changing conditions

3. *Jewish synagogue practice*: innovation (things included in the Jewish synagogue practice which were not contained in the OT)

4. *Historic Christian practice*: cultural, fluid, in line with Scripture

D. Doxological Theology (cf. Robert Webber)

1. How Jewish and Christian worship can inform theology

2. Explaining precisely what is the tie between theology and worship, Phil. 2.5-11

3. Historical outline of theology through detailed study of worship

E. Key subject of liturgical theology: the liturgical calendar (the story of God in the service of the Church)

1. Judaism

   a. Elaborate calendar of holy days in Judaism (similar in some respects to the Catholic calendar)

   b. One weekly (Sabbath), one monthly (the new moon)

   c. Leviticus 23 as biblical description of some of the key festivals and feasts

   d. All days of festival included feasts except the Day of Atonement (a fast)

   e. Feast of Purim added later, along with Dedication (cf. John 10.22)

   f. Worship as ritual drama (remembrance and re-enactment)

2. Gentile Christianity (after the first century)

   a. Exempted from literal law obedience (the council of Jerusalem, Acts 15)

   b. Destruction of the Temple in AD 70, prominence of Gentile form

   c. Christian calendar consisted of Christian holy-days shortly thereafter

   d. The Lord's Day, Sunday

   e. Fasts on Wednesday and Friday (opposed to Jewish on Monday and Thursday)

   f. Borrowed from Judaism – Easter (*Pascha*, i.e., the Passover)

   g. Ascension Day, Epiphany, and Christmas

   h. Trinity Sunday (10th c., western)

F. Summary of Liturgical Theology: celebrates the course of the Revelation story culminating in the life, death, exaltation, and return of Christ

The Ministry of Praise and Worship (continued)

IV. To Be an Effective Worship Leader One Must Comprehend Specifically and Biblically the Power and Significance of Music

A. The power of music

1. As a spiritual force

2. As a cultural phenomenon

3. As an emotional response

4. As a form of communication

5. As a artistic expression

B. Love music as an expression of your heart to the Lord: Psalm 150 (worship is to be unbroken, undiluted, high-energy, wholehearted, and uncompromising)

C. Learning to be a member of a band: the power of contribution

1. Band vs. individual

2. Contribution's elements

a. Developing an ear for "our sound:" playing a role on a team

b. Dashes and pinches: the "Lazy Susan" approach to contribution

c. Learning to downshift: providing sound only when it contributes

d. Your goal: "I intend to play on my instrument all that and no more which each song requires to give the overall sense and impression that we together intend to make."

D. Master and employ to the full the *Basic Building Blocks* of music.

1. Rhythm - Beat

2. Tempo

3. Melody

4. Harmony

5. Lyrics

6. Dynamics

E. The importance of regular practice

1. Alone

2. Together

F. Familiarity: becoming best friends with your instrument

V. To Be an Effective Worship Leader One Must Concentrate on Developing Mastery in Musicianship and Identify Gifts and Passions in Worship

A. Mastery comes with discipline: 1 Tim. 4.7-8

B. Identify what your best gifts are (under the scrutiny of loving critique!)

1. Is it my voice?

2. Is it my instrumentation?

3. Is it both? Is it neither? Is it something else altogether?

C. Design your worship themes, sets of music, and approaches to the service

1. In conjunction with the theme: forming links, connections, and associations

a. Invocation and opening praise: beckoning the saints to worship ("Come, Now is the Time to Worship")

The Ministry of Praise and Worship (continued)

        b. Joyous celebration in the presence of the Lord ("We Bring the Sacrifice of Praise")

        c. Adoration and worship ("We Declare Your Majesty")

        d. Commitment and benediction ("Lift Up Your Hearts")

    2. In conjunction with the proclaimed Word of the Lord

    3. In conjunction with the styles

    4. In conjunction with your time constraints

D. Shaping each song within your music set

    1. A song as a story: introductions, middles, transitions, and ends

    2. The art of transposition, changed tempo, voices dropping out, etc.

    3. From trickle to stream to rapids to ocean

    4. Avoiding the "wall of sound" problem associated with young musicians

E. Learning to help every worship team member make their unique contribution to the worship experience through who they are and what they do

    1. Don't simply play or sing; listen to yourself and contribute

    2. The cycle of unending noise

        a. We're playing loud; I cannot hear myself

        b. I turn myself up; others can't hear themselves, they turn themselves up

        c. We're all playing even louder now; I cannot hear myself

        d. Etc.

F. Note the difference between merely playing well vs. enhancing the body's worship

    1. Between performing a concert and leading worship

    2. Between highlighting your play and contributing to the feeling and mood of the song

    3. Between beautifying our song together and playing your instrument

G. Obtain and use the Appropriate Gear

    1. Make the financial and emotional investment

        a. From the church: becoming a part of the church's budget

        b. From the musician: investing wisely in the right materials

    2. Quality

        a. Avoid the cheapest gear

        b. Don't go broke on the high end

        c. Middle-of-the-road is not bad today: modest investments can produce CD quality return

    3. Tastiness: the art of tweaking

    4. "Less is more:" If in doubt, dumb down for greatest impact

VI. To Be an Effective Worship Leader One Must Know How to Build and Sustain a Focused Worship Team

A. The many voices, contributions, and gifts in coordination = greatest worship experience for the congregation

B. The importance of worship as a *community event*

The Ministry of Praise and Worship (continued)

C. The Trinitarian Principle applied to worship: unity, diversity, and equality

1. The symphony as model for worship in the Church of Jesus Christ

2. European styles dominate in American churches

3. The Nicene Creed: the Church is one, holy, apostolic, and catholic

    a. Hundreds of styles of praise

    b. Offered to God in scores of languages

    c. Ethno-musicology - the science of human music and learning

    d. No form is superior; all forms are acceptable if done in conjunction with the biblical edicts

4. Dangerous to ignore this principle: hegemony of European styles and power

D. Have clear standards and policies for everyone involved

E. Be careful not to become too professional; emphasize quality but allow for full participation by the body

F. Offer clear and encouraging leadership at all times

G. Recruit from a broad base of people

H. Organize for maximum success and effectiveness

VII. To Be an Effective Worship Leader One Must Creatively Use Resources to Blend the Old and New (the Ancient and the Modern) in Worship and Praise

A. The broadness of expression in the Church of Jesus Christ

1. The biblical plethora: Revelation 5 (from every tribe, language, kindred, and nation)

2. Within these many different styles are reflected, expressed, and enjoyed

a. Differences according to time: traditional styles versus contemporary styles

b. Differences according to culture: southern gospel to hip-hop

c. Differences according to volume

d. Differences according to meanings of music

3. The "fight" is real and meaningful

4. Not "either/or" but "both/and"

B. Why is a blended worship approach so important?

1. Variety is truly the spice of life, and the nature of God's person and working

2. To hear the Lord's voice afresh: the case for contemporary

3. To remember the Lord's work in our past: the case for traditional

C. One person's garbage is another person's wealth: the tyranny and phases of ethnocentrism (see Acts 10: Peter and the Jewish band's reaction to Cornelius)

1. Phase one: ours is *preferred* over theirs

2. Phase two: ours is *better* than theirs

3. Phase three: ours is *right*, theirs is somewhat iffy

The Ministry of Praise and Worship (continued)

4. Phase four: mine is God-ordained and *superior*, and everyone else's is odd and wrong

D. Blending: an affirmation of the importance of difference of expression and the holding of tradition in our worship experience in God. How do you blend?

1. In the songs you select

2. In the styles you play

3. In the instrumentation you select

4. In the vocal arrangements you choose

E. Respecting difference while allowing for preferences and self-expression: the constant challenge of the worship leader

1. Integrate the service with genuine appreciation of styles

2. Tease out meaning by playing the same music in differing styles

VIII. The Summary of Worship: Glorifying God in God-Pleasing Harmony

A. Members of the household of God: worship as the expression of saved spirits

B. Built on the foundation of the apostles and prophets, with Jesus Christ as the Chief and Precious Cornerstone: worship as the response to God's historical self-revelation through his Word

C. Joined together as a holy temple in the Lord: worship as the people of God becoming a holy sanctuary where his praises dwell

D. Built together into a dwelling place for God by the Spirit: we ourselves are the place where God's praises originate and where he dwells

E. All that we are and do can harmonize together as leaders, congregation, and worship team into a praise offering sweet and pure enough for our God to dwell!

Eph. 2.19-22 (ESV)
So then you are no longer strangers and aliens, but you are fellow citizens with the saints and members of the household of God, [20] built on the foundation of the apostles and prophets, Christ Jesus himself being the cornerstone, [21] in whom the whole structure, being joined together, grows into a holy temple in the Lord. [22] In him you also are being built together into a dwelling place for God by the Spirit.

APPENDIX 40

The Church Year (Western Church)

The Urban Ministry Institute

The purpose of the liturgical calendar is to relive the major events in Jesus' life in real time.

Date	Event	Purpose
Begins late Nov. or early Dec.	Advent	A season of anticipation and repentance which focuses on **the First and Second Comings of Christ**. The dual focus means that Advent both begins and ends the Christian year (Isa. 9.1-7, 11.1-16; Mark 1.1-8).
Dec. 25	Christmas	Celebrates **the Birth of Christ** (Luke 2.1-20).
Jan. 6	Epiphany	The Feast of Epiphany on January 6 commemorates the coming of the Magi which reveals Christ's mission to the world. The entire season of Epiphany then emphasizes **the way in which Christ revealed himself to the world as the Son of God** (Luke 2.32; Matt. 17.1-6; John 12.32).
The seventh Wednesday before Easter	Ash Wednesday	A day of fasting and repentance that reminds us that we are disciples about to begin **the journey with Jesus that ends in the cross** (Luke 9.51). Ash Wednesday begins the observance of Lent.
40 days before Easter (excluding Sundays)	Lent	A time for reflection on **the suffering and death of Jesus**. Lent also emphasizes "death to self" so that, like Jesus, we prepare ourselves to obey God no matter what sacrifice it involves. Lenten observance calls for people to fast as a way of affirming this attitude of obedience (Luke 5.35; 1 Cor. 9.27; 2 Tim. 2.4; Heb. 11.1-3).
Moveable depending on the date of Easter Sunday which occurs in March or April	Holy Week	*Palm Sunday* The Sunday before Easter which commemorates **the Triumphal Entry of Christ** (John 12.12-18). *Maundy* Thursday* The Thursday before Easter which commemorates the giving of **the New Commandment and the Lord's Supper** prior to Christ's Death (Mark 14.12-26; John 13). (* From the Latin *mandatum novarum* - "new commandment.") *Good Friday* The Friday before Easter which commemorates **the crucifixion of Christ** (John 18-19). *Easter Sunday* The Sunday which celebrates **the resurrection of Christ** (John 20).
40 days after Easter	Ascension Day	Celebrates **the Ascension of Christ** to heaven at which time God "seated him at his right hand in the heavenly realms, far above all rule and authority, power and dominion, and every title that can be given, not only in the present age but also in the one to come" (Eph. 1.20b-21; 1 Pet. 3.22; Luke 24.17-53).
7th Sunday after Easter	Pentecost	The day which commemorates the coming of the Holy Spirit to the Church. **Jesus is now present with all his people** (John 16; Acts 2).
Nov. 1st	All Saints Day	A time to remember those heroes of the faith who have come before us (especially those who died for the Gospel). **The living Christ is now seen in the world through the words and deeds of his people** (John 14.12; Heb. 11; Rev. 17.6).

The Church Year (continued)

The Church Year Follows the Ordering of the Gospels and Acts

- It begins with the birth of Christ (Advent to Epiphany).

- It then focuses on the revelation of his mission to the world (Epiphany).

- It reminds us that Jesus set his face toward Jerusalem and the cross (Ash Wednesday and Lent).

- It chronicles his final week, his crucifixion and his resurrection (Holy Week).

- It affirms his Ascension to the Father's right hand in glory (Ascension Day).

- It celebrates the birth of his Church through the ministry of his Spirit (Pentecost).

- It remembers the history of his Church throughout the ages (All Saints Day).

- Advent both ends the cycle and begins it again. It looks forward to his Second Coming as the conclusion of the Church year but also prepares to remember again his first coming and thus starts the Church year afresh.

Birth
⇩
Ministry
⇩
Passion
⇩
Ascension
⇩
Descent of the Spirit
⇩
The Church through the Ages
⇩
Second Coming

Colors Associated With the Church Year

Christmas Season (Christmas Day through start of Epiphany) - *White and Gold*

Epiphany Season - *Green*

Ash Wednesday and Lent - *Purple*

Holy Week

> *Palm Sunday* - *Purple*

> *Maundy Thursday* - *Purple*

> *Good Friday* - *Black*

> *Easter Sunday* - *White and Gold*

Ascension Day - *White and Gold*

Pentecost - *Red*

All Saints Day - *Red*

Advent Season (Fourth Sunday before Christmas through Christmas Eve) - *Purple*

The Meaning of the Colors

Black
Mourning, Death

Gold
Majesty, Glory

Green
Hope, Life

Purple
Royalty, Repentance

Red
Holy Spirit (flame)
Martyrdom (blood)

White
Innocence,
Holiness, Joy

APPENDIX 41

A Guide to Determining Your Worship Profile

Taken from Robert Webber, Planning Blended Worship, Nashville: Abingdon Press, 1998

1. Which of the following categories best describes your church?

   _____ Affected by Catholic and mainline worship renewal

   _____ Affected by the Pentecostal, charismatic, or praise and worship renewal

   _____ Affected by the movement to blend traditional and contemporary worship

   _____ Not affected by any of the worship renewal movements

2. Identify the age make-up of the people in your church

   _____% of people in our church are boosters (born before 1945)

   _____% of people in our church are boomers (born between 1945 and 1961)

   _____% of people in our church are from generation X (born after 1961)

3. Of the 8 common elements of worship renewal, which ones have made an impact on the worship of your church? Evaluate each of the areas on a scale of 1 (least impact) to 10 (most impact). Then take time to discuss those areas that are weakest.

   a. Our church draws from a biblical understanding of worship. 1 2 3 4 5 6 7 8 9 10

   b. The worship of our church draws from the past, especially the early Church. 1 2 3 4 5 6 7 8 9 10

   c. Our church has experienced a new focus on Sunday worship. 1 2 3 4 5 6 7 8 9 10

   d. Our church draws from the music of the whole Church. 1 2 3 4 5 6 7 8 9 10

   e. Our church has restored the use of the arts. 1 2 3 4 5 6 7 8 9 10

   f. Our church follows the calendar of the Christian year effectively. 1 2 3 4 5 6 7 8 9 10

   g. Our church has experienced the restoration of life in the sacred actions of worship. 1 2 3 4 5 6 7 8 9 10

   h. The worship of our church empowers its outreach ministries. 1 2 3 4 5 6 7 8 9 10

A Guide to Determining Your Worship Profile (continued)

4. Evaluate the content, structure, and style of your worship. Again, use a scale of 1 ("That does not describe our church at all.") to 10 ("Yes, that is our church!"). Discuss areas of greatest weakness.

   a. The content of our worship is the full story of Scripture.   1 2 3 4 5 6 7 8 9 10

   b. The structure of our worship is the universally accepted fourfold pattern.   1 2 3 4 5 6 7 8 9 10

   c. The style of our worship is appropriate to our congregation and to the people we attract.   1 2 3 4 5 6 7 8 9 10

5. Answer the following:

   a. The approach to worship in our church is based upon: Conceptual language/Symbolic language

   b. The communication style of our church will relate best to: Boosters/Boomers/Generation X

   All of the above

6. I would describe our church as: An old paradigm church/A new paradigm church

7. Draw from each of the previous questions to create a worship profile of the church. Do so by completing each of the following sentences:

   a. Our church has been affected by (which stream of worship renewal)

   b. Our age group is primarily

   c. Of the eight aspects of worship renewal, we draw on

   d. The content of our worship is

   e. The structure of our worship is

   f. The style of our worship is

   g. Our approach to communication is

8. To complete this study, comment on the kinds of changes you would like to see occur in the worship of your church.

APPENDIX 42

Understanding Leadership as Representation

The Six Stages of Formal Proxy

Don L. Davis

Leadership As Representation

The Revealed Will of God

Consent of Your Leaders

The Fulfillment of the Task and Mission

CONVICTION

CONSCIENCE

CHARACTER

Commissioning [1]

Formal Selection and Call to Represent

- Chosen to be an emissary, envoy, or proxy
- Confirmed by appropriate other who recognize the call
- Is recognized to be a member of a faithful community
- Calling out of a group to a particular role of representation
  - Calling to a particular task or mission
  - Delegation of position or responsibility

Luke 10.1 (ESV) After this the Lord appointed seventy-two others and sent them on ahead of him, two by two, into every town and place where he himself was about to go. . .

Luke 10.16 (ESV) "The one who hears you hears me, and the one who rejects you rejects me, and the one who rejects me rejects him who sent me."

John 20.21 (ESV) Jesus said to them again, "Peace be with you. As the Father has sent me, even so I am sending you."

Equipping [2]

Appropriate Resourcing and Training to Fulfill the Call

- Assignment to a supervisor, superior, mentor, or instructor
- Disciplined instruction of principles underlying the call
- Constant drill, practice, and exposure to appropriate skills
  - Recognition of gifts and strengths
  - Expert coaching and ongoing feedback

Entrustment [3]

Corresponding Authorization and Empowerment to Act

- Delegation of authority to act and speak on commissioner's behalf
- Scope and limits of representative power provided
- Formal deputization (right to enforce and represent)
- Permission given to be an emissary (to stand in stead of)
- Release to fulfill the commission and task received

Mission [4]

Faithful and Disciplined Engagement of the Task

- Subordination of one's will to accomplish the assignment
- Obedience: carrying out the orders of those who sent you
  - Fulfilling the task that was given to you
- Freely acting within one's delegated authority to fulfill the task
  - Maintaining loyalty to those who sent you
  - Using all means available to do one's duty, whatever the cost
- Full recognition of one's answerability to the one(s) who commissioned

---

Reckoning [5]

Official Evaluation and Review of One's Execution

- Reporting back to sending authority for critical review
  - Formal comprehensive assessment of one's execution and results
  - Judgment of one's loyalties and faithfulness
  - Sensitive analysis of what we accomplished
  - Readiness to ensure that our activities and efforts produce results

---

Reward [6]

Public Recognition and Continuing Response

- Formal publishing of assessment's results
- Acknowledgment and recognition of behavior and conduct
  - Corresponding reward or rebuke for execution
  - Review made basis for possible reassignment or recommissioning
  - Assigning new projects with greater authority

APPENDIX 43

Capturing God's Vision for His People

The "Enduring Solidarity" of Our Search for the Land of Promise

Heb. 11.13-16 (ESV) - These all died in faith, not having received the things promised, but having seen them and greeted them from afar, and having acknowledged that they were strangers and exiles on the earth. [14] For people who speak thus make it clear that they are seeking a homeland. [15] If they had been thinking of that land from which they had gone out, they would have had opportunity to return. [16] But as it is, they desire a better country, that is, a heavenly one. Therefore God is not ashamed to be called their God, for he has prepared for them a city.

A whole galaxy of auxiliary images oscillate around the analogy of "the people of God" for Christians and the Christian church. These include in the Pauline letters the following: "God's elect" (Rom. 8.33; Eph. 1.4; Col. 3.12), "Abraham's descendants" (Rom. 4.16; Gal. 3.29; 4.26-28), "the true circumcision" (Phil. 3.3; Col. 2.11), and even "Israel of God" (Gal. 6.16). All of these images assert, in some manner, an enduring solidarity of the people of the church with the people of Israel, whose history provides the church with an authoritative account of the principles and actions of God's past redemptive working. It is the task of exegesis and theology to spell out the nature of this relationship.

~ Richard Longenecker, ed.
Community Formation in the Early Church and in the Church Today.
Peabody, MA: Hendrickson Publishers, 2002. p. 75.

Readings on the Church

The People of God: Living the Adventure of the *Ekklesia*

1 Pet. 2.9-12 (ESV) - But you are a chosen race, a royal priesthood, a holy nation, a people for his own possession, that you may proclaim the excellencies of him who called you out of darkness into his marvelous light. [10] Once you were not a people, but now you are God's people; once you had not received mercy, but now you have received mercy. [11] Beloved, I urge you as sojourners and exiles to abstain from the passions of the flesh, which wage war against your soul. [12] Keep your conduct among the Gentiles honorable, so that when they speak against you as evildoers, they may see your good deeds and glorify God on the day of visitation.

The identification of Christians as "the people of God" appears a number of times in the New Testament (e.g. Luke 1.17; Acts 15.14; Titus 2.14; Heb. 4.9; 8.10; 1 Pet. 2.9-10; Rev. 18.4; 21.3). But it is used by Paul with special significance in Romans 9.25-26; 11.1-2; 15.10, and 2 Corinthians 6.16 to set the Christian church in the context of the long story of God's dealing with his chosen people Israel. "People of God," a covenant expression, speaks of God's choosing and calling a particular people into covenantal relationship (Exod. 19.5; Deut. 7.6; 14.2; Ps. 135.4; Heb. 8.10; 1 Pet. 2.9-10; Rev. 21.3). They are God's gracious initiative and magnanimous action in creating, calling, saving, judging, and sustaining them. And as God's people, they experience God's presence among them.

~ Richard Longenecker, ed.
Community Formation in the Early Church and in the Church Today.
Peabody, MA: Hendrickson Publishers, 2002. p. 75.

Where Biblical Study of Leadership Begins: The Church as Context for World Change

[A] biblical study on leadership must begin with the story of the church that came into existence on the Day of Pentecost. The term *ekklesia* is used more than one hundred times in the New Testament. In fact, it's virtually impossible to understand God's will for our lives as believers without comprehending this wonderful "mystery of Christ" that has "been revealed by the Spirit to God's holy apostles and prophets" (Eph. 3.4-5).

Readings on the Church (continued)

Beyond the Gospels, most of the NT is the story of "local churches" and how God intended them to function. True, Jesus Christ came to lay the foundation and to build his *ekklesia* (Matt. 16.18) and when he said to Peter, "I will build my *church*," He was certainly thinking more broadly than establishing a "local church" in Caesarea Philippi where this conversation took place (Matt. 16.13-20). . . .

On the other hand, Jesus was also anticipating the multitude of *local churches* that would be established in Judea and Samaria and throughout the Roman Empire--and eventually all over the world as we know it today. This story begins in the book of Acts and spans a significant period during the first century (approximately from A.D. 33 to A.D. 63). Furthermore, during this time frame, most of the New Testament letters were written to these local churches--or to men like Timothy and Titus who were helping to establish these churches.

~ Gene Getz. **Elders and Leaders**. Chicago: Moody, 2003. pp. 47-48.

A World to Change, a World to Win

If anyone is going to change the world for the better, it may be argued, it ought to be the Christians, not the Communists. For myself, I would say that if we started applying our Christianity to the society in which we live, then it would be we, indeed, who would change the world. Christians, too, have a world to change and a world to win. Had the early Christians gone in for slogans these might well have been theirs. They might be ours too. There is no reason at all why they should be the monopoly of the Communists *[and the Muslims, and the atheists, and the hedonists, and the secular humanists, and the . . .]*

~ Douglas Hyde, **Dedication and Leadership**, pp. 32-33

Those Who Turn the World Upside Down Have Themselves Been Turned Inside Out

The bitterest foe became the greatest friend. The Blasphemer became the preacher of Christ's love. The hand that wrote the indictment of the disciples of Christ when he brought them before magistrates and into prison now penned epistles of God's redeeming love. The heart that once beat with joy when Stephen sank beneath the bloody stones now rejoiced in scourgings and stonings for the sake of Christ.

From this erstwhile enemy, persecutor, blasphemer came the greater part of the New Testament, the noblest statements of theology, the sweetest lyrics of Christian love.

~ C. E. Macartney in **Dynamic Spiritual Leadership** by J. Oswald Sanders. pp. 33-34

Readings on Pastoral Care

Rev. Dr. Don L. Davis

Pastoral Care Demands Spiritual Discernment

The pastor was becoming greatly concerned that things were not "happening" in the church as he believed the Lord wanted at this critical time of the church's growth. Seeking the counsel of one of his leading deacons, the pastor asked, "What is wrong with our church? Is it *ignorance* or *apathy*?

The deacon responded, "*I don't know*, and *I don't care!*"

Pastoral Care Focuses on Growth to Maturity

Paul's vision of the church and its ministry *works against the trends of the past century.* Because his ecclesial vision is *apostolic*, it stands in judgment of our pastoral methods and offers to any generation a foundation for church and ministry appropriate to any person, church, or era.

While our pastoral work involves an incredibly wide variety of tasks and responsibilities, and while our role in the church and community offers us many opportunities to use our gifts and abilities, all our labors are merely *means to a divine end.* We ourselves are a means God uses to accomplish a *divine purpose. God calls pastors to grow or to build the church.*

When I came to my current pastorate, I joined a long line of pastors who serve the same end. *We are all different, and we have different emphases, opportunities, gifts, and results; but our goal is singular: We exist to build the temple of the Holy Spirit. We are called to grow Christ's church.* It is easy to confuse means and ends. Every individual and church does it. Yet the result can be tragic.

~ David Fisher. **The 21st Century Pastor**.
Grand Rapids: Zondervan, 1996. p. 192.

Discerning and Addressing the Root Issues Is Key to All Pastoral Care

1 Thess. 5.14-15 (ESV) - And we urge you, brothers, admonish the idle, encourage the fainthearted, help the weak, be patient with them all. [15] See that no one repays anyone evil for evil, but always seek to do good to one another and to everyone.

Admonish the idle

Encourage the Fainthearted

Help the weak

Be patient with all

Repay evil to none

Do good to one another and to everyone

APPENDIX 46

The Method of the Master

Faithful Servants Representin'

[Jesus'] concern was not with programs to reach the multitudes, but with men whom the multitudes would follow. Remarkable as it may seem, Jesus started to gather those men before he ever organized an evangelistic campaign or even preached a sermon in public. Men were to be his method of winning the world to God. . . . Jesus devoted most of his remaining life on earth to these few disciples. He literally staked his whole ministry on them. The world could be indifferent toward him and still not defeat his strategy. It even caused him no great concern when his followers on the fringes of things gave up their allegiance when confronted with the true meaning of the Kingdom (John 6.66). But he could not bear to have his close disciples miss his purpose. They had to understand the truth and be sanctified by it (John 17.17), else all would be lost. Thus he prayed "not for the world," but for the few God gave him "out of the world (John 17.6, 9). Everything depended on their faithfulness if the world would believe in him "through their word" (John 17.20).

~ Robert Coleman, **The Master Plan of Evangelism**. pp. 27, 31.

A P P E N D I X   4 7
Readings on Servanthood

Jesus' Concept of Servanthood

When Jesus speaks to his disciples of servanthood, he has two aspects in mind. First is the service rendered *to God as the supreme authority to whom they owe their allegiance*, and the second is the service which they render *to people as an expression of humility and love.*

~ David Bennett. **Metaphors of Ministry**. p. 25

Taking Our Cues from the Master Himself: Jesus as Servant

It is with an issue like [servanthood] that I see one distinguishing characteristic that sets Christians apart from the world: we serve because Christ was a servant and clearly told us to do this in memory of him.

We are not to serve because it makes us feel good or serves as some kind of therapy. We are not to serve because it is a good example for our children. We are not to serve because it will make the wheels of society turn more smoothly.

We serve because Christ was a servant.

~ Kenneth H. Carter, Jr. **The Gifted Pastor**. p. 495

Dynamics of Credible Spiritual Vision
Rev. Dr. Don L. Davis

Vision originates in calling

Vision presumes gifting

Vision assures confirmation

Vision inspires commitment

Vision identifies opportunity

Vision demands strategy

Vision requires resources

Calling

+

Gifting

+

Confirmation

+

Commitment

+

Opportunity

+

Strategy

+

Resources

=

Results for God

APPENDIX 49

The Church Leadership Paradigm
The Case for Biblical Leadership
Rev. Dr. Don L. Davis

1. The *Kingdom of God* has come in the person of *Jesus of Nazareth*, and is now manifest through the Spirit in the Church.

2. The cities of the world, as strongholds of the devil, desperately need the *presence* and *witness* of the Church.

3. The Church cannot thrive and provide witness without *leadership*.

4. Authentic leadership in the Church must be *called by God, represent Jesus Christ, be gifted by the Spirit, and confirmed by others* in the body.

5. Called, endowed, and confirmed leaders must be given *authority, resources, and opportunity* in order to facilitate maturity and equip the saints for ministry.

Watch What You Image Forth

Images are powerful. They shape what we see, by highlighting certain features and moving others into the background. They dominate our patterns of analysis and reflection. They suggest explanations of why we relate to one another the way we do, or why certain structures exist. They support particular understandings of the past, interpretations of the present, and scenarios for the future. They promote some values and discourage others. They suggest priorities, and awaken emotions.

The choice to emphasize a given metaphor and to put aside another can set the direction of a community and its leadership. Therefore, we must become aware of the images we use, and how we are using them. In particular, *we must examine the metaphors we use in the development of our future leaders.*

~ David Bennett. **Metaphors of Ministry**. p. 199.

APPENDIX 51

Roles of Representational Leadership

Rev. Dr. Don L. Davis

Things that may or may not have any bearing on the personal representation of another:

Roles of Representational Leadership

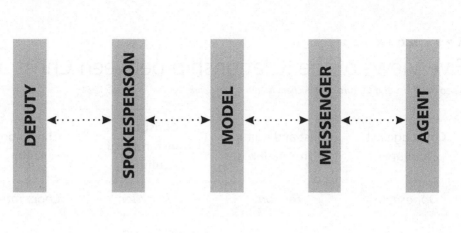

DEPUTY ◄┄┄► SPOKESPERSON ◄┄┄► MODEL ◄┄┄► MESSENGER ◄┄┄► AGENT

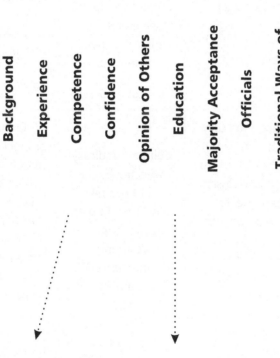

Background

Experience

Competence

Confidence

Opinion of Others

Education

Majority Acceptance

Officials

Traditional Ways of Promotion and Demotion

Seniority

Voting Habits

Has someone granted to you the right and responsibility to stand for them in this situation?

What precisely have you been authorized to do and entrusted to steward or accomplish on behalf of the person who granted these rights to you?

What is at stake in my faithful accomplishment of my entrusted status--what will I gain or what will I forfeit with this charge?

Five Views of the Relationship between Christ and Culture

Based on **Christ and Culture** by H. Richard Niebuhr, New York: Harper and Row, 1951

Christ against Culture	Christ and Culture in Paradox	Christ the Transformer of Culture	Christ above Culture	The Christ of Culture
Opposition	*Tension*	*Conversion*	*Cooperation*	*Acceptance*
Therefore come out from them and be separate, says the Lord. Touch no unclean thing, and I will receive you. - 2 Cor. 6.17 (cf. 1 John 2.15)	Give to Caesar what is Caesar's, and to God what is God's. - Matt. 22.21 (cf. 1 Pet. 2.13-17)	In putting everything under him, God left nothing that is not subject to him. Yet at present we do not see everything subject to him. - Heb. 2.8 (cf. Col. 1.16-18)	Indeed, when Gentiles, who do not have the law, do by nature things required by the law, they are a law for themselves. - Rom 2.14 (cf. Rom. 13.1, 5-6)	Every good and perfect gift is from above, coming down from the Father of the heavenly lights, who does no change like shifting shadows. - James 1.17 (cf. Phil. 4.8)
Culture is radically affected by sin and constantly opposes the will of God. Separation and opposition are the natural responses of the Christian community which is itself an alternative culture.	Culture is radically affected by sin but does have a role to play. It is necessary to delineate between spheres: Culture as law (restrains wickedness), Christianity as grace (gives righteousness). Both are an important part of life but the two cannot be confused or merged.	Culture is radically affected by sin but can be redeemed to play a positive role in restoring righteousness. Christians should work to have their culture acknowledge Christ's Lordship and be changed by it.	Culture is a product of human reason and is part of a God-given way to discover truth. Although culture can discern real truth, sin limits its capacities which must be aided by revelation. Seeks to use culture as a first step toward the understanding of God and his revelation.	Culture is God's gift to help man overcome his bondage to nature and fear and advance in knowledge and goodness. Human culture is what allows us to conserve the truth humanity has learned. Jesus' moral teaching moves human culture upward to a new level.
Tertullian Menno Simons Anabaptists	Martin Luther Lutherans	St. Augustine John Calvin Reformed	Thomas Aquinas Roman Catholic	Peter Abelard Immanual Kant Liberal Protestant

A Theology of the Church in Kingdom Perspective

Terry Cornett and Don Davis

APPENDIX 54

The Picture and the Drama

Image and Story in the Recovery of Biblical Myth

Don L. Davis

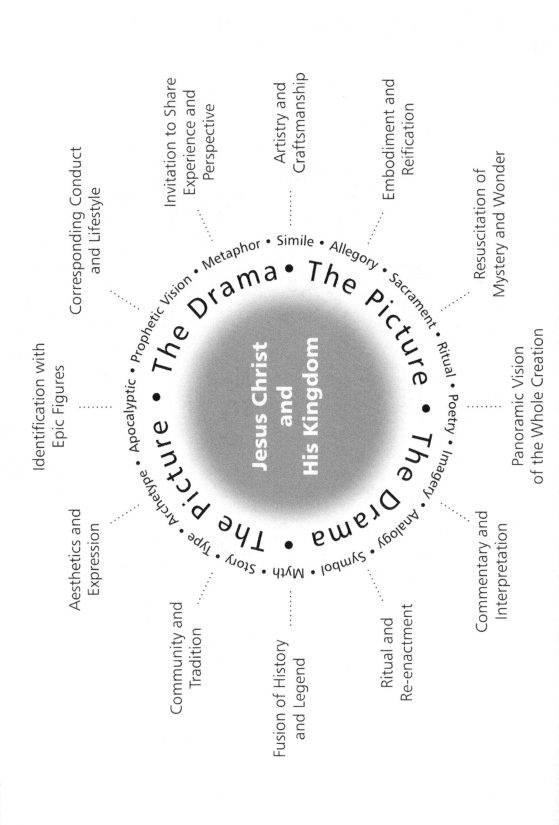

The Drama • The Picture • The Drama • The Picture • The Drama • The Picture

Prophetic Vision • Metaphor • Simile • Allegory • Sacrament • Ritual • Poetry • Imagery • Analogy • Symbol • Myth • Story • Type • Archetype • Apocalyptic •

Jesus Christ and His Kingdom

Invitation to Share Experience and Perspective

Artistry and Craftsmanship

Embodiment and Reification

Resuscitation of Mystery and Wonder

Corresponding Conduct and Lifestyle

Panoramic Vision of the Whole Creation

Identification with Epic Figures

Commentary and Interpretation

Aesthetics and Expression

Ritual and Re-enactment

Community and Tradition

Fusion of History and Legend

APPENDIX 55

Fit to Represent

Multiplying Disciples of the Kingdom of God

Rev. Dr. Don L. Davis • Luke 10.16 (ESV) - The one who hears you hears me, and the one who rejects you rejects me, and the one who rejects me rejects him who sent me.

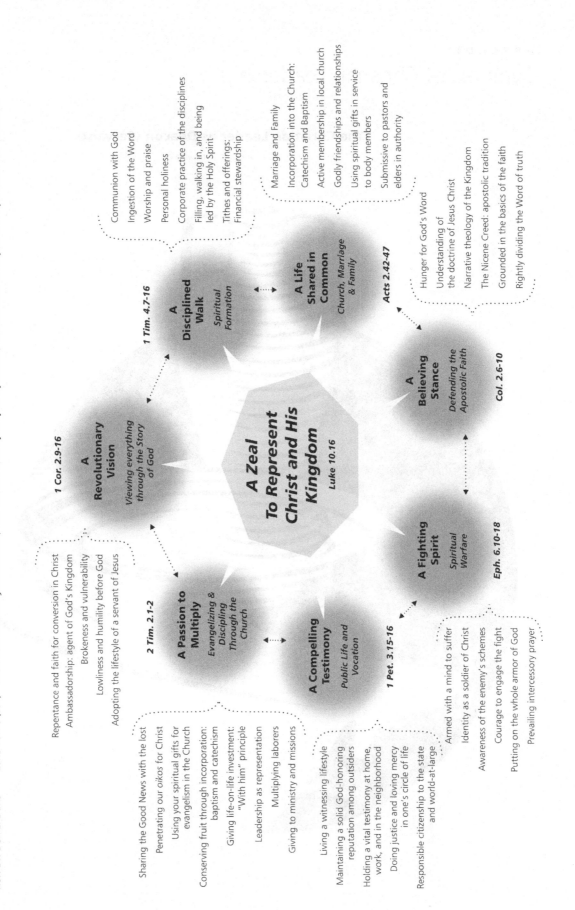

A Zeal To Represent Christ and His Kingdom
Luke 10.16

A Revolutionary Vision
Viewing everything through the Story of God
1 Cor. 2.9-16

- Repentance and faith for conversion in Christ
- Ambassadorship: agent of God's Kingdom
- Brokeness and vulnerability
- Lowliness and humility before God
- Adopting the lifestyle of a servant of Jesus

A Disciplined Walk
Spiritual Formation
1 Tim. 4.7-16

- Communion with God
- Ingestion of the Word
- Worship and praise
- Personal holiness
- Corporate practice of the disciplines
- Filling, walking in, and being led by the Holy Spirit
- Tithes and offerings: Financial stewardship

A Life Shared in Common
Church, Marriage & Family
Acts 2.42-47

- Marriage and Family
- Incorporation into the Church: Catechism and Baptism
- Active membership in local church
- Godly friendships and relationships
- Using spiritual gifts in service to body members
- Submissive to pastors and elders in authority

A Believing Stance
Defending the Apostolic Faith
Col. 2.6-10

- Hunger for God's Word
- Understanding of the doctrine of Jesus Christ
- Narrative theology of the Kingdom
- The Nicene Creed: apostolic tradition
- Grounded in the basics of the faith
- Rightly dividing the Word of truth

A Passion to Multiply
Evangelizing & Discipling Through the Church
2 Tim. 2.1-2

- Sharing the Good News with the lost
- Penetrating our *oikos* for Christ
- Using your spiritual gifts for evangelism in the Church
- Conserving fruit through incorporation: baptism and catechism
- Giving life-on-life investment: "With him" principle
- Leadership as representation
- Multiplying laborers
- Giving to ministry and missions

A Compelling Testimony
Public Life and Vocation
1 Pet. 3.15-16

- Living a witnessing lifestyle
- Maintaining a solid God-honoring reputation among outsiders
- Holding a vital testimony at home, work, and in the neighborhood
- Doing justice and loving mercy in one's circle of life
- Responsible citizenship to the state and world-at-large

A Fighting Spirit
Spiritual Warfare
Eph. 6.10-18

- Armed with a mind to suffer
- Identity as a soldier of Christ
- Awareness of the enemy's schemes
- Courage to engage the fight
- Putting on the whole armor of God
- Prevailing intercessory prayer

APPENDIX 56
Symbols of Christian Leadership

The Christian Leader as Deacon (Servant)

Illustrated by Tim Ladwig

The Christian Leader as Elder

Illustrated by Tim Ladwig

Symbols of Christian Leadership (continued)

The Christian Leader as Pastor

Illustrated by Tim Ladwig

Symbols of Christian Leadership (continued)

The Christian Leader as Bishop

Illustrated by Tim Ladwig

A P P E N D I X   5 7

Picking Up on Different Wavelengths
Integrated vs. Fragmented Mindsets and Lifestyles
Dr. Don L. Davis

A Fragmented Mindset and Lifestyle	An Integrated Lifestyle and Mindset
Sees things primarily in relation to one's own needs	Sees all things as one and whole
Sees something other than God as a substitute point of reference and coordination for meaning and truth	Sees God in Christ as the ultimate point of reference and coordination for all meaning and truth
Seeks God's blessing upon one's own personal enhancement	Aligns personal goals with God's ultimate plan and purposes
Understands the purpose of life to experience the greatest level of personal fulfillment and enhancement possible	Understands the purpose of life to make the maximum contribution possible to God's purpose in the world
Only relates to others in connection to their effect upon and place within one's individual personal space	Deeply identifies with all people and things as an integral part of God's great plan for his own glory
Defines theology as seeking to express someone's perspective on some religious idea or concept	Defines theology as seeking to comprehend God's ultimate designs and plans for himself in Jesus Christ
Applications are rooted in seeking right responses to particular issues and situations	Applications are byproducts of understanding what God is doing for himself in the world
Focuses on the style of analysis (to discern the processes and make-up of things)	Focuses on the style of synthesis (to discern the connection and unity of all things)
Seeks to understand biblical revelation primarily from the standpoint of one's private life ("God's plan for my life")	Seeks to understand biblical revelation primarily from the standpoint of God's plan for whole ("God's plan for the ages")
Governed by pressing concerns to ensure one's own security and significance in one's chosen endeavors ("My personal life plan")	Decision making is governed by commitment to participate as co-workers with God in the overall vision ("God's working in the world")
Coordinates itself around personal need as a working paradigm and project	Connects and correlates itself around God's vision and plan as a working paradigm
Sees mission and ministry as the expression of one's personal giftedness and burden, bringing personal satisfaction and security	Sees mission and ministry as the present, practical expression of one's identity vis-a-vis the panoramic vision of God
Relates knowledge, opportunity, and activity to the goals of personal enhancement and fulfillment	Relates knowledge, opportunity, and activity to a single, integrated vision and purpose
All of life is perceived to revolve around the personal identity and needs of the individual	All of life is perceived to revolve around a single theme: the revelation of God in Jesus of Nazareth

Scriptures on the Validity of Seeing All Things as Unified and Whole

Ps. 27.4 (ESV) - One thing have I asked of the Lord, that will I seek after: that I may dwell in the house of the Lord all the days of my life, to gaze upon the beauty of the Lord and to inquire in his temple.

Luke 10.39-42 (ESV) - And she had a sister called Mary, who sat at the Lord's feet and listened to his teaching. [40] But Martha was distracted with much serving. And she went up to him and said, "Lord, do you not care that my sister has left me to serve alone? Tell her then to help me." [41] But the Lord answered her, "Martha, Martha, you are anxious and troubled about many things, [42] but one thing is necessary. Mary has chosen the good portion, which will not be taken away from her."

Phil. 3.13-14 (ESV) - Brothers, I do not consider that I have made it my own. But one thing I do: forgetting what lies behind and straining forward to what lies ahead [14] I press on toward the goal for the prize of the upward call of God in Christ Jesus.

Ps. 73.25 (ESV) - Whom have I in heaven but you? And there is nothing on earth that I desire besides you.

Mark 8.36 (ESV) - For what does it profit a man to gain the whole world and forfeit his life?

Luke 18.22 (ESV) - When Jesus heard this, he said to him, "One thing you still lack. Sell all that you have and distribute to the poor, and you will have treasure in heaven; and come, follow me."

John 17.3 (ESV) - And this is eternal life, that they know you the only true God, and Jesus Christ whom you have sent.

1 Cor. 13.3 (ESV) - If I give away all I have, and if I deliver up my body to be burned, but have not love, I gain nothing.

Gal. 5.6 (ESV) - For in Christ Jesus neither circumcision nor uncircumcision counts for anything, but only faith working through love.

Picking Up on Different Wavelengths (continued)

Col. 2.8-10 (ESV) - See to it that no one takes you captive by philosophy and empty deceit, according to human tradition, according to the elemental spirits of the world, and not according to Christ. [9] For in him the whole fullness of deity dwells bodily, [10] and you have been filled in him, who is the head of all rule and authority.

1 John 5.11-12 (ESV) - And this is the testimony, that God gave us eternal life, and this life is in his Son. [12] Whoever has the Son has life; whoever does not have the Son of God does not have life.

Ps. 16.5 (ESV) - The Lord is my chosen portion and my cup; you hold my lot.

Ps. 16.11 (ESV) - You make known to me the path of life; in your presence there is fullness of joy; at your right hand are pleasures forevermore.

Ps. 17.15 (ESV) - As for me, I shall behold your face in righteousness; when I awake, I shall be satisfied with your likeness.

Eph. 1.9-10 (ESV) - making known to us the mystery of his will, according to his purpose, which he set forth in Christ [10] as a plan for the fullness of time, to unite all things in him, things in heaven and things on earth.

John 15.5 (ESV) - I am the vine; you are the branches. Whoever abides in me and I in him, he it is that bears much fruit, for apart from me you can do nothing.

Ps. 42.1 (ESV) - As a deer pants for flowing streams, so pants my soul for you, O God.

Hab. 3.17-18 (ESV) - Though the fig tree should not blossom, nor fruit be on the vines, the produce of the olive fail and the fields yield no food, the flock be cut off from the fold and there be no herd in the stalls, [18] yet I will rejoice in the Lord; I will take joy in the God of my salvation.

Matt. 10.37 (ESV) - Whoever loves father or mother more than me is not worthy of me, and whoever loves son or daughter more than me is not worthy of me.

Ps. 37.4 (ESV) - Delight yourself in the Lord, and he will give you the desires of your heart.

Ps. 63.3 (ESV) - Because your steadfast love is better than life, my lips will praise you.

Ps. 89.6 (ESV) - For who in the skies can be compared to the Lord? Who among the heavenly beings is like the Lord

Phil. 3.8 (ESV) - Indeed, I count everything as loss because of the surpassing worth of knowing Christ Jesus my Lord. For his sake I have suffered the loss of all things and count them as rubbish, in order that I may gain Christ

1 John 3.2 (ESV) - Beloved, we are God's children now, and what we will be has not yet appeared; but we know that when he appears we shall be like him, because we shall see him as he is.

Rev. 21.3 (ESV) - And I heard a loud voice from the throne saying, "Behold, the dwelling place of God is with man. He will dwell with them, and they will be his people, and God himself will be with them as their God.

Rev. 21.22-23 (ESV) - And I saw no temple in the city, for its temple is the Lord God the Almighty and the Lamb. [23] And the city has no need of sun or moon to shine on it, for the glory of God gives it light, and its lamp is the Lamb.

Ps. 115.3 (ESV) - Our God is in the heavens; he does all that he pleases.

Jer. 32.17 (ESV) - Ah, Lord God! It is you who has made the heavens and the earth by your great power and by your outstretched arm! Nothing is too hard for you.

Dan. 4.35 (ESV) - all the inhabitants of the earth are accounted as nothing, and he does according to his will among the host of heaven and among the inhabitants of the earth; and none can stay his hand or say to him, "What have you done?"

Eph. 3.20-21 (ESV) - Now to him who is able to do far more abundantly than all that we ask or think, according to the power at work within us, [21] to him be glory in the Church and in Christ Jesus throughout all generations, forever and ever. Amen.

APPENDIX   5 8

A Theological Overview of the Equipping Gifts Described in Ephesians 4.11

Rev. Terry Cornett, M.A., M.A.R.

I. Evangelists

A. Linguistic Considerations

Euaggelistes

"A preacher of the gospel" (*Strong's Greek Dictionary of New Testament Words*)

"The word translated in the NT 'evangelist' is a noun from the verb *euangelizomai* 'to announce news' and usually rendered . . . as 'preach the gospel'" (D.B. Knox, "Evangelist," *New Bible Dictionary*, 2nd Edition, J. D. Douglas and others, eds. Leicester, England-Downers Grove, IL: InterVarsity Press, 1982, p. 356).

"The Greek word for evangelist (Eph. 4.11) is a compound of two words. The first Greek word means "well, good, kind, right, and proper," eu. The second word means "messenger, envoy, one sent, an angel of God," *aggelos*. Evangelist conveys one who is a good messenger, a messenger who comes to bring good news–news that will fill a listeners heart with joy and thanksgiving" (Harley H. Schmitt, *Many Gifts, One Lord*, Fairfax, VA: Xulon Press, 2002, p. 76).

B. Relevant Theological Quotes

1. "An evangelist knew the gospel narrative thoroughly and was capable of explaining it, as Philip the evangelist did to the eunuch. . . . Originally, *euaggelistes* denoted a function rather than an office. There could have been little difference between an apostle and an evangelist, all the apostles being evangelists, but not all evangelists being apostles" (Spiros Zodhiates, *The Complete Word Study Dictionary*: New Testament, Chattanooga, TN: AMG Publishers, 1992, pp. 670-671).

2. "All Christians are called to play their part in fulfilling Jesus' Great Commission, but some believers have a special call to, and a spiritual gift for, communicating Christ and leading others to him. These we call

A Theological Overview of the Equipping Gifts Described in Ephesians 4.11 (continued)

evangelists, as does the New Testament" (The Amsterdam Declaration, published in *Christianity Today*, August 7, 2000, [Amsterdam 2000 was a world-wide gathering of evangelicals in mission called by the Billy Graham Evangelistic Association with a special focus on itinerant evangelists and their role in world mission]).

3. "It will be seen then that though the apostles were evangelists, not all evangelists were apostles. This distinction is confirmed in Ephesians 4.11, where the office of 'evangelist' is mentioned after 'apostle' and 'prophet,' and before 'pastor' and teacher.' From this passage it is plain that the gift of evangelism was a distinct gift within the Christian church; and although all Christians doubtless performed this sacred task, as opportunity was given to them, there were some who were pre-eminently called and endowed by the Holy Spirit for this work (D.B. Knox, "Evangelist," *New Bible Dictionary*, 2nd Edition, J. D. Douglas and others, eds. Leicester, England-Downers Grove, IL: InterVarsity Press, 1982, pp. 356-57).

4. "Such individuals were not specifically called to serve a specific congregation, but moved about from place to place, proclaiming the gospel to people wherever they had opportunity. . . .Evangelists share the gospel of Jesus Christ in such a manner that it becomes good news to the hearers. The hearers respond and become faithful and committed followers of Jesus Christ. The evangelist also has a specific anointing "to equip the saints, for the work of ministry for building up the body of Christ" (Eph. 4.12). The official recognition of such individuals within the congregation and in the church at large enables the process of bringing people to faith in Christ" (Harley H. Schmitt, *Many Gifts, One Lord*, Fairfax, VA: Xulon Press, 2002, p. 77).

5. "The evangelist of the Scriptures is, without question, the messenger to the unevangelized, preparing the way for the pastor and teacher in his more constant ministry in the church" (Lewis Sperry Chafer, *True Evangelism*, Grand Rapids: Zondervan, 1967, p. 6).

6. "It will be seen that as an order in the ministry, the evangelist precedes that of the pastor and teacher, a fact which harmonizes with the character of the work each is still recognized as doing. The evangelist has no fixed place of residence, but moves about in different localities,

A Theological Overview of the Equipping Gifts Described in Ephesians 4.11 (continued)

preaching the gospel to those ignorant of it before. As these are converted and united to Jesus Christ by faith, the work of the pastor and teacher begins, to instruct them further in the things of Christ and build them up in the faith" (J. M. Gray, *The International Standard Bible Encyclopedia*, Vol. 2, Geoffrey W. Bromily, Gen. ed. Grand Rapids: Eerdmans, 1982, p. 204).

C. Summary

1. Like the apostolic and prophetic ministries, the primary function of the evangelistic office is itinerant and missionary in nature. The evangelistic office recognizes that while Christianity spreads naturally through the *oikos* (family and friends) of converted individuals, it often comes across barriers (culture, geography, resistant religions, etc.) that the ordinary spread of the Gospel will not quickly overcome. It is the unique function of the evangelist to break open ground that the Gospel can then spread in through more ordinary means.

2. The gift of evangelism ensures that a special endowment of the Spirit's wisdom and power is present so that the evangelist is unusually effective at receiving a hearing for the Gospel, even in hostile environments. The office of evangelist both frees the gifted person for itinerant ministry in a way that can be underwritten by the larger church, and mandates for this person a special responsibility to stimulate and train evangelists in the local congregations created by missionary outreach, since like all the offices of Ephesians 4.11, it exists to "equip the saints for the work of ministry."

3. Although the evangelist plays a distinct function in mission, the task of the evangelist is not to be separated from the task of church planting. This is seen clearly in Acts 8, where Philip's evangelistic success in Samaria culminates in a visit from the apostles who confirm the conversions, baptize the new believers, ensure that the presence of the Holy Spirit is understood and experienced by the new community of Christians, use the laying on of hands as a formal recognition of the new converts legitimacy, exercise teaching and church discipline (correcting Simon the former sorcerer), and extend the outreach of the mission by preaching in other Samaritan towns. In other words, evangelists are the first stage in a process of church planting and discipleship, not an

A Theological Overview of the Equipping Gifts Described in Ephesians 4.11 (continued)

independent office which exists for an isolated exercise of its own ministry gifts.

II. Pastors[1]

A. Linguistic Considerations

Poimen

"A shepherd" (literally or figuratively) (*Strong's Greek Dictionary of New Testament Words*).

"Herdsman, shepherd, is an Indo-European word which is frequently used in metaphorical senses: leader, ruler, commander. . . .Plato reminds us of the religious use of the word when he compares the rulers of the city-state to shepherds who care for their flock" (E. Beyreuther, *The New International Dictionary of New Testament Theology*, Vol. 3, Colin Brown, Gen. ed., Grand Rapids: Zondervan, 1986, p. 564).

"[Shepherd is] a word naturally of frequent occurrence in Scripture. Sometimes the word "pastor" is used instead (Jer. 2.8; 3.15; 10.21; 12.10; 17.16). This word is used figuratively to represent the relation of rulers to their subjects and of God to his people (Ps. 23.1; 80.1; Isa. 40.11; 44.28; Jer. 25.34, 35; Nahum 3.18; John 10.11, 14; Heb. 13.20; 1 Pet. 2.25; 5.4). The duties of a shepherd in an unenclosed country like Palestine were very onerous. "In early morning he led forth the flock from the fold, marching at its head to the spot where they were to be pastured. Here he watched them all day, taking care that none of the sheep strayed, and if any for a time eluded his watch and wandered away from the rest, seeking diligently till he found and brought it back. In those lands sheep require to be supplied regularly with water, and the shepherd for this purpose has to guide them either to some running stream or to wells dug in the wilderness and furnished with troughs. At night he brought the flock home to the fold, counting them as they passed under the rod at the door to assure himself that none were missing. Nor did his labours always end with sunset. Often he had to guard the fold through the dark hours from the attack of wild beasts, or the wily attempts of the prowling thief" (see 1 Sam. 17.34) ("Shepherd," *Easton's Bible Dictionary*).

[1] Because Paul in Ephesians 4.11 omits the definite article before the word "teachers," it has long been debated in the Church whether he intended to describe only one office, "pastor-teacher" or two "pastors" and "teachers." John Calvin outlines the debate when he says, "Pastors and Teachers are supposed by some to denote one office. . . . Chrysostom and Augustine are of this opinion. . . . I partly agree with them, that Paul speaks indiscriminately of pastors and teachers as belonging to one and the same class, and that the name teacher does, to some extent apply to all pastors. But this does not appear to me a sufficient reason why two offices, which I find to differ from each other, should be confounded. Teaching is, no doubt, the duty of all pastors; but to maintain sound doctrine requires a talent for interpreting Scripture, a man may be a teacher who is not qualified to preach" ("Epistle to the Ephesians," Calvin's Commentaries, vol. XXI, Grand Rapids: Baker, 1981, pp. 279-280). This paper follows Calvin in supporting the possibility of two separate offices, while understanding practically that both offices are often combined in the same individual.

B. Relevant Theological Quotes

1. "Apostles and evangelists had a particular task in planting the church in every place; prophets, for bringing a particular word of God to a situation. Pastors and teachers were gifted to be responsible for the day-to-day building up of the church" (Francis Foulkes *The Epistle of St. Paul to the Ephesians, Tyndale New Testament Commentaries*, Grand Rapids: Eerdmans, 1956, p. 119).

2. "'Pastors' may readily be identified with the ministers who are elsewhere called 'elders' (*presbyteroi*) or 'bishops' (*episkopoi* rendered 'guardians' in our preceding citation of Acts 20.28: 'shepherd the flock of God that is in your charge' is the injunction given to elders by a 'fellow elder' in 1 Pet. 5.2). (It is fitting that this injunction should be ascribed to the apostle whose final commission from the Lord, according to John 21.15-17, was 'Feed my sheep.'") (F. F. Bruce, "Epistle to the Colossians, to Philemon, and to the Ephesians," *The New International Commentary on the New Testament*, Vol. 10., Grand Rapids: Eerdmans, 1984, pp. 348).

3. "The ministry of a pastor is a ministry of love. No man can perform this ministry without a shepherd's heart as a gift from God. . . .Jesus pointed out that the disposition of a true shepherd is to lay down his life for his sheep. . .When a man has been given the heart of a true shepherd, he is there for the best interest of the flock regardless of personal cost. . . .The duties of the pastor are varied but most can be grouped under three general headings. In the first place, the pastor must oversee and feed the flock of God. . . .Secondly, he has the responsibility of guarding and instructing the people. . . .Thirdly, the pastor must be a teacher of the Word by precept and example" (Joe H. Cothen, *Equipped for Good Work*, Gretna, LA: Pelican Publishing, 1996, pp. 13-15).

4. "In addition to whatever else it may be, the gift of pastoring is a catalyst geared to release the gift potential of those in the flock" (Kenneth O. Gangel, *Unwrap Your Spiritual Gifts*, Wheaton, IL: Victor Books, 1983, p. 72).

5. "The apostles preached the gospel before they planted churches and gave their converts further teaching; they were in effect evangelists (as

A Theological Overview of the Equipping Gifts Described in Ephesians 4.11 (continued)

well as pastors and teachers) though they are not specifically called so" (F. F. Bruce, "Epistle to the Colossians, to Philemon, and to the Ephesians," *The New International Commentary on the New Testament*, Vol. 10., Grand Rapids: Eerdmans, 1984, p. 347).

C. Summary

Pastors organize, nurture, train, and protect Christian communities and their members. The ultimate goal of the pastoral task is to present everyone "complete in Christ" so that the community of believers acts and speaks in the world just as Christ would. The core task of the pastor is not "doing ministry" but "equipping members to do ministry" by training them in the Word of God and by recognizing their spiritual gifts and helping them to put these gifts into action for ministry and mission. Missionaries with pastoral gifts have a special responsibility to train indigenous leaders to take over the work from their charge.

III. Teachers

A. Linguistic Considerations

didaskalos

"An instructor" (*Strong's Greek Dictionary of New Testament Words*).

"Acts 13.1 refers to *didáskaloi*, teachers with *prophetai*, prophets. From this it is concluded that in the Christian church the *didáskaloi*, teachers appear as having a special function (Acts 13.1; 1 Cor. 12.23,29; Eph. 4.11; James 3.1). These *didáskaloi* answer to the Jewish *grammateís* (pl.), scribes, and are to be viewed as in a special sense acquainted with and interpreters of God's salvation (Matt. 13.52; Luke 2.46). To them fell the duty of giving progressive instruction of God's redeeming purpose, a function which, according to Eph. 4.11, may have been united with *poimen*, pastor, in one person. Notwithstanding, linguists have debated the precise relationship between teachers and pastors in that text. There is a growing consensus that pastors are a sub-group within the larger body of teachers" (Spiros Zodhiates, *The Complete Word Study Dictionary: New Testament*, Chattanooga, TN: AMG Publishers, 1992).

A Theological Overview of the Equipping Gifts Described in Ephesians 4.11 (continued)

B. Relevant Theological Quotes

1. "The words *pastor* and *teacher* are grouped as though this were one single office, and in many ways it is. However, there may be teachers who are not called to be pastors. The teacher is one who instructs, especially in doctrine" (Joe H. Cothen, *Equipped for Good Work*, Gretna, LA: Pelican Publishing, 1996, p. 301).

2. "The content of the teaching was wide-ranging: it included the teaching of Jesus with its implications for Christian belief and conduct. In Acts 2.42 it is called 'the apostles' teaching,' to which the primitive church of Jerusalem is said to have devoted itself. . . . Paul assumes, in writing to Rome, that the 'form of teaching' which the Christians of that city had received was sufficiently clear and comprehensive to enable them to detect and reject propaganda which was incompatible with it (Rom. 6. 17; 16.17)" (F. F. Bruce, "Epistle to the Colossians, to Philemon, and to the Ephesians," *The New International Commentary on the New Testament*, Vol. 10., Grand Rapids: Eerdmans, 1984, pp. 348-349).

3. "Let us remember that Jesus was not only *the* pastor or shepherd, but He was *the* teacher (even as He was *the* apostle, *the* prophet, and *the* evangelist). . . . His teaching was the life-giving word of God. Early in His ministry, in response to a temptation by Satan, Jesus declared, "Man shall not live by bread alone, but by every word that proceeds from the mouth of God" (Matt. 4.4). . . . Thus the primary purpose of all Christian teaching is to feed people with the same life-giving word. . . .Recall that Peter was commanded by Jesus not only to tend His sheep–referring essentially to overseeing and guarding–but also to feed His lambs and feed His sheep. This feeding can occur only through "every word that proceed from the mouth of God"–and it is the teacher's responsibility to enable people to understand and receive this word" (J. Rodman Williams, *Renewal Theology: Systematic Theology from a Charismatic Perspective, Vol. 3: The Church, the Kingdom and Last Things*, Grand Rapids: Zondervan, 1996, pp. 180-81).

4. "In 1 Cor. 12.28 *didaskalos* is mentioned as the third charismatic office of a triad (alongside apostles and prophets). Men holding this office had the task of explaining the Christian faith to others and of providing a Christian exposition of the OT. . . . Jas. 3.1, warning against too strong

A Theological Overview of the Equipping Gifts Described in Ephesians 4.11 (continued)

[2] While it is useful to understand the linguistic and social context of the Greek world which informs the word Paul uses here, it is probably that there is relatively little overlap between the prophecy common to the Hellenistic world and Paul's much more Judeo-Christian use of the term. Christopher Forbes makes a strong case for these differences in his book *Prophecy and Inspired Speech in Early Christianity and its Hellenistic Environment* (Peabody: Hendrickson, 1997). Among other things, Forbes points out that the social forms that defined Christian prophecy differed dramatically from Greek prophecy. "The early Christian groups . . . had no priestly hierarchies, no consciously formalized prophetic ritual beyond a few simple rules of procedure . . . no oracular places, and no procedure for securing an oracle should one be required. . . . prophecy in early Christianity took a very different overall form from that which it took in the wider Hellenistic world" (p. 319). As opposed to the divination prophecy of Greek culture, "Early Christian prophecy was characteristically spontaneous in at least this sense: one did not approach the prophet with an inquiry. The prophet addressed the congregation, without prior inquiry, in the confidence that his revelation as God's word for their need, whether or not that need had yet been perceived" (p. 289).

an influx into the teaching office (an office which the writer himself appears to hold) points out that the failures of teachers will incur severe penalties in the judgment" (K. Wegenast, *The New International Dictionary of New Testament Theology*, Vol. 3, Colin Brown, Gen. ed., Grand Rapids: Zondervan, 1986, p. 768).

C. Summary

The core of the teaching office is the ability to explain the Scriptures in such a way that "the deposit of faith" is passed on to congregations and the individuals in them, and to oppose false doctrine with scriptural truth. Because they guard sound doctrine, it is important that those who hold the teaching "office" be formally recognized and authorized to speak on behalf of the congregation. Missionaries with teaching gifts must constantly work to entrust sound doctrine to "faithful men who will be able to teach others also" (2 Tim. 2.2 ESV).

IV. Prophets

A. Linguistic Considerations

Prophetes

"A foreteller" ("prophet"); by analogy, an inspired speaker; by extension, a poet (*Strong's Greek Dictionary of New Testament Words*)

"'One who speaks forth openly,' 'a proclaimer of the divine message'. . . . In general, 'the prophet' was one upon whom the Spirit of God rested . . . one, to whom and through whom, God speaks" (W. E. Vine, *Vine's Complete Expository Dictionary of Old and New Testament Words*, Nashville: Thomas Nelson, 1996, p. 493).

In ancient Greek[2] culture, the term *prophet* could describe an oracle prophet such as the one at Delphi, where it was clearly used to describe an official position (office). "The oracle prophet enjoys such social esteem that he may be invited to fulfill representative functions like leading delegations and serving as a spokesman for them. The official character of his position is plain from the fact that it was common to name the year after his period of office" (*Theological Dictionary of the New Testament*, Vol.6, Gerhard Kittel,

A Theological Overview of the Equipping Gifts Described in Ephesians 4.11 (continued)

ed., Grand Rapids: Wm. B. Eerdmans, 1964, p. 792). However, it could also be used to describe much more informal prophets such as those engaging in prophetic manticism, and poets who created under the influence of their Muse. The majority of prophecy in the Greek world was in the form of divination in which a person approached the prophet with an inquiry which the prophet answered. In Greek thought, "The prophet occupies a mediatorial role. He is the mouthpiece of the god and he is also man's spokesman to the god." (*Theological Dictionary of the New Testament*, Vol.6, Gerhard Kittel, ed., Grand Rapids: Wm. B. Eerdmans, 1964, p. 794).

B. Relevant Theological Quotes

1. "All may agree that there appears no new revelation to be expected concerning God in Christ. But there appears to be no good reason why the living God, who both speaks and acts (in contrast to dead idols), cannot use the gift of prophecy to give particular local guidance to a church, nation or individual, or to warn or encourage by way of prediction as well as by reminders, in full accord with the written word of Scripture, by which all such utterances must be tested. Certainly the NT does not see it as the job of the prophet to be a doctrinal innovator, but to deliver the word the Spirit gives him in line with the truth once for all delivered to the saints (Jude 3), to challenge and encourage our faith" (J. P. Baker, "Prophecy," *New Bible Dictionary*, 2nd Edition, J. D. Douglas and others, eds., Leicester, England-Downers Grove, IL: InterVarsity Press, 1982, p. 985).

2. "The prophet knows something of the divine mysteries. . . . Nevertheless, primitive Christian prophecy does not consist only of the disclosure of future events. . . . The prophet speaks out on contemporary issues. He does not say only what God intends to do; he also proclaims what God would have done by men. . . . The prophet admonishes the indolent and weary and consoles and encourages those under assault, 1 Co. 14.3; Ac. 15.32. Through his preaching he brings to light the secret wickedness of men, 1 Co. 14.25. Since he speaks with a sense of God-given authority, he gives authoritative instruction, though he is not above criticism" (Gerhard Kittel, ed., *Theological Dictionary of the New Testament*, Vol.6, Grand Rapids: Wm. B. Eerdmans, 1964, p. 848).

A Theological Overview of the Equipping Gifts Described in Ephesians 4.11 (continued)

3. "At all times [*in the history of the church*] there have not been lacking persons having the spirit of prophecy, not indeed for the declaration of any new doctrine of faith, but for the direction of human acts" (Thomas Aquinas, *Summa Theologica*, Vol. IV., Westminster, MD: Christian Classics, © Benziger Brothers, 1948, p. 1906).

4. "[Prophecy] was given unquestioned authority only after it was vetted (cf. 1 Thes. 5.19-21). Even when it was recognized to be a divine word, it did not necessarily become a canonical word. Prophecy had (and has) important uses for its immediate recipients but it was given canonical status only when it was recognized also to be normative revelation for future generations and a touchstone by which future prophecies might be tested" (E. E. Ellis, "Prophecy, Theology of," *New Dictionary of Theology*, Sinclair Ferguson, David F. Wright, and J. I. Packer, eds., Downers Grove, IL/Leicester, England: InterVarsity Press, 1988, p. 538).

5. Wayne Gruden argues in his book *The Gift of Prophecy in the New Testament and Today*, (Wheaton, IL: Crossway Books, 2000) that Old Testament prophets and New Testament Apostles (in the narrow sense of the Twelve plus Paul) are functionally equivalent in that they are the *only* people authorized to give immediate revelation from God that cannot be broken. What is true of Old Testament prophets is also true of New Testament apostles in that both of these speak with an authority that surpasses that of New Testament prophets. In other words, a New Testament prophet is not speaking for God in the same way as an Old Testament prophet or a New Testament apostle (narrowly defined). This view is shared by D.A. Carson who writes that,

> "it can be argued rather compellingly that the true NT analogue of the OT prophet is not the NT prophet but the NT apostle (in the narrow sense). . . . It is virtually impossible to conceive of 1 Cor. 14.29 being applied to OT prophets (once their credentials were accepted) or to NT apostles." (See "Church, Authority in," *The Evangelical Dictionary of Theology*, Walter A. Elwell, ed, Grand Rapids: Baker Book House, 1984, pp. 228-229.)

Graham Houston nuances this view further by arguing that even in the Old Testament there was a distinction between types of prophecy. There was the authoritative word from the Lord which had a uniquely binding character (like the NT Apostles) but there were also many instances *"where a type of prophecy is described which seems to have been regarded differently, not so much as a revelation of God's secrets but as a powerful sign of his presence with his people at crucial times in the unfolding of God's purposes"* (*Prophecy: A Gift for Today?* Downers Grove, IL: InterVarsity Press, 1989, p. 35). Among instances of this less authoritative, secondary-type prophecy could be named King Saul's sudden bout of prophecy that changed his mind about pursing David and the prophecy of the seventy elders in Numbers 11 which did not result in a specific recorded message but was a confirming sign of God's presence with them. Likewise, Moses' desire that all of God's people become prophets (Num. 11.29) seems to suggest by necessity this second-order prophecy focused on God's presence and leading rather than authoritative pronouncements of the Divine will and corresponds closely to Joel's prophetic vision of a time when the Spirit would be poured out in such a way that all of God's people both young and old, male and female, would receive prophetic words and visions (Joel 2.28).

C. Summary

Prophecy is the open proclamation of a revealed message from God which prepares the Church for obedience to him and to the Scriptures. In New Testament practice the prophetic message is received spontaneously and declared immediately (i.e. it is not something prepared in advance). New Testament prophecy is associated with a variety of spiritual functions including guidance, comfort, exhortation, and prediction. It is not itself a proclamation of the Gospel but rather a means by which the principles of Scripture can be more clearly understood in regard to a particular situation. Its purpose is always to strengthen the Church.

All Christian traditions have some means by which people can affirm, "I believe that God is saying to us that . . . ." Whenever God's voice is discerned to be speaking among us, a prophetic word has been given. Prophecy encourages, guides, and motivates obedience to God among a particular people facing particular situations. It is always judged by it conformity to

A Theological Overview of the Equipping Gifts Described in Ephesians 4.11 (continued)

the written Word of God (and in some traditions preaching and prophecy are held to be synonymous). This prophetic leadership and its development may employ a number of different forms in regard to how the voice of the Holy Spirit that guides into all truth is discerned, evaluated, and obeyed. Baptists, Pentecostals, Mennonites, and Presbyterians have very different traditions as to the language and means that are employed in this process but all of them take seriously that the Church must hear specifically what God is saying to them in the present.

V. Apostles

A. Linguistic Considerations

Apostolos

A *delegate*; specially, an *ambassador* of the Gospel; officially a commissioner of Christ (*Strong's Greek Dictionary of New Testament Words*).

"*A delegate, messenger, one sent forth with orders.* . . . specifically applied to the twelve disciples whom Christ selected, out of the multitude of his adherents, to be his constant companions and the heralds to proclaim to men the kingdom of God. . . . In a broader sense the name is transferred to other eminent Christian teachers; as Barnabas, Acts xiv. 14., and perhaps also Timothy and Silvanus," (1 Th. ii. 7, cf. too Ro. xvi. 7). (Joseph Henry Thayer, *A Greek-English Lexicon of the New Testament*, Grand Rapids: Baker, 1977, p. 68).

Linguistic authorities generally agree that there is relatively little in common between the way that classical Greek or intertestamental Judaism used the term *apostle* and the significance that it came to have in the ministry of Jesus or the post-Pentecost Church.[3]

B. Relevant Theological Quotes

1. [Paul] then, in a general way, calls those in this place [Rom. 16.7][4] Apostles, who planted Churches by carrying here and there the doctrine of salvation . . ." (John Calvin, "Romans," *Calvin's Commentaries*, Vol. XIX, Grand Rapids: Baker Book House, 1981, p. 546).

[3] See, for example, the article on "Apostolos" in *Theological Dictionary of the New Testament*, vol. 1, Gerhard Kittel, ed. Grand Rapids: Wm. B. Eerdmans, 1964, pp. 398-420.

[4] Romans 16.7 refers to Andronicus and Junias, who were not part of the twelve, but were spoken of as apostles by Paul.

A Theological Overview of the Equipping Gifts Described in Ephesians 4.11 (continued)

2. "The titles 'apostle' and 'prophet' occur in the NT with both wide and narrow meanings. Sometimes the term 'apostle' is filled with connotations of special election and authority; in these cases it is restricted to the twelve disciples of Jesus and Paul. On other occasions it is used in a wider sense: every witness of the resurrected Christ and anyone delegated by a church for mission work can bear the same title (Matt. 10.1-5; Gal. 1.1,17, 19; 1 Cor. 9.1-2; 2 Cor. 8.23)" (Karl Barth, *Ephesians 4-6*, Garden City, N.Y.: Doubleday & Co., 1974, p. 314 quoted in Harley H. Schmitt, *Many Gifts, One Lord*, Fairfax, VA: Xulon Press, 2002).

3. "[Apostle] is a comprehensive term for "bearers of the NT message." The name is first borne by the circle of the twelve, i.e., the original apostles. . . . Yet the name is also applied to the first Christian missionaries or their most prominent representatives, including some who did not belong even to the wider groups of disciples" (Gerhard Kittel, ed., *Theological Dictionary of the New Testament*, Vol. 1, Grand Rapids: Wm. B. Eerdmans, 1964, p. 422).

4. "The term *apostles* designates three different groups of people. Initially, only the original disciples (meaning "students, learners") of Jesus were called apostles (meaning "those sent forth with a mission"). Later, the name was given to missionaries involved in church planting who were also eyewitnesses of Christ's resurrection, such as Paul himself (1 Cor. 9.1-1) and a group of Jesus' followers other than the Twelve (1 Cor. 15.5,7). Finally, the designation was extended to people who had never seen Christ but who were involved with apostles in pioneer missionary efforts—Apollos (1 Cor. 4.6,9); Epaphroditus (Phil. 2.25); Silvanus and Timothy (1 Thess. 1.1, cf. 2.6). The definition of "apostles" as one of the higher gifts to be desired bears evidence to the continued accessibility to this ministry for qualified individuals (1 Cor. 12.28, cf. 31). Corinthian Christians could aspire to become apostles, prophets, or teachers. The term *apostle* was still used in this broad sense in the post-apostolic writings of the Didache" (Gilbert Bilezikian, *Beyond Sex Roles: What the Bible says about a Woman's Place in Church and Family*, Grand Rapids, MI: Baker Book House, 1986).

A Theological Overview of the Equipping Gifts Described in Ephesians 4.11 (continued)

5. "Most evangelicals feel very uncomfortable using the term *apostle* to describe any office or leader in the church today. Is it possible, however, for us to conceive of a separation of gift and office after the first century? Rather than assigning this gift to the history of the early church, can we not recognize the broad sense of the verb form *apostello*? Could it not be that in the time between the 1st and 20th centuries the Holy Spirit has given this gift to God's people in what we have come to call *missionary service*? . . . Many have chosen the option of locking several of the spiritual gifts into the first century, lest some explanation be required for their presence in the church today. I would prefer to allow the Holy Spirit the broadest latitude to produce in Christ's body any gift in any age as He sees fit. It seems quite safe to say that the *office* of the apostles was restricted to the establishing of the New Testament church. But . . .we may be justified in seeing evidence of "apostleship" not only as a gift, but as a gift which has operated in the church throughout all the years of its history" (Kenneth O. Gangel, *Unwrap Your Spiritual Gifts*, Wheaton, IL: Victor Books, 1983, pp. 26-27).

6. "A distinction may be made between the foundational ministry of apostle, that is, the apostleship, and the ongoing ministry of others who are called apostles. In this broader sense an apostle is one *sent, commissioned*, and therefore is not affixed to a particular location or church. He does not have the authority of a foundational apostle nor are his words equally inspired. Such an apostle operates in translocal manner, but he does not operate independently. He is church-based, representing a particular church, but ministering largely in a field beyond. *Such apostles are always essential to the life of a church that realizes its call to reach out beyond itself in the mission of the gospel*" (J. Rodman Williams, *Renewal Theology: Systematic Theology from a Charismatic Perspective, Vol. 3: The Church, the Kingdom and Last Things*, Grand Rapids: Zondervan, 1996, pp. 169-70).

7. "The word is occasionally applied in a less restrictive sense in the N.T. to men of apostolic gifts, graces, labors, and successes. It is so notably of Barnabas, who was sent forth with Paul (Acts 13.3; 14.4, 14). Similarly one still meets with such expressions, as Judson, the apostle of Burma" ("Apostle," *The Westminster Dictionary of the Bible*, John D. Davis, ed. Philadelphia: The Westminster Press, 1944, p. 36).

A Theological Overview of the Equipping Gifts Described in Ephesians 4.11 (continued)

8. "One of the principal functions—indeed, the primary function–of an apostle (in the special Christian use of the word) was the preaching of the gospel. The apostles, as an order of ministry in the church, were not perpetuated beyond the apostolic age, but the various functions which they discharged did not lapse with their departure, but continued to be performed by others-notably by the evangelists and the pastors and teachers listed here [in Ephesians 4.11] . . . The apostles preached the gospel before they planted churches and gave their converts further teaching; they were in effect evangelists (as well as pastors and teachers) though they are not specifically called so" (F. F. Bruce, "Epistle to the Colossians, to Philemon, and to the Ephesians," *The New International Commentary on the New Testament*, Vol. 10., Grand Rapids: Eerdmans, 1984, pp. 346-347).

9. "The word *apostle* means *one who is sent*, and is used for others in addition to the original twelve. Today, he is the missionary to new areas" (Avery Willis, Jr. *Biblical Basis of Missions*, Baptist Doctrine Series, Nashville: Convention Press, 1979, p. 108).

10. "In light of [Ephesians] 2.20 and 3.5 and the fact that Paul himself functioned as both apostle and prophet, the first three designations [apostles, prophets and evangelists] refer primarily though in the case of prophets and evangelists not exclusively, to itinerant ministries among the early churches. Itinerant workers founded churches by evangelizing and built them up through prophetic utterances. There can be little question that this is the understanding of the term "apostle" in Paul's letters" (Gordon D. Fee, *God's Empowering Presence*, Peabody, MA: Hendrickson, 1994, p. 707).

C. Summary

The idea that the broad sense of apostleship used in the Pauline letters and the modern term missionary are functionally equivalent has widespread support in current biblical and theological scholarship and this understanding is commonly (although not universally) found both in the Reformed and the Arminian sectors of evangelical theology.[5] In this wide sense the apostolic gifting is strongly associated with those called to a ministry of *itinerant* church-planting mission.

[5] *Likewise, Roman Catholicism which promotes an active office of apostle in a way that Protestants do not (i.e. the bishops of the church are successors of the Apostles narrowly defined and exercise their office authoritatively through a direct line of apostolic succession), nevertheless, also retain a distinction between the narrow and wide sense of the term "apostle." Thus, the Catholic Church can teach the existence of a wider kind of apostolic ministry in the broad sense of missionary and ministry outreach saying, "Indeed, we call an apostolate 'every activity of the Mystical Body' that aims 'to spread the Kingdom of Christ over all the earth'" (Catechism of the Catholic Church, Liguori, MO: Liguori Publications, 1994, p. 229).*

A Theological Overview of the Equipping Gifts Described in Ephesians 4.11 (continued)

In spite of this, however, it is probably best to restrict the idea of an "Apostolic office" to the more narrow sense of the Twelve (substituting Matthias for Judas) plus Paul. Hence, missionary is a better term than apostle for the modern cross-cultural church planter because it retains the linguistic sense of one sent out in mission without detracting from the *special authority* retained by the original Apostles who were directly commissioned by the Risen Lord. Nonetheless, it should be recognized that the nature of the missionary task is to be "little apostles" bearing witness to Christ and exercising authority over the formation of their congregations within the bounds of Scripture. The original Apostles could speak authoritatively to the whole church, missionaries can speak authoritatively to the churches they have planted within the bounds of Scripture. Ultimately, for both Apostles and missionaries, the issue of authority is not one of control but of developing congregations and leaders that can themselves hear and obey Christ.[6]

The missionary (apostolic) gifting, defined in this way, indicates that:

- a person feel an urgent call to the unreached,

- they will constantly press on to new unreached groups,

- they will aggressively adapt themselves to new cultures in order to win as many as possible,

- and, they will raise up leadership for the new churches they establish so that they functionally serve as a "pastor to pastors."

[6] *All legitimate Christian authority is based on its ability to edify (cf. 2 Cor. 10.8). Blessing, not control, is the point of authority. Even the direct "submission to leaders" language of Hebrews 13.17 is predicated on the fact that it brings "advantage" to the follower. Christians submit to leaders because they are God's gift to provide edification and protection. Any Christian leader who claims an authority that is separated from obedience to Christ, submission to the Scripture, the growth of Christ's Church, or the edification of its members is no longer exercising biblical authority. Paul will make this idea plain in the upcoming portions of the text when he writes that the "equipping of the saints for ministry" is intended to result in "building up (edifying) the body of Christ" (Eph. 4.13).*

A P P E N D I X   5 9

Wei Ji

Chua Wee Hian, **The Making of a Leader***. Downers Grove: InterVarsity Press, 1987, p. 151.*

"Crisis"

"Opportunity"

APPENDIX 60

Documenting Your Work

A Guide to Help You Give Credit Where Credit Is Due
The Urban Ministry Institute

Avoiding Plagiarism

Plagiarism is using another person's ideas as if they belonged to you without giving them proper credit. In academic work it is just as wrong to steal a person's ideas as it is to steal a person's property. These ideas may come from the author of a book, an article you have read, or from a fellow student. The way to avoid plagiarism is to carefully use "notes" (textnotes, footnotes, endnotes, etc.) and a "Works Cited" section to help people who read your work know when an idea is one you thought of, and when you are borrowing an idea from another person.

Using Citation References

A citation reference is required in a paper whenever you use ideas or information that came from another person's work.

All citation references involve two parts:

- Notes in the body of your paper placed next to each quotation which came from an outside source.

- A "Works Cited" page at the end of your paper or project which gives information about the sources you have used

Using Notes in Your Paper

There are three basic kinds of notes: parenthetical notes, footnotes, and endnotes. At The Urban Ministry Institute, we recommend that students use parenthetical notes. These notes give the author's last name(s), the date the book was published, and the page number(s) on which you found the information. Example:

> In trying to understand the meaning of Genesis 14.1-24, it is important to recognize that in biblical stories "the place where dialogue is first introduced will be an important moment in revealing the character of the speaker . . ." (Kaiser and Silva 1994, 73). This is certainly true of the character of Melchizedek who speaks words of blessing. This identification of Melchizedek as a positive spiritual influence is reinforced by the fact that he is the King of Salem, since Salem means "safe, at peace" (Wiseman 1996, 1045).

Documenting Your Work (continued)

A "Works Cited" page should be placed at the end of your paper. This page:

Creating a Works
Cited Page

- lists every source you quoted in your paper

- is in alphabetical order by author's last name

- includes the date of publication and information about the publisher

The following formatting rules should be followed:

1. Title

The title "Works Cited" should be used and centered on the first line of the page following the top margin.

2. Content

Each reference should list:

- the author's full name (last name first)

- the date of publication

- the title and any special information (Revised edition, 2nd edition, reprint) taken from the cover or title page should be noted

- the city where the publisher is headquartered followed by a colon and the name of the publisher

3. Basic form

- Each piece of information should be separated by a period.

- The second line of a reference (and all following lines) should be indented.

- Book titles should be underlined (or italicized).

- Article titles should be placed in quotes.

Example:

Fee, Gordon D. 1991. *Gospel and Spirit: Issues in New Testament Hermeneutics.* Peabody, MA: Hendrickson Publishers.

4. Special Forms

A book with multiple authors:

> Kaiser, Walter C., and Moisés Silva. 1994. *An Introduction to Biblical Hermeneutics: The Search for Meaning.* Grand Rapids: Zondervan Publishing House.

An edited book:

> Greenway, Roger S., ed. 1992. *Discipling the City: A Comprehensive Approach to Urban Mission.* 2nd ed. Grand Rapids: Baker Book House.

A book that is part of a series:

> Morris, Leon. 1971. *The Gospel According to John.* Grand Rapids: Wm. B. Eerdmans Publishing Co. The New International Commentary on the New Testament. Gen. ed. F. F. Bruce.

An article in a reference book:

> Wiseman, D. J. "Salem." 1982. In *New Bible Dictionary.* Leicester, England - Downers Grove, IL: InterVarsity Press. Eds. I. H. Marshall and others.

(An example of a "Works Cited" page is located on the next page.)

For Further Research

Standard guides to documenting academic work in the areas of philosophy, religion, theology, and ethics include:

> Atchert, Walter S., and Joseph Gibaldi. 1985. *The MLA Style Manual.* New York: Modern Language Association.

> *The Chicago Manual of Style.* 1993. 14th ed. Chicago: The University of Chicago Press.

> Turabian, Kate L. 1987. *A Manual for Writers of Term Papers, Theses, and Dissertations.* 5th edition. Bonnie Bertwistle Honigsblum, ed. Chicago: The University of Chicago Press.

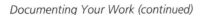

Documenting Your Work (continued)

Works Cited

Fee, Gordon D. 1991. *Gospel and Spirit: Issues in New Testament Hermeneutics*. Peabody, MA: Hendrickson Publishers.

Greenway, Roger S., ed. 1992. *Discipling the City: A Comprehensive Approach to Urban Mission*. 2nd ed. Grand Rapids: Baker Book House.

Kaiser, Walter C., and Moisés Silva. 1994. *An Introduction to Biblical Hermeneutics: The Search for Meaning*. Grand Rapids: Zondervan Publishing House.

Morris, Leon. 1971. *The Gospel According to John*. Grand Rapids: Wm. B. Eerdmans Publishing Co. *The New International Commentary on the New Testament*. Gen. ed. F. F. Bruce.

Wiseman, D. J. "Salem." 1982. In *New Bible Dictionary*. Leicester, England-Downers Grove, IL: InterVarsity Press. Eds. I. H. Marshall and others.

Made in the USA
Monee, IL
11 February 2025

12078396R00171